Education, Philosophy and Well-being

John White is one of the leading philosophers of education currently working in the Anglophone world. Since first joining the London Institute of Education in 1965, he has made significant contributions to the landscape of the discipline through his teaching, research and numerous publications. His academic work encompasses a broad range of rich philosophical issues, ranging from questions surrounding the child's mind, through the moral and pedagogical obligations of teachers and schools, to local and national questions of educational policy.

In this volume, international contributors address key issues in the philosophy of education, touching on significant contemporary concerns and demonstrating the breadth and influence of John White's work. Each chapter critically examines, builds on, and pays tribute to John White's unique contribution, considering how his work has impacted on the discipline of education as we know it today.

Topics covered include:

- policy and the role of philosophy of education
- liberal education
- the aims of education
- moral education
- leadership.

Education, Philosophy and Well-being will appeal to postgraduate students and academics in the fields of history, policy, education studies and philosophy, as well as to policy-makers, educational administrators and teachers.

Judith Suissa is Reader in Philosophy of Education at the Institute of Education, University of London, UK.

Carrie Winstanley is Principal Lecturer in the School of Education, Roehampton University, London, UK.

Roger Marples is Principal Lecturer in the School of Education, Roehampton University, London, UK.

Routledge Research in Education

For a complete list of titles in this series, please visit www.routledge.com.

91 **Language, Literacy, and Pedagogy in Postindustrial Societies**
The Case of Black Academic Underachievement
Paul C. Mocombe and Carol Tomlin

92 **Education for Civic and Political Participation**
A Critical Approach
Edited by Reinhold Hedtke and Tatjana Zimenkova

93 **Language Teaching Through the Ages**
Garon Wheeler

94 **Refugees, Immigrants, and Education in the Global South**
Lives in Motion
Edited by Lesley Bartlett and Ameena Ghaffar-Kucher

95 **The Resegregation of Schools**
Education and Race in the Twenty-First Century
Edited by Jamel K. Donnor and Adrienne D. Dixson

96 **Autobiographical Writing and Identity in EFL Education**
Shizhou Yang

97 **Online Learning and Community Cohesion**
Linking Schools
Roger Austin and Bill Hunter

98 **Language Teachers and Teaching**
Global Perspectives, Local Initiatives
Edited by Selim Ben Said and Lawrence Jun Zhang

99 **Towards Methodologically Inclusive Research Syntheses**
Expanding Possibilities
Harsh Suri

100 **Raising Literacy Achievement in High-Poverty Schools**
An Evidence-Based Approach
Eithne Kennedy

101 **Learning and Collective Creativity**
Activity-Theoretical and Sociocultural Studies
Annalisa Sannino and Viv Ellis

102 **Educational Inequalities**
Difference and Diversity in Schools and Higher Education
Edited by Kalwant Bhopal and Uvanney Maylor

103 **Education, Social Background and Cognitive Ability**
The Decline of the Social
Gary N. Marks

104 **Education in Computer Generated Environments**
Sara de Freitas

105 **The Social Construction of Meaning**
Reading Literature in Urban English Classrooms
John Yandell

106 **Global Perspectives on Spirituality in Education**
Edited by Jacqueline Watson, Marian de Souza and Ann Trousdale

107 Neo-liberal Educational Reforms
A Critical Analysis
Edited by David A. Turner and Hüseyin Yolcu

108 The Politics of Pleasure in Sexuality Education
Pleasure Bound
Edited by Louisa Allen, Mary Lou Rasmussen, and Kathleen Quinlivan

109 Popular Culture, Pedagogy and Teacher Education
International Perspectives
Edited by Phil Benson and Alice Chik

110 Teacher Training and the Education of Black Children
Bringing Color into Difference
Uvanney Maylor

111 Secrecy and Tradecraft in Educational Administration
The Covert Side of Educational Life
Eugenie A. Samier

112 Affirming Language Diversity in Schools and Society
Beyond Linguistic Apartheid
Edited by Pierre Wilbert Orelus

113 Teacher Leadership: New Conceptions for Autonomous Student Learning in the Age of the Internet
Kokila Roy Katyal and Colin Evers

114 Test Fraud
Statistical Detection and Methodology
Edited by Neal M. Kingston and Amy K. Clark

115 Literacy, Play and Globalization
Converging Imaginaries in Children's Critical and Cultural Performances
Carmen Liliana Medina and Karen E. Wohlwend

116 Biotechnology, Education and Life Politics
Debating Genetic Futures from School to Society
Pádraig Murphy

117 Vernaculars in the Classroom
Paradoxes, Pedagogy, Possibilities
Shondel Nero and Dohra Ahmad

118 Professional Uncertainty, Knowledge and Relationship in the Classroom
A Psycho-social Perspective
Joseph Mintz

119 Negotiating Privilege and Identity in Educational Contexts
Adam Howard, Aimee Polimeno, and Brianne Wheeler

120 Liberty and Education
A Civic Republican Approach
Geoffrey Hinchliffe

121 Constructing Narratives of Continuity and Change
A Transdisciplinary Approach to Researching Lives
Edited by Hazel Reid and Linden West

122 Education, Philosophy and Well-being
New Perspectives on the Work of John White
Edited by Judith Suissa, Carrie Winstanley and Roger Marples

123 Chinese Students' Writing in English
Implications from a Corpus-driven Study
Maria Leedham

Education, Philosophy and Well-being

New perspectives on the work of John White

Edited by Judith Suissa,
Carrie Winstanley and Roger Marples

Routledge
Taylor & Francis Group
LONDON AND NEW YORK

First published 2015
by Routledge
2 Park Square, Milton Park, Abingdon, Oxfordshire OX14 4RN

and by Routledge
711 Third Avenue, New York, NY 10017

First issued in paperback 2016

Routledge is an imprint of the Taylor & Francis Group, an informa business

British Library Cataloguing in Publication Data
A catalogue record for this book is available from the British Library

Library of Congress Cataloging-in-Publication Data
Education, philosophy and well-being : new perspectives on the work of John White / edited by Judith Suissa, Carrie Winstanley, and Roger Marples.
pages cm – (Routledge research in education)
1. White, John, 1934 November 7- 2. Education–Philosophy. 3. Moral education. I. Suissa, Judith, 1966- editor of compilation. II. Winstanley, Carrie, editor of compilation. III. Marples, Roger, editor of compilation.
LB880.W482E38 2014
371.001–dc23
2014011033

ISBN 13: 978-1-138-29088-4 (pbk)
ISBN 13: 978-1-138-02134-1 (hbk)

Typeset in Galliard
by Deer Park Productions

Contents

Contributors

Richard Aldrich is Emeritus Professor of the History of Education at the Institute of Education, University of London and a past president of ISCHE and the UKHES. He is the fortunate recipient of two *Festschriften* while *Lessons from History of Education: The Selected Works of Richard Aldrich* was published in Routledge's World Library of Educationalists series in 2006.

David Bridges is Emeritus Professor of Education at the University of East Anglia, where he was previously Pro Vice Chancellor and Director of Research (Kazakhstan and Mongolia) at the University of Cambridge Faculty of Education and Emeritus Fellow of St Edmund's and Homerton Colleges. He is an Honorary Vice President of the PESGB.

Eamonn Callan is Pigott Family Professor in the Graduate School of Education and (by courtesy) Professor of Philosophy at Stanford University. He has published widely in the philosophy of education.

Penny Enslin is Chair of Education at the University of Glasgow and Professor Emeritus in the School of Education at the University of the Witwatersrand, Johannesburg. Her research interests and publications are in political philosophy and education with particular reference to democratic theory, citizenship, cosmopolitan justice and gender in education.

Michael Fielding is currently Emeritus Professor of Education at the Institute of Education, University of London. Michael Fielding taught for 19 years in some of the UK's pioneer radical secondary comprehensive schools and for a similar period and with identical commitments at the universities of Cambridge, London and Sussex.

Michael Hand is Professor of Philosophy of Education at the University of Birmingham and editor of the IMPACT pamphlet series. His research interests are in the areas of moral, political, religious and philosophical education. His publications include *Is Religious Education Possible?* (Continuum, 2006), *Philosophy in Schools* (Continuum, 2008) and *Patriotism in Schools* (Wiley, 2011).

Roger Marples was a secondary school teacher for ten years, during which time he was introduced to philosophy by John White who later became his PhD supervisor. Until recently he was Principal Lecturer in Education at Roehampton University, London. He edited *The Aims of Education* (Routledge, 1999) and his current research interests include moral education, multiculturalism and the aims of education.

Janet Orchard is a former schoolteacher and Co-Programme Director of the PGCE in the Graduate School of Education, University of Bristol. She is a member of the Executive Committee of the PESGB and the editorial board of IMPACT. Her PhD thesis was supervised by John White at the Institute of Education, University of London.

Richard Pring is Professor of Education, University of Winchester, previously having been Professor of Educational Studies at the University of Oxford and director of the Department of Educational Studies, 1989–2003, and lead director of the Nuffield Review of 14–19 Education and Training for England and Wales, 2003–9. He has recently published *Life and Death of Secondary Education for All* (Routledge, 2012) while his *John Dewey: Philosopher of Education for the 21st Century* (Continuum, 2004) is currently being published in paperback.

Michael J. Reiss is Pro-Director: Research and Development and Professor of Science Education at the Institute of Education, University of London and an Academician of the Academy of Social Sciences. The former Director of Education at the Royal Society, he has researched and written extensively about curricula, pedagogy and assessment.

Doret de Ruyter is Professor of Philosophy of Education at VU University Amsterdam. She is associate editor of *Journal of Philosophy of Education* and *Theory and Research in Education* and member of the editorial board of *Journal of Moral Education*. Her main research interests are ideals in education, human flourishing and happiness, moral education, the rights of children and the duties of parents and the state.

Harvey Siegel is Professor of Philosophy at the University of Miami. His areas of interest include epistemology, philosophy of science and philosophy of education.

Judith Suissa is Reader in Philosophy of Education at the Institute of Education, University of London. She is the author of *Anarchism and Education* (Routledge, 2006) and co-author, with Stefan Ramaekers, of *The Claims of Parenting: Reasons, Responsibility and Society* (Springer, 2012).

Mary Tjiattas has taught philosophy in the Department of Philosophy and the School of Education at the University of the Witwatersrand, Johannesburg. She now teaches applied ethics at North Carolina State University. Her research interests are in social and political philosophy, moral psychology, and philosophy of social science and psychoanalysis. Her most recent research focuses on global justice and its educational implications.

Carrie Winstanley is an Executive Council member of the Philosophy of Education Society of Great Britain and has organised the annual conference and Summer School programmes for almost a decade. She is Principal Lecturer in education at Roehampton University, London, and is interested in pedagogy and creating challenge for diverse learners, and in social justice. Her most recent monograph is *The Ingredients of Challenge* (Trentham Books, 2010) following on from the co-edited collection considering the role of *Philosophy in Schools* (with Michael Hand, Bloomsbury, 2008).

Editorial preface

Anyone coming into the field of philosophy of education cannot fail to encounter the work of John White. Indeed, for many of us who were students of the discipline during the last 20 years or more, John White's work was probably our first introduction to the systematic philosophical treatment of central educational issues such as knowledge, the curriculum and the aims of education. Yet for several years John White has been far more than just a leading scholar within a niche academic discipline. Not only has his academic work extended far beyond the confines of institutional boundaries, engaging with practitioners, policy-makers and academics from different disciplines, but his commitment to the field of education has made him a prominent figure in the activities of the wider community of philosophy of education. There is hardly an educational debate or discussion about pressing issues of educational policy and practice on which John White's voice has not been heard. John has, for over fifty years, tirelessly defended the role of philosophy in education, and has exemplified through his many writings the need for clear thinking on educational issues combining philosophical rigour and clarity with powerful moral arguments expressed in straightforward and accessible language.

The decision to put together a collection of writings in honour of John White was, then, an obvious and easy one. What was less easy was selecting, from the wide range of philosophical and educational issues on which John has written over the years, a list of topics that would make for a manageable editorial task. In making our selection, we were guided by two key considerations: the desire to put together a volume that would address issues of lasting and topical relevance to readers both within philosophy of education and within the wider world of educational practice; and the desire to showcase the work of colleagues who have themselves engaged with similar issues, whether through an agreement with or a challenge to John's ideas. The list of international scholars, ex-colleagues and ex-students, senior, junior, younger and older, who were keen to contribute to this project is testament to the esteem and affection in which John is held. Inevitably, we could not include everybody, but we feel that the following chapters give a sense of the lively way in which philosophy of education continues – to use a word close to John's heart – to flourish, and offer readers a chance to revisit some of the central philosophical questions about education that John's work has addressed so thoroughly.

We would like to thank all the contributors for their willingness to be a part of this project and for their hard work in meeting the commitments which they so cheerfully made all those months ago when the idea of the *Festschrift* was first mooted. Thanks too to Clare Ashworth and the entire editorial team at Routledge for their help, efficiency and endless patience during the preparation of the manuscript. We would like to say a special thank you to Patricia White for her enthusiastic and unstinting advice and support throughout the process of working on this book and for her impressive success at keeping it a secret. Finally, thanks must go to John himself for his many years of intellectual inspiration, collegiality and friendship. We hope that readers find this collection of papers stimulating.

Judith Suissa
Carrie Winstanley
Roger Marples
March 2014

John White – biography

Professor John White, at the Philosophy of Education Society of Great Britain annual conference at New College, Oxford, March 2014.

John White is Emeritus Professor of Philosophy of Education at the Institute of Education University of London, where he has worked since 1965, before which time he taught in secondary schools and colleges in Britain and France.

His interests are in the mind of the learner and in interrelationships among educational aims and applications to school curricula. Until the early 1980s he saw his work, in teaching and writing, as playing a part in the educational reform movement, built around the comprehensive ideal, that had begun in the mid-1960s. A central interest was in the ethical underpinnings of a common, nationwide school curriculum to fit that ideal.

After that time, in the face of political reaction to the earlier reforms, including the creation of a backward- rather than forward-looking national curriculum, his work increasingly blended philosophically orientated policy critique with his earlier, more constructive, project. He was active, on the Institute's behalf, in forging links with Russian and other East European scholars at the end of the Soviet Union, but was surprised – again – by the evaporation of liberal-democratic expectations.

The arrival of the computer in the 1980s, coupled with retirement from full-time work after 2000, have enabled him to write much more. As well as philosophical and policy-orientated work on his central project on school aims, he has recently drawn on his early training in psychology and in history to connect that project with ideas on intelligence, the origins of the traditional school curriculum, and examinations.

At the end of this volume is a full list of John White's publications.

Chapter 1

Liberal education and its aims

Richard Pring

Context: a bit of history

The 1960s were a revolutionary period in Britain for the philosophy of education, spearheaded by the creation of the four-year BEd degree and the transformation of training colleges into colleges of education. That revolution was signalled by the address given by Richard Peters in the 1964 ATCDE-DES conference in Hull when he argued that there was a need to get rid of the 'mush' from educational theory. There was a new dawn – profoundly influenced by the analytic tradition within mainstream philosophy.

Why was this thought to be necessary? The change from 'training colleges' to 'colleges of education' offering university degrees in 'educational studies' required greater 'academic respectability'. Usually that meant a 'three plus one' structure – the first three years focusing predominantly on the professional and practical needs of teaching and the final year providing the academic and theoretical depth provided by the major disciplines of education, namely philosophy, sociology, psychology and history.

The dominant mover in this (and the key to its rapid and successful development) was the Institute of Education of London University. The Institute had within its responsibility about thirty training colleges, now colleges of education, each of which was offering the BEd degree validated by the Institute. There was a need for a national staff development programme, and this was provided at the Institute by diploma courses within the respective educational disciplines. Richard Peters, who succeeded Louis Arnaud Reid as Professor of Philosophy of Education at the Institute in 1963, set the tone with his inaugural lecture 'Education as Initiation' (1964) and with his edited book *The Concept of Education* in 1967, to which John White contributed a paper on 'Indoctrination'.

What Peters did was to create a powerful group of philosophers around him – Paul Hirst, Robert Dearden, John and Patricia White, Joan Cooper and later Ray Elliott, who together provided the influential books and papers within the analytic tradition of philosophy which were to shape the course of academic educational studies.

The need for such a tradition was manifest in the respective critiques of the major report on primary education, namely the Plowden Report, *Children and*

Their Primary Schools (Central Advisory Council for Education 1967). A certain toughness of language was required in the use of such concepts, central to the Report, as 'growth', 'needs', 'happiness', 'creativity', 'educational aims' and 'curriculum'. It was here that the Institute philosophers led the way, not least through John White's closely argued paper, 'Creativity and Education', published in the *British Journal of Educational Studies* (1968). This together with the papers by Dearden on 'happiness', Peters on 'growth', Hirst on 'liberal education' and Patricia White on 'socialisation' were published in the collection edited by Dearden *et al.*, *Education and the Development of Reason* (1972).

Meanwhile, the Philosophy of Education Society of Great Britain was established with an annual meeting. The proceedings of these annual meetings, from 1967 onwards, have provided a continuous record of philosophy of education thinking arising from the early work of Richard Peters and his colleagues at the Institute. The proceedings demonstrate both the continuity of the interests initially established and yet their inevitable expansion and deeper analysis. Perhaps the analytic tradition is not quite so dominant, but it remains, ploughing its furrow through the undergrowth of policies and practices, sharpening the thinking (one hopes) of policy-makers, lecturers, teachers and students, recalling the programme set by Wittgenstein: 'My aim is to teach you to pass from a piece of disguised nonsense to something that is patent nonsense' (Wittgenstein 1958: I.464).

It is within that expanding tradition that one needs to see the power and value of John White's contribution to educational thinking over a period of 50 years.

Liberal education and its aims

At the centre of the philosophical deliberations about education in the period referred to above, and in which John White played a significant part, was the meaning of 'education' itself – or, more precisely, the question 'What counts as an educated person?' (See, for example, Richard Peters' paper 'Education and the Educated Man' in the 1972 collection edited by Dearden *et al.* already referred to.) We know, of course, what is meant when a person asks 'Where were you educated?' One answers by giving them the name of the school or the university. But it would be perfectly intelligible then to receive the reply: 'but that surely was not an education'. Rather, in the words of John Dewey, it might be better described as a 'mis-education'; one ended up bored, ignorant, never wanting to read a book again, put off learning.

From observations such as these, it was clear that one needs to distinguish between education as a purely descriptive word (the learning which takes place, or the place where it is pursued) and education as an evaluative word (that sort of learning which, in certain respects, makes one a better person). In that latter evaluative sense, 'education' was likened to 'reform'. A reformed person is one who has changed for the better – for example, shed his or her criminal activity and is now living an honest life. Similarly, the educated person is, in certain particular respects, now a better person. Indeed, it would seem that the descriptive sense is derivative from the evaluative, such that, in noting the failure to nurture the qualities which would make the learners more educated, one might wish to withdraw the description of school or university as a place of *education*.

As Richard Peters argued, such conceptual analysis, in one sense, leaves everything as it is, but it opens up significant lines of enquiry and criticism. If the person judged to be educated is thereby understood to be a better person, what are the distinctively human qualities by which he or she is judged to be better? This line of questioning does, of course, take us into ethics, and one might therefore see education and its aims as a branch of ethics. 'What makes us human?' asked Jerome Bruner (1966). 'How did he become so?' 'How can he become more so?'

'Educated' might not readily capture all the qualities which we want to associate with the 'fully developed' human being, and that is important when we consider later the limitations of the *process* of educating. But 'educated' captures crucial ones, namely the development of knowledge and understanding – the wherewithal by which persons might operate intelligently within the physical, social and moral worlds they inhabit. It would seem to be contradictory to say of someone that he or she was highly educated yet profoundly ignorant. It was appropriate therefore that the major collection of essays, to which Peters contributed 'Education and the Educated Man', was entitled *Education and the Development of Reason*, in which Paul Hirst's most influential paper, 'Liberal Education and the Nature of Knowledge' was reprinted. If educated persons are those who have developed the capacity to think and act intelligently, to reason appropriately, to understand and make sense of the physical and social and moral worlds they have inherited, then they need to be initiated into the different forms of knowledge and understanding. It is no good talking about general mental capacities (such as creativity, sound judgment, effective thinking, communication skills, discrimination) without reference to the logical characteristics specific to the successful creation of this or that, or to the kind of thinking one is engaged in, or to the nature of that within which one is being asked to discriminate. There are logical as well as psychological aspects of creating, thinking, valuing and discriminating. (See Hamlyn (1967) in the collection of papers, edited by Peters, in which John White's 'Indoctrination' was first published.)

A general education, therefore, would enable the learners to master these logical features of reasoning, knowing and understanding – the key concepts through which experience and thinking are organised in particular ways, the distinctive modes of enquiring, and the different ways in which the truth of statements is tested and verified. Educated persons need to be able to think like scientists, like historians, like mathematicians, at least to a certain level – to have the foundations, at least, for an intelligent grasp of the complex world in which they live and have to act, and to be able to progress to more specialist understanding and active engagement should they so choose.

John White's paper, 'Creativity and Education: A Philosophical Analysis' (in the 1972 volume referred to) both drew upon this general analysis of 'the educated person' and contributed significantly to it, especially as teaching children to be creative was at the time (and remains) a rhetorical cry of so-called progressive and child-centred education (what White referred to as 'the cult of creativity ... adopted by teachers in Colleges of Education and elsewhere' (p. 132). However, to be creative is to produce something of value, seen as such because it meets the logical characteristics for doing that sort of thing well. To be a creative physicist is to be original – but in the context of what it means to do physics.

> A creative thinker is one whose thinking leads to a result which conforms to criteria of value in one domain or another.
>
> (Ibid.: 135)

To be educated, therefore, in this evaluative sense, is to have learnt how to think and reason, to have been initiated therefore into the different and distinctive forms of knowledge through which we make sense of the world and of the social and personal contexts of our lives. As Michael Oakeshott argues in the same collection of essays,

> Education ... is the transaction between the generations in which newcomers to the scene are initiated into the world which they are to inhabit. This is a world of understandings, imaginings, meanings ... states of mind in which the human condition is to be discerned ... To be initiated into this world is learning to become human.
>
> (Ibid.: 47)

Learning to be human, human flourishing and the aims of education

There needs here, however, to be a warning shot across the bows. Cannot a person be initiated into the world of understandings and meanings, enabled to employ the language of science, of history, of philosophy, of poetry, and yet not live a distinctively human life? The principal of the American High School (one of the Just Community Schools working with Lawrence Kohlberg), having seen in the concentration camp 'what no man should witness – gas chambers built by learned engineers, children poisoned by educated physicians', was 'suspicious of education'. Hence:

> My request is: Help your students become human. Your efforts must never produce learned monsters, skilled psychopaths, educated Eichmans. Reading, writing, arithmetic are important but only if they serve to make our children more human.
>
> (Strom 1981)

There would, it seems, be more to becoming human than the development of reason in its different forms and than the engagement with what Oakeshott described as 'the conversation between the generations of mankind', although that would seem to be an essential component. Much of John White's subsequent writing has, therefore, been to widen the debate both theoretically and practically in his engagement with policy makers. To that end, he has emphasised and explored the related ideas of 'human flourishing', 'the good life', 'autonomy' and 'personal well-being'.

Too often, it would seem, the educational programme of schools starts off with 'the given' – the traditional subjects which make up the curriculum, especially in the secondary school, and which are enshrined within England and Wales' National Curriculum, established through Act of Parliament in 1988. These subjects looked remarkably like Hirst's eight 'forms of knowledge' with geography added on, although the equation of the forms of knowledge with subjects was not made by Hirst. None the less, given that there are different ways of thinking, reasoning, appreciating and problem-solving shaped by logically different forms, then it makes good sense to focus for at least part of the curriculum upon these distinctive concepts and methodological approaches, distinguishing different modes of testing the truth of the claims made. And, indeed, Her Majesty's Inspectorate's publication *A View of the Curriculum* (1980), though not equated with subjects as such, drew upon the 'forms of knowledge' to argue for the different areas which the curriculum should cover in one way or another – a sort of checklist. To understand key concepts in physics, for example, such as 'force' or 'gravity' (let alone more abstract ones such as 'atom' or 'electron') required systematic initiation, starting with modes of understanding at an elementary level and, through what Bruner (1960) referred to as a 'spiral curriculum', reaching more abstract and theoretical levels.

However, in thus starting with 'the given' (in part reflecting historical and therefore socially originated conditions), there can so easily be a failure to provide an education appropriate for young people in this day and age – in the social and economic conditions in which young people are helped to enter adulthood and lead what White refers to as 'flourishing lives'. He has argued, therefore, since his inaugural lecture in 1975 entitled 'Education and Personal Well-being in a Secular Society', reprinted in *The Curriculum and the Child* (2005), for a prior and explicit consideration of the aims of education. What are we trying to do in compelling all young people to undertake full-time education, especially one which is so rigidly timetabled into totally distinct subjects? And he observes how little, if any, attention is given to this question in all the curriculum developments led by the government since their interventions from 1988 onwards.

Such an explicit and public consideration of aims would seem to be crucial. As White argues, such macro-decisions about school aims cannot be left totally to the individual teacher, since such aims go beyond personal preferences to issues about the kind of society we should be promoting. Those with long memories will remember the problems at the William Tyndale school in the 1960s and the verdict of the Auld Report (1976). As White argues in *Rethinking the School*

Curriculum, 'they are political decisions touching on the good life for individuals and society' (p. 21). They therefore require political rather than professional control.

There are three issues here which require further and close examination: first, the meaning of 'human flourishing' as an aim of education; second, the political framework and process within which such aims might be thrashed out and made a requirement for all schools; and, third, the role of the teacher in all this.

Human flourishing

A key premise in White's continuing argument has been that to be human is to be able to become 'autonomous', able to make up one's own mind as to what is the life worth living, as opposed to having such a life determined by others. Such a life would be one which caused pleasure, met one's desires, gave life meaning. And such a life might be found in many different ways – developing particular skills (skateboarding, reading books, enjoying relationships, eating and drinking, being a scientist), so long as harm does not thereby come to others. It is not possible to say objectively what constitutes such a worthwhile life other than the fact that it gives the person a sense of value, a sense of life worth living.

Of course, as a matter of fact, one knows with some degree of certainty what does give people that sense of value and dignity. These would include having work which is satisfying, belonging to a community and contributing to its welfare, having sufficient nourishment and warmth. Moreover, one might argue, as White argues in several places (for example, in White 2003: 22) that pursuing and enjoying such activities requires the development of certain virtues such as patience, courage, friendliness. Again, knowledge and reasoning power are needed for one to be able to choose wisely, to know alternatives, and to manage one's life intelligently. In particular, it requires social and political knowledge so that one can help create and maintain the sort of society, essentially democratic, where an individual's autonomous choices can be pursued, free from constraint, yet compatible with respect for those of others.

To understand the fairly radical nature of this position, it is helpful to contrast it with what prevails in practice, and indeed with what philosophically has been argued to justify the 'traditional subject-based curriculum'. Richard Peters, for example, in *Ethics and Education* (1966: ch.5), famously produced the 'transcendental argument' for justifying the kinds of knowledge as a basis for the curriculum, without which one could not really pursue questions about what is of most worth. To ask such a question seriously presupposes an acquaintance with those forms of knowledge which enable one to answer that very question. White accepts this to some extent. It is impossible to imagine a flourishing life in the absence of the capacity to understand basic physical facts, to exercise moral judgment, to appreciate visual and aural images, or to have some sense of where one comes from. The forms of knowledge are constitutive of basic everyday thinking, deliberating and appreciating. Formal schooling has the task of extending and deepening such knowledge, at least as far as each young person might be able to manage his or her life more intelligently. But narrow concentration on the subjects which embody directly not just the core concepts and disciplinary features of such forms, but also the abstract 'modes of representation' (to borrow Bruner's phrase) developed within them, is to commit two mistakes.

First, the subsequent knowledge remains too abstracted from the concrete reality of the young people and the experiences which they bring with them to school. Connections are not made. Their everyday world is not illuminated.

Second, so much of the knowledge which young people need 'to manage life intelligently' is left out. Many leave school without the necessary knowledge and understanding to meet basic needs and to make the sort of choices which will enable them to live healthy lives, to find satisfying employment, to enjoy aesthetically the world around them, to enter into meaningful relationships, to realise the importance of democratic society if one is to enjoy the autonomous life to which one aspires.

Therefore the aims of education need to start from elsewhere, while never ignoring the ever deepening understanding of those forms of knowledge through which those aims might be more fully realised. Here it was seen to be important to distinguish between, on the one hand, providing the knowledge related to 'basic needs' and, on the other, enabling young people to discover (and to be able to realise more richly) 'worthwhile activities and goals' – what Raz (2003), quoted with approbation by White (2006), refers to as 'wholehearted engagement in valuable activities and relationships'.

With regard to basic needs, a list of aims would consist of such matters as basic hygiene, healthy eating, relevant exercise, cooking, personal finance. Indeed, one might well ask how it is that, at the end of formal education, so many have failed to make a connection between their curriculum learning and what is needed to survive healthily and safely – for example, protected through relevant knowledge from the enticements of the financial advisers and lenders.

With regard to 'worthwhile activities', there are greater, though by no means insuperable, difficulties, for it is up to autonomous individuals to discover or to work out for themselves what is worthwhile – what gives enduring satisfaction, a sense of a 'meaningful life', a sense of personal worth. And this may be found in a wide range of activities – gardening, playing sport, cooking, engaging in politics or enjoying a deep relationship with another. There are no objective criteria, so it is argued, for saying that one lifetime pursuit is more worthwhile than another. As White argued in 'Wellbeing and Education: Issues of Culture and Authority' (2007), what is seen to be a worthwhile mode of living cannot be derived from our understanding of human nature – 'ought' does not follow from 'is', as David Hume argued. Thus released from authorities on 'worthwhileness' with the right to impose their views of what is valuable on another, each is thrust upon his or her own resources to find what is worthwhile, except that such pursuit of what is worthwhile would have to be compatible with, first, respect for others as they pursue what they believe to be worthwhile and, second, the very conditions of autonomy, namely engagement in a democratic form of community or society.

This requires further explanation and understanding, possibly with reference to two philosophers in whose respective traditions John White seems to sit – John Stuart Mill and John Dewey, although my invocation of the latter might come as a surprise to John White.

Are not some activities which bring pleasure and satisfaction objectively superior to others which also bring an equal amount of pleasure? Are not the most valuable actions those which bring the greatest amount of pleasure not just to the person himself, but to the greatest number of persons, as Jeremy Bentham argued? John White seems very much within this utilitarian tradition, responding in a similar way to that of John Stuart Mill in Chapter 2 of his book *Utilitarianism*. Reflecting on the very same problem, Mill had misgivings with Bentham's assessment of the quantity of pleasure. Surely some pleasures are qualitatively, not just quantitatively, superior to others. For, as Mill argued:

> It is better to be a human being dissatisfied than a pig satisfied; better Socrates dissatisfied than a fool satisfied. And if the fool, or the pig, are of a different opinion, it is because they only know their own side of the question. The other party to the question knows both sides.
>
> (Mill 1859: 9)

Once you have tasted real coffee, it is difficult to go back to Nescafé. Once you have come to appreciate a good malt, you see the greater pleasure it affords over blended whisky. Increasing capacity to discriminate visually enables the onlooker to appreciate the finer points in a work of art. Experience, a wider acquaintance with other sources of pleasure, a more refined understanding of that experience widens the gap between the educated person and the fool. There are, White argues (2007), values which are intrinsic to particular activities which have evolved and remain as these activities become part of everyday life. One can imagine how a group skateboarding over a period of time evolves the rules or criteria for high-standard skateboarding, the attainment of which becomes intrinsic to the pleasure – the sense of achievement – obtained.

As a further example, the good art teacher initiates the neophyte into a tradition of appreciation which increases the intensity of the pleasure obtained. It enhances the autonomy of the individual to make choices about the life worth living. In this way White feels able to distinguish what is desirable from what is merely desired.

Or again, one particular duty in a school which adopted White's understanding of the meaningful and flourishing life would be that of providing the 'information, advice and guidance' from an early age through which the learner could explore the various training and employment possibilities, matched to the learner's interests and aspirations and to the wide economic context. Such knowledge of context would be matched with the growing consciousness of one's own abilities, interests and aspirations. 'Know thyself' as Socrates instructed.

There are further consequences for the role of the school other than the ones which have been mentioned in passing, in particular the importance of appreciating what John White (2002) refers to as 'the child's mind'. The child, through the acquisition of language, develops increasing self-consciousness and is enabled to form a narrative of his or her life and project that into the future. Experience is crucial. The capacity to reflect on that experience opens up further experiences. Through reflection on such experiences one discovers what will hold one's attention, giving a sense of meaning to one's life.

Are there not shades of John Dewey in all this, which were articulated so well by Pat Wilson whose paper to the Philosophy of Education Society in 1974, 'Interests and Educational Values', received such a frosty reception? An interest, as Wilson argued with reference to John Dewey, is what holds the attention, which is pursued, thereby leading to a deepening of that interest, to further understanding, to the acquisition perhaps of the requisite skills to pursue the interest further. Schools are important therefore in opening up possible interests to young people, in enabling them to pursue these interests more intelligently, in showing what further interests they might lead to. Indeed, Wilson, in a memorable criticism of Peters' transcendental argument developed in *Ethics and Education* to justify certain activities as intrinsically worthwhile (namely the pursuit of knowledge in its different forms), wrote in defence of bingo as a worthwhile pursuit where the dedicated bingo player found in it a deep interest, indeed an interest which led to a satisfying and meaningful life (Wilson 1967), to which Peters wrote a response 'In Defence of Bingo: A Rejoinder' (1967).

Political control

Ensuring that the curriculum meets the aims which John White has argued for (namely meeting basic human needs for flourishing in today's world and society, and having the necessary experiences, guidance, knowledge and opportunities to find what activities and ways of life will give the deep satisfaction and sense of meaning both presently and in the future) cannot be left in the hands of the teachers themselves. 'Teachers are no more professionally equipped to make such choices than computer operators or shop assistants.' Teachers have to work within a framework of aims which have been developed with the wider social context in view. It becomes a political matter. That is, agreement about these aims needs to be made within a democratic political order. Preparation for such a political order therefore is one element in a school's responsibilities. To come to see each and everyone as a political equal should be part of ongoing moral education.

This proposal, however, requires considerable thought. The 1944 Education Act was carefully formulated in order to prevent political control over what is learnt in schools and to mitigate political interference. Memories of Germany and Italy were too recent. The maintained system of education, therefore, ensured local control through representative governing bodies and local education authorities. Indeed, when Dr Marjorie Reeves, distinguished medieval historian, was invited to join the Central Advisory Committee for Education in 1947, she was told by the Permanent Secretary that the main duty of a member of the Advisory Committee was to be prepared 'to die at the first ditch as soon as politicians get their hands on education.'[1] And surely that advice has proved correct, as we see the Secretary of State for Education, ignoring professional advice, dictating in detail the history curriculum from ages 5 to 16. Admittedly he changed it (for instance, removing Clive of India from the compulsory curriculum and reducing what 5–11 year olds should know to a mere 700 years up to 1066 and all that – but without the jokes) following the public criticism at the Telegraph Hay Festival from Simon Schama (2013), referring as he did to Clive of India as a 'sociopathic corrupt thug'.

Therefore, in what way might the deliberation of educational aims and their embodiment in the curriculum become 'a political matter', no longer 'left in the hands of the teachers themselves'?

It may well be worth reflecting on how decisions were once eventually made about the aims, structure and (to some extent content) of education at its different levels. The process was indeed set up by politicians, but transcended political fighting and the whimsical decisions from the transient Ministers or Secretaries of State. In the nineteenth century, Royal Commissions were established where major decisions had to be made about the creation of an effective system of national education. For example, the Newcastle Royal Commission (1858) and Taunton School Inquiry Commission (1868) led to the Foster Act 1870, which established the universal system of elementary schools and school boards accountable to the local councils while the Bryce Commission Report (1895) led to the 1902 Balfour Act and 1904 regulations for secondary schools. There were, until comparatively recently, similar commissions and consequent reports, established by government to address major problems as they had arisen within the educational system, but conducted by the independent Central Advisory Councils (established under the 1944 Act). For example, the 1962 Robbins Report led to the growth and shape of higher education, and the 1959 Crowther Report, *15 to 18*, led to the reform of county colleges and the further education system. Characteristic of these reports was that, although established by government (in that sense 'political'), they remained strictly independent of it, having as members key representatives from all sectors affected by the problems identified and the solutions proposed. They met for a couple of years or more, gathering information, consulting widely, initiating necessary research. Above all they addressed the question of aims (witness the extremely detailed and thorough account of the aims of higher education in the Robbins Report). A further feature of such reports was the time span between publication and subsequent legislation or policy. For example, by contrast with the 'quick-fix' solution to currently perceived problems with regard to public examinations at 16 and 18, the recommendations of the Waddell Commission, appointed in March 1977 and reporting in July1978, were not implemented until 1982 by Sir Keith Joseph after much debate and further consultation. Despite difficulties which inevitably arise in any examination system, the quite revolutionary creation of a single examination at 16 has survived for over 30 years.

Perhaps the now abandoned system of Royal or Advisory Commissions should be the way ahead in which the framework of curriculum aims argued for by John White might meet his requirement for deliberation and decision within a 'democratic political order'.

Bring back teaching

However, should such a 'political order' mean that 'teachers are no more professionally equipped to make such choices [concerning educational aims] than computer operators or shop assistants'?

It may be worth reflecting here upon the once successful attempt to enable teachers, with their distinctive experience and expertise, to contribute through deliberation, practice and research to the formulation of educational values through engagement in curriculum development. The Schools Council was established in 1962, dominated by teachers but with considerable representation from local education authorities, government, employers and the community. Its purposes were, first, to support curriculum development based on deliberations about the values embodied in different activities and areas of experience and, second, to propose the kind of examinations which reflected those values and learning. Any curriculum embodies a view, often unexamined, as to what counts as *educational* development, in this case made particularly urgent by the imminent raising of the school-leaving age. Therefore there evolved a radical review of science teaching (in cooperation with the Nuffield Foundation), the creation of the Humanities Curriculum Project through which students discussed socially controversial issues in the light of historical, sociological, literary (etc.) evidence, the development of Geography for the Young School Leaver, and many others. Teachers were at the heart of the deliberations about values and the embodiment of these in the educational advancement of all students at the time when many more would be remaining in education until the age of 16.

But in what ways may teachers be 'more professionally equipped to make such choices [concerning educational aims] than computer operators or shop assistants'? Perhaps Dewey may be accused of exaggeration when he claimed that teachers are the 'usherers in of the kingdom of God', but behind such a claim was the belief that teachers have a special role in society, namely that of custodians of the cultural achievements we have inherited and the conveyors of these to 'the child's mind' – not in the sense of 'transmitting knowledge' but in showing the relevance of such achievements to the concerns, growing self-consciousness, aspirations and search for a meaningful life of the young learner.

As Derek Morrell, in effect the architect of the Schools Council, argued, there is an 'urgent demand for help in thinking about the nature of the human condition, and the purpose of life itself'. This meant shifting the curriculum emphasis from the impersonal to the personal. The classroom becomes the place where this dialogue takes place between the learner (trying to make sense of experience) and the teacher (with wider and deeper cultural understanding) – where, in the light of that inherited wisdom within literature, the arts or science, the teacher 'shares his humanity' with the pupils (Morrell 1966: 7).

Note

1 Personal conversation with the author.

References

Auld Report (1976) *William Tyndale Junior and Infants Schools Public Enquiry.* London: ILEA.

Bruner, J. (1960) *The Process of Education.* Cambridge, MA: Harvard University Press.

Bruner, J. (1966) 'Man: a course of study', *Towards a Theory of Instruction.* Cambridge, MA: Harvard University Press.

Central Advisory Council for Education (1967) *Children and Their Primary Schools* ('The Plowden Report'). London: HMSO.

Dearden, R., Hirst, P. and Peters, R. S. (1972) *Education and the Development of Reason.* London: Routledge & Kegan Paul.

Hamlyn, D. W. (1967) 'The logical and psychological aspects of learning', in R. S. Peters (ed.), *The Concept of Education.* London: Routledge & Kegan Paul.

Mill, J. S. (1863) *Utilitarianism.* London: Everyman Edition.

Morrell, D. (1966) *Education and Change*, Joseph Payne Memorial Lecture. London: College of Preceptors.

Peters, R. S. (1965) *Ethics and Education.* London: Routledge & Kegan Paul.

Peters, R. S. (1967) 'In defence of bingo: a rejoinder', *British Journal of Educational Studies*, 15 (2): 188–94.

Peters, R. S. (ed.) (1967) *The Concept of Education.* London: Routledge & Kegan Paul.

Raz, J. (2003) *The Practice of Value.* Oxford: Clarendon Press.

Schama, S. (2013) *Our Children, Our History*, The Telegraph Hay Festival, Event 286.3, 30 May.

Strom, M. (1981) 'Facing history and ourselves: integrating a Holocaust unit into the curriculum', *Moral Education Forum*, Summer.

White, J. (1968) 'Creativity and education', *British Journal of Educational Studies*, XVI (2): 123–37.

White, J. (2002) *The Child's Mind.* London: Routledge.

White, J. (ed.) (2003) *Rethinking the School Curriculum: Values, Aims and Purposes.* London: RoutledgeFalmer.

White, J. (ed.) (2004) *Rethinking the School Curriculum: Values, Aims and Purposes.* London: RoutledgeFalmer.

White, J. (2005) *The Curriculum and the Child: The Selected Works of John White.* London: RoutledgeFalmer.

White, J. (2006) 'Autonomy, human flourishing and the curriculum', *Journal of Philosophy of Education*, 40 (3): 381–90.

White, J. (2007) 'Wellbeing and education: issues of culture and authority', *Journal of Philosophy of Education*, 41 (1): 17–28.

Wilson, P. S. (1967) 'In defence of bingo', *British Journal of Educational Studies*, 15 (1): 5–27.

Wilson, P. (1971) *Interest and Discipline in Education.* London: Routledge & Kegan Paul.

Wittgenstein, L. (1958) *Philosophical Investigations.* London: Basil Blackwell.

Chapter 2

From philosophy to history

Some turning points

Richard Aldrich

Introduction

It is both a privilege and a pleasure to contribute to this volume for John White. When I came to the Institute of Education as a member of staff in 1973, Philosophy of Education was in the ascendant, not least in the PGCE Education course. Indeed, John White's pioneering volume, *Towards a Compulsory Curriculum*, was published in that very year. My interest in this area was much enhanced and ever since then I have followed John's career and work with great interest and profit. We were colleagues for some 30 years and in retirement have shared rooms in our roles as Emeriti Professors. We alternated as Head of Department when History and Philosophy were brought together with Humanities into a single department, taught on courses at initial training, master and doctoral levels, and contributed to Institute publications (Aldrich 1988; Aldrich and White 1998; White 1988). Over the years I have come to place a very high value indeed on John's scholarship and friendship.

Richard Rogers, who with Su Brumwell and Renzo Piano designed the Pompidou Centre in Paris, is convinced that 'Architecture is too complex to be solved by any one person.' Education, which has been well described by César Manrique as 'a country's biggest business', is infinitely more complex than architecture. The purpose of this article is to complement the analysis in John White's recent book, *The Invention of the Secondary Curriculum* (2011). Four main points are made in the introductory chapter to this work. The first is the prevalence of the traditional academic curriculum of subjects in secondary schools, not only in England but also in many countries around the world. The second is that for a hundred years and more dissatisfaction has been expressed with the inappropriate nature of this curriculum, especially for those who are indeed 'less academic'. Third, in looking back on the 1960s and 1970s and in a departure from his previous position, John judges that 'The London philosophers, Hirst, Peters, Dearden, and White all argued for a broad, academic curriculum based on types of knowledge or understanding. All their arguments fail, whether they favor an intrinsic justification or an extrinsic one' (p. 121). Finally, he turns from justification to explanation, 'from philosophy to history. If I could not find any good, validating reasons for this curriculum in terms of wider aims and values, I might at least explore, empirically, the reasons why we have come to rely on it' (p. 3). John White locates the origins of the current curriculum in 'radical Protestant ideas and practices, in and after the seventeenth century' (p. 4). He concludes that while the pedagogical revolution brought about by Ramus and his successors was highly successful in challenging contemporary orthodoxies, including the prevalence of the study of Greek and Latin, it is now part of a new orthodoxy that needs to be replaced (p. 162). Following this Introduction the next five chapters of the book provide a historical account of curriculum development from 1550 to 1988. The final two chapters, entitled 'Into the Twenty-First Century' and 'Beyond the Traditional Curriculum', build on the sixth chapter to provide a critique and a series of recommendations.

This chapter is organised under two broad headings – the past on the one hand and present and future on the other. The first section provides some methodological perspectives upon the historical dimensions of *The Invention of the Secondary Curriculum*. The second brings historical perspectives to bear upon its contemporary arguments and proposals for the future.

Past

History is the study of human events with particular reference to the dimension of time – past, present and future. This may be reflected in the study of a particular period and area – 'Ancient Rome', 'Tudor England', Twentieth-Century China'. Alternatively there may be more emphasis on a particular person or theme – 'Julius Caesar', 'Mahatma Gandhi', the 'Spanish Armada', the 'Second World War', the 'History of Medicine'. In both cases, the treatment is likely to be chronological, starting at the more distant moment in time and ending at the more recent. Historians, including those engaged in the study of the history of education, bring widely different approaches to the relationship between past and present events. There are those who believe that the past should be studied for its own sake. There is clearly a danger of studying, and even glorifying, only those elements in the past that appear to have led to the present in a continuous line of development. These dangers, with particular reference to the notion of progress in history, were highlighted, although not always subsequently heeded, by Herbert Butterfield in his famous study, *The Whig Interpretation of History* (1931). The eminent Belgian historian, Marc Depaepe, is the principal contemporary critic of 'presentism' in relation to educational history (Depaepe 2010). Others, myself included, while recognising these dangers, emphasise that every moment in time is in turn a future, a present and a past, and that the interests of the present will influence many, but not all, of the questions we ask of the past.

Line of development

The Invention of the Secondary Curriculum is a classic example of line of development history – one that traces a particular topic or phenomenon through the past into the present. Line of development is widely practised and is frequently to be found when history is divided into various subjects or areas, for example constitutional history, diplomatic history, military history, the history of parliament, the history of education. One of the most influential books on this historical approach was *History in Schools: The Study of Development* (1939) by M. V. C. Jeffreys, who taught history and religious education at the Institute of Education 1932–9. The traditional historical syllabus, both in elementary and secondary schools, was chronological in nature and largely political in content. Jeffreys argued that younger pupils in particular had little interest in and less understanding of such complex issues as Greek democracy and the Renaissance and Reformation. In contrast, line of development would enable more practical topics, for example food, homes or transport, to be studied chronologically by younger pupils. Jeffreys' concept of development was not simply to be equated with progress. Indeed he argued that pupils 'should study some fields of human activity (such as the arts) in which progress is obviously not a general tendency' (Jeffreys 1939: 21). But perhaps the most interesting element in Jeffreys' book is that after acknowledging and responding to potential criticisms of line of development, he concluded by arguing that the line of development approach could contribute to the reorganisation of the curriculum as a whole with particular reference to 'education for active citizenship' (ibid.: 91).

> If we are to educate citizens, the work in school must have reality and purpose – that is to say it must be intelligibly related to the problems of actual life. To that end, there must be some rearrangement of the content of the curriculum; the formal division into 'subjects' must give way in the interests of research into problems of real and present importance
>
> (ibid.: 91).

In *The Invention of the Secondary Curriculum* John White is as careful as was Jeffreys to counter the major criticism frequently levelled at any line of development approach such as history of parliament or history of education, namely that history cannot be compartmentalised in this way. He acknowledges the danger and explains that in looking for the origins of the contemporary subject-based academic curriculum in secondary schools, and in seeking to show how it has become an apparently immoveable phenomenon, he is avoiding any mono-causal explanation.

> As I shall be at pains to emphasise, the historical forces that have shaped it must be legion, and I cannot begin to claim that I have come to grips with them all. This is not, in fact, my intention. It is, rather, to explore *one route*, albeit it seems a major one, by which the traditional curriculum has come down to us.
>
> (White 2011: 2)

Problems with the line of development approach

The major problem with the line of development approach is that human life is not lived in compartments of this nature and educational developments cannot be studied in complete isolation from other factors. Two examples from the work of contemporary Institute colleagues are relevant here. The French scholar, Vincent Carpentier, has brought an important new dimension to the study of history of education in the UK with his work on the relationship between education and economics (Carpentier 2001, 2003). The inexorable rise of public expenditure on education in the UK during the nineteenth and twentieth centuries is well known. By drawing on the contentious theory of Kondratiev cycles, however, Carpentier demonstrates that 'prior to 1945, in relative terms educational expenditure seems to have increased during periods of economic downturn and decreased when the economy was strong' (2003: 7). After 1945 the situation was reversed. Educational expenditure increased during the period of growing prosperity following the Second World War, but decreased in relative terms during the economic downturn triggered by the oil crisis of 1973. This pattern, moreover, was repeated in both France and Germany and suggests that educational systems may be driven by international forces such as the endogenous accumulation of knowledge and the rise of lifelong learning.

A second example of the dangers of line of development with reference to the history of education is provided by a study of the organisation of German secondary education by the Danish scholar, Susanne Wiborg (2010). This is a particularly pertinent piece as the *Realschulen* are cited by John White as 'the first successful attempt to offer a vocational training to bourgeois and artisan families whose sons were not intended for the university and for whom the Latin schools were inappropriate' (White 2011: 87). Explanations of the resistance of Germany to the introduction of comprehensive secondary schools have focused upon the protection of the classically oriented *Gymnasium* by the educated elite, and the continuing popularity of the *Realschule*, the secondary technical school, among industrialists and the skilled working classes (Ertl and Phillips 2000). The commitment of Germany to substantial provision for pupils of average and below average ability is of long standing and was noted by several distinguished British visitors, including Matthew Arnold who in the 1860s investigated secondary education in Prussia on behalf of the Taunton Commission (White 2011: 71). During the following decades concerns about the inadequacies of British education increased as the economy went into relative decline while that of Germany steadily advanced. Wiborg acknowledges the force of traditional educational explanations but draws upon Scandinavian experience to argue that the failure to introduce comprehensive secondary schooling in Germany was essentially the result of a failure of political development. 'It is the absence of a similar powerful social democracy that can explain, comparatively, why comprehensive education failed in Germany' (Wiborg 2010: 555).

Turning points

Line of development history may be modified or complemented by a 'patch' approach involving 'turning points'. Given the impossibility of providing detailed studies across large tracts of time, historians frequently identify turning points in history – events or periods that signify, or appear to signify, fundamental changes. These may range from the birth and spread of new faiths, for example Christianity and Islam, to moments of high political and intellectual drama, as with the French and Russian revolutions. How might this approach be applied to the organisation, ownership and professionalisation of knowledge in relation to secondary school curricula?

The end of the nineteenth century and the birth of the twentieth, symbolised in British history by the death of Queen Victoria in January 1901 following a reign of more than 60 years, was also a turning point in the history of secondary school curricula in this country. In 1902 the Balfour Education Act transferred control over all types of maintained schooling to county and county borough councils and empowered these bodies to establish secondary schools. As John White notes (2011: 101), the *Regulations for Secondary Schools* of 1904 set out the course of subjects that has lasted largely unchanged from that day to this and was confirmed by the National Curriculum of 1988.

Several forces were at work to strengthen that continuity. In the nineteenth century English elementary school teachers, in common with their primary successors in the twentieth and twenty-first centuries, were customarily trained to teach across a number of curriculum areas. Secondary school teachers, on the other hand, have become subject specialists – geographers, historians, mathematicians, physicists, etc. – and key factors were at work to create this situation. For centuries, masters in grammar and public schools had been qualified to teach by reason of their university degrees. This tradition continued into the county secondary schools established under the 1902 Act, although initially there was a distinct shortage of women graduates for posts in girls' secondary schools. In May 1890, Circular 287 had set out detailed procedures enabling universities and university colleges to provide day training facilities for teachers, and students in these colleges were permitted to attend other lectures in the university. These arrangements allowed for some subject specialisation, although even in 1925–6 there were 4,602 students in the university sector formally preparing for elementary teaching as opposed to only 917 for secondary. Many of the elementary trained, however, subsequently proceeded to secondary schools while college staff increasingly included secondary subject method specialists. Key examples at the London Day Training College, the Institute's predecessor, included James Fairgrieve in Geography in 1912, John Johnston Bell in History in 1922, M. Gladys Calthrop in Modern Languages in 1923 and Marion Richardson in Art in 1924 (Aldrich 2002: 48, 73–7).

History provides a classic example of subject and community development at the end of the nineteenth century. The *Regulations for Secondary Schools* of 1904 made history a compulsory subject at secondary school level. A growing sense of community was assiduously promoted by the Historical Association, founded in 1906, in which university dons, secondary school teachers and teacher trainers were bound together in their commitment to the subject. 'Its first council, which included 11 university staff, 9 from secondary schools and 4 from training colleges, reflected the status which history had achieved throughout the educational system and provided a forum for collaboration amongst its practitioners' (Aldrich 2006: 173).

Turning points at one period in time – for example at the turn of the twentieth century the strengthening of secondary school subjects by such diverse factors as central government legislation and regulation and the development of subject communities including academics, school teachers and teacher trainers – may be linked to a consideration of more fundamental themes. One such is the substantial change that has occurred in the amount, nature and codification of knowledge. The explosion of knowledge that has occurred since the late eighteenth century in Europe has been tellingly, if mischievously, represented in the title of Andrew Robinson's biography of Thomas Young (1773–1829) whom he hails as *The Last Man Who Knew Everything: Thomas Young, The Anonymous Polymath Who Proved Newton Wrong, Explained How We See, Cured the Sick and Deciphered the Rosetta Stone, Among Other Feats of Genius* (2006). The development of subjects with distinctive limits and procedures has been essential to the development of knowledge. To take a single example, astronomy, which for centuries and across many cultures was a matter of religious belief, is now a science. The very word 'scientist' was invented by William Whewell (1794–1866) and as Pamela H. Smith has shown 'The human engagement with nature that has come to be codified in the natural sciences has brought into being structures and systems of knowledge, of belief, of education, and of communities, and has come to provide a means of arbitrating competing knowledge claims' (Smith 2012: 269). The obvious danger of such an explosion and codification of knowledge is that academics, and others, become isolated specialists, or groups of specialists, who know more and more about less and less and that this culture permeates down into the secondary school.

Present and future

John White's approach to the replacement of the current subject-based orthodoxy is formulated in terms of a commission to determine the curriculum, the importance of beginning with aims based on liberal-democratic values, and an end to fragmentation in arrangements for learning. He advocates 'schools where children spend their time thoroughly absorbed in worthwhile pursuits, with plenty of opportunities for them to choose from what is offered that which suits them most' (2011: 161).

Can there be agreement on educational aims and values in a liberal-democratic society? To whom do schools belong? The secondary school curriculum has been a contested site between various groups in society: central and local governments and their politicians and administrators, faiths and sects, teachers, parents, employers and pupils themselves. There has been no agreement on the key question 'What knowledge is of most worth?' Should traditional subjects prevail or greater priority be given to vocational, artistic, humanist or child-centred approaches? In his search for worthwhile pursuits and opportunities for choice, John White has challenged the place of even the most central of existing secondary school subjects, including mathematics (White 2000). But are such decisions to be made purely on rational grounds? For the great majority of the last two thousand years it was widely believed in Britain that the most worthwhile element in education was the promotion of Christianity. This would ensure both a good life on this earth and the attainment of salvation hereafter. From the sixteenth century even this notion of worthwhile would be subject to fierce controversies between members of the different Christian sects. In twenty-first-century England Christian beliefs are increasingly complemented and challenged both by secularists and by adherents of other faiths.

Young School Leavers

A classic example of the contested curriculum, in this case between the values of head teachers and teachers on the one hand and parents and pupils on the other, became apparent in 1968. In that year the Schools Council produced a report entitled *Young School Leavers*, also known as *Schools Council Enquiry I*. Over a period of some two years interviews were conducted with 4,618 13–16 year olds, 4,546 of their parents and 1,489 of their teachers and head teachers. A further 3,421 former pupils aged 19–20 from the same schools were also interviewed. Of course the educational landscape of the 1960s differed from that of today in several respects. This survey pre-dated the raising of the compulsory school age to 16, while the Certificate of Secondary Education (CSE) had only recently been introduced. Many youngsters, therefore, left school without taking any exams or securing any qualifications. Nevertheless a startling contrast was revealed.

Among the 15-year-old leavers, both boys and girls placed the following three objectives at the top of a list of 27 curriculum alternatives, albeit in a slightly different order:

> Teach you things which will help you to get as good a job or career as possible.
> Teach you things which will be of direct use to you in your job.
> Teach you how to manage your money when you are earning, and about things like rates and income tax.

The bottom three in descending order were identical:

> Take you on outings to places like art galleries, the theatre, museums or castles.
> Do drama in school, that is acting or reading plays.
> Study poetry in school and read or learn poems.
>
> (Schools Council, 1968: 33–4)

Parents of these 15-year-old leavers, both boys and girls, also put drama and poetry in the bottom two places. Their three priorities were: 'writing easily', 'good job/career as possible' and 'speaking well' (ibid.: 39).

This emphasis of pupils and parents upon learning about things of direct use in jobs and of getting as good a job or career as possible was at odds with the values and purposes of those who were teaching them. Both head teachers and teachers chose a top three of 'personality and character', 'speaking well' and 'independence' from a similar list of 24 objectives. Head teachers, indeed, placed 'good job/career as possible', 'plenty of subjects to widen interest', 'examination achievement' and 'things of direct use in jobs' at the very bottom of their list. Teachers' choices were almost identical but they substituted 'poetry' for 'good career/job as possible' (ibid.: 42).

Ninety-three per cent of boys in this group rated maths as being a useful subject, followed by English (90 per cent), metalwork and engineering (71 per cent), woodwork (68 per cent), science (60 per cent) and technical drawing (57 per cent). Only 8 per cent of boys thought music was a useful subject, with religious instruction (22 per cent) next. Girls chose English (94 per cent), maths (92 per cent), housecraft (91 per cent), commercial subjects and typing (81 per cent) and needlework (73 per cent) as the most useful subjects. They also placed music (11 per cent) at the bottom of the list with art and handicraft (22 per cent) next (ibid.: 57). These choices indicate not only perceived usefulness, but also the more diverse range of subjects available to secondary modern pupils of that time.

While current pupils and their parents wanted a more vocational approach to school curricula, the former pupils, 19–20 year olds born between 1 September 1945 and 31 August 1947 who would generally have had some experience of work and/or further education, and possibly of marriage, took a different view.

> It was noted in Chapter 2 that 19 to 20 year olds gave substantially less support than 13 to 16 year olds to the idea that they should learn things in school which would be of direct use to them in their jobs ... In considering whether and, if so, to what extent specific vocational training should form part of the secondary school course, it seems important to bear in mind also that during these youngsters' lifetimes a large proportion of existing jobs may disappear and be replaced by totally new ones.
>
> (Ibid.: 71)

Since the 1960s considerable changes have indeed taken place with respect to the nature of employment. For example, manufacturing jobs have declined in numbers, to be replaced by those in the service industries, but it is arguable that future prosperity may require a reversal in that trend.

Young School Leavers also revealed marked gender differences in pupil and parental choices of useful subjects. Boys' parents placed English, maths and metalwork, woodwork, technical drawing and other technical subjects at the top, with typing, shorthand, bookkeeping and commercial subjects at the bottom and cookery, housecraft, mothercraft, etc. next. On the other hand girls' parents placed cookery, housecraft, mothercraft, etc. at the top of the list, and metalwork, woodwork, technical drawing and other technical subjects at the bottom (ibid.: 63). Since the 1960s considerable changes have taken place with respect to gender stereotyping and the roles of men and women. Nevertheless there is little sign of unanimity on the place of domestic subjects in school curricula, even within the current coalition government. For example, in July 2013 the Prime Minister, David Cameron, was reported as calling for the return of old-fashioned home economics for all, boys and girls alike, when saying that 'Above all, we need to teach children about food, as well as how to cook.' This statement came weeks after the Secretary of State for Education, Michael Gove, was persuaded by business leaders that plans for regular lessons on cooking and nutrition were inappropriate in a new Design and Technology curriculum. These plans were accordingly modified so that more emphasis could be placed upon high-tech design and robotics (Bennett 2013: 18).

Lifelong learning

Schools Council Enquiry I demonstrates the complexity of curriculum construction and choice. In 1968 pupils, parents and teachers had different notions of usefulness and interest. Former pupils, now aged 19 and 20, did not have exactly the same perception of their school curricula as when they were 15. There is little reason to expect a greater unanimity today. Changes since that date suggest an increase in uncertainties and that the secondary curriculum must be not only reformed but also relocated within a much broader series of contexts.

The first and most important of these is the concept of lifelong learning. The secondary school curriculum cannot be treated in isolation, but as one element in a lifetime of education. Some of this will be located within formal educational institutions, but much of it will take place outside. It is not simply, as the authors of the 1968 report noted, that there is less likelihood of jobs for life. The Internet has changed the extent, availability and ownership of knowledge and the very nature and location of employment. Over a period of fewer than 20 years a new communications revolution has seen the birth of the digital age. Toddlers now manipulate cell phones with greater assurance than their grandparents, while teenagers have become screenagers. Recent developments in neuroscience may have considerable implications for the organisation of formal education, including the curricula of primary and secondary schools. For example, it is suggested that the best time to learn a second language is in infancy and that the brains of infant and primary school children are twice as active as the adult brain. Nevertheless, it is also clear that the adult brain itself continues to change and adapt throughout life (Aldrich 2013: 400).

International dimensions

Since 1988 education in England has become increasingly national and directed from the centre, at a time when other dimensions of life are increasingly international, as in the case of online learning. What effect can these changes have upon the curricula of secondary schools? Two examples are provided here.

Global issues, for example overpopulation and shortages of food, water and energy, need to be considered in an international curricular framework. Since 2006, Rescue!History, an independent network of radical academics, independent researchers and committed campaigners, have sought to inform academics, students and the wider public about 'anthropogenic climate change, the most urgent but also all-encompassing of challenges now facing humanity' (Levene *et al.* 2010: 11). Similarly Lord Rees, the Astronomer Royal, has argued that 'the odds are no better than fifty-fifty that our present civilisation on Earth will survive to the end of the present century without a serious setback' (Rees 2003: 61). Are we to be 'passive spectators at the self-inflicted demise of our species' (Levene *et al.* 2010: 32–3) or should the most important aim of education, and hence of the secondary school curriculum, be human survival (Aldrich 2010)?

Education and employment are becoming increasingly international, not least within the boundaries of the European Union. Universities are one of the few surviving institutions from the European Middle Ages. Their requirements strongly influence the curricula of English secondary schools. Nevertheless, universities are currently undergoing rapid transformations. Indeed, hundreds of courses are now freely available on line (http://openculture.com/freeonline, accessed 6 March 2012). Rapid expansion may soon be followed by contraction and diversification. Increased fees have brought a heightened sense among students and their parents of the need for value for money, especially in terms of preparation for future employment. Chris Haskins has recently drawn attention to the situation in Germany where only 20 per cent attend university and argues that too many young people in England (some 40 per cent) are encouraged to go to university where they often study courses that are of no use to a future employer. For example, he draws attention to an alarming skills gap in the Humber region, an area composed of well-to-do parts such as East Yorkshire and rural North Lincolnshire, and cities such as Grimsby and Hull that have experienced decades of social deprivation and relative economic decline. This is contrasted with skill supply in Germany, where the education system at school and post-school levels is bolstered by the commitment of businesses, both large and small, to vocational training in general and apprenticeships in particular. Big companies such as BMW and Siemens in Munich and Volkswagen in Saxony are fully involved in their local communities, both in terms of education and employment (Haskins 2013: 45).

Conclusion

For more than 40 years John White has been the leading thinker and important activist in respect of secondary school curricula in England. While this work has principally been approached from a philosophical perspective, *The Invention of the Secondary Curriculum* delves back into history to trace the origins of the existing curriculum and concludes that it is now ripe for replacement. It is certainly true that secondary school curricula in England, and in many other countries, are principally organised along subject lines. In consequence whereas primary school pupils are usually based in one classroom and with one teacher for a majority of the school day, secondary school pupils tend to move from teacher to teacher and from room to room. It is also true that for many years commentators have questioned the nature of this subject-based curriculum and its attendant learning styles. John White begins his book by quoting Cyril Norwood's dissatisfaction expressed in 1937. An even more apposite example is provided by A. N. Whitehead who not only urged an end to 'the fatal disconnection of subjects which kills the vitality of the modern curriculum' (Whitehead 1949: 10) but also, like John White, reserved a special disdain for 'the scraps of gibberish, which in their school-days were taught to them in the name of algebra' (ibid.: 12).

In this chapter I have tried to complement John White's analysis of the historically contested nature of the school curriculum by considering other factors to amplify his line of development approach. The subject-based curriculum is underpinned by the very proliferation and subdivision of areas of knowledge that has taken place since the late eighteenth century, and by the twentieth-century development of specific subject communities. As the curricular choices of pupils, former pupils, parents, teachers and head teachers in *Young School Leavers* demonstrated, it is not easy in a democratic and increasingly pluralistic society to secure agreement upon what is worthwhile in education. Nevertheless, other factors suggest that we may be at a turning point. The communications revolution that has occurred over the last 20 years has transformed the generation, transmission and ownership of knowledge. These changes, coupled with others in the nature of employment and increased globalisation may have a considerable impact, not only on the organisation of the secondary school curriculum, but on the very nature of education itself.

References

Aldrich, R. (1988) 'The National Curriculum: an historical perspective', in D. Lawton and C. Chitty (eds), *The National Curriculum*. London: Institute of Education, pp. 21–33.

Aldrich, R. (2002) *The Institute of Education 1902–2002. A Centenary History*. London: Institute of Education.

Aldrich, R. (2006) *Lessons from History of Education: The Selected Works of Richard Aldrich*. London: Routledge.

Aldrich, R. (2010) 'Education for survival: an historical perspective', *History of Education*, 39: 1–14.

Aldrich, R. (2013) 'Neuroscience, education and the evolution of the human brain', *History of Education*, 42: 396–410.

Aldrich, R. and White, J. (1998) *The National Curriculum: The QCA and the Aims of Education*. London: Institute of Education.

Bennett, R. (2013) 'Cookery lessons for every child, pledges Cameron', *The Times*, 26 July, pp. 18–19.

Butterfield, H. (1931) *The Whig Interpretation of History*. London: Bell.

Carpentier, V. (2001) *Système Éducatif et Performances Économiques au Royaume-Uni: 19ème et 20ème siècles*. Paris: L'Harmattan.

Carpentier, V. (2003) 'Public expenditure and economic growth in the UK, 1833–2000', *History of Education*, 32: 1–15.

Depaepe, M. (2010) 'The ten commandments of good practices in history of education research', *Zeitschrift für padagogische historiographie*, 16: 31–4.

Ertl, H. and Phillips, D. (2000) 'The enduring nature of the tripartite system of secondary schooling in Germany: some explanations', *British Journal of Educational Studies*, 48: 391–412.

Haskins, C. (2013) 'Making us useful', *Journal of the Royal Society of Arts*, Summer, pp. 44–5.

Jeffreys, M. V. C. (1939) *History in Schools: The Study of Development*. London: Pitman.

Levene, M., Johnson, R. and Roberts, P. (eds) (2010) *History at the End of the World? History, Climate Change and the Possibility of Closure*. Penrith: Humanities-Ebooks, LLP.

Rees, M. (2003) *Our Final Century: Will Civilisation Survive the Twenty-First Century?* London: Heinemann.

Robinson, A. (2006) *The Last Man Who Knew Everything: Thomas Young, the Anonymous Polymath Who Proved Newton Wrong, Explained How We See, Cured the Sick and Deciphered the Rosetta Stone, Among Other Feats of Genius*. New York: Pi Press.

Schools Council (1968) *Young School Leavers*. London: HMSO.

Smith, P. H. (2012) 'Science', in U. Rublack (ed.), *A Concise Companion to History*. Oxford: Oxford University Press, pp. 268–97.

White, J. (1973) *Towards a Compulsory Curriculum*. London: Routledge & Kegan Paul.

White, J. (1988) 'An unconstitutional National Curriculum', in D. Lawton and C. Chitty (eds), *The National Curriculum*. London: Institute of Education, pp. 113–22.

White, J. (2000) 'Should mathematics be compulsory for all until the age of 16?', in S. Bramall and J. White (eds), *Why Learn Maths?* London: Institute of Education, pp. 71–84.

White, J. (2011) *The Invention of the Secondary Curriculum*. New York: Palgrave Macmillan.

Whitehead, A. N. (1949) *The Aims of Education and Other Essays*. London: Ernest Benn.

Wiborg, S. (2010) 'Why is there no comprehensive education in Germany? A historical explanation', *History of Education*, 39: 539–56.

Chapter 3

The curriculum and subject knowledge

Michael J. Reiss

Before I came to the IOE in January 2001, I knew only the members of the science education team and, by reputation, a handful of other academics, including Peter Aggleton, Gunther Kress, John White and Geoff Whitty. For many years John and I hardly spoke to one another (the IOE is a large place and we are in different departments) and then back in 2009 for some reason we had lunch together. Considering that one of us is a leading philosopher of education and an active member of the British Humanist Association and the other a science educator and a priest in the Church of England we got on extremely well. We found ourselves in agreement that atheism should be taught properly in schools and immediately wrote a short piece together (Reiss and White 2009). That might have been the extent of our collaboration but two and a half years later John e-mailed me:

> ... I don't know if you would be interested in co-authoring a piece of around 20–25K words, perhaps to be submitted to IOE for possible publication, on <The Aims-based Curriculum>? I've written a lot of it already, around 15K, but it is still unpolished stuff, and needs much more doing to it. I'm particularly incapable on matters to do with science and mathematics and would welcome your help on this. But the whole thing would benefit by co-writing, so as to make the argument less subjective and give it more weight ...
>
> (E-mail to M. Reiss, 21 December 2011)

I responded enthusiastically and the result was Reiss and White (2013). I consider myself extremely fortunate. Not only have I enjoyed and learnt a great deal from our co-authorship, but it has helped push me into broader issues than those on which I usually write, which is good for me.

Towards a compulsory curriculum

John's first book, *Towards a Compulsory Curriculum*, was published in 1973 (White 1973). In it he advanced a number of arguments that he then developed over the next forty years. I'll explore some of the developments of the major themes in his writings below but in this book, which preceded the National Curriculum in England and Wales by some 16 years, there is a central presumption – the point is hardly argued – that education must be for the benefit of individual learners and take them as its starting point:

> It is at this point that notions of a 'child-centred' education and an 'integrated' education meet: the child must be at the centre of all he learns; education cannot be 'subject-centred' in this sense.
>
> (White 1973: 51)

This presumption, which seems to me entirely correct, of the fundamental requirement for education to be child-centred in the true sense of the term (by true, I mean that child-centredness does not, for instance, entirely equate with acceding all control of children's education to them – something that would be as wise as allowing children repeatedly to hit younger siblings, should they so wish) leads to a number of related points being made. These points are of particular significance when constructing a compulsory curriculum, and yet have been consistently overlooked since England introduced a compulsory (national) curriculum. First, adopting a Millian perspective, White argues: 'It would be right to constrain a child to learn such and such only if (a) he is likely to be harmed if he does not do so, or (b) other people are likely to be harmed' (White 1973: 6). Secondly, and relatedly: 'It follows from the insistence on the principles of liberty in this essay that the presumption is that the pupil should be obliged to study as little as possible' (White 1973: 67). This latter point allows John to espouse a curriculum in which a high proportion of the curriculum is voluntary, and his interest in matters Russian (Crace 2006) shows in his enthusiasm for the Young Pioneer movement in eastern Europe where compulsory education takes place in the morning with children 'left free in the afternoon to join, if they want to, the various Pioneer "circles" or groups, organized either on the school premises or in Pioneer Houses and Palaces serving several schools' (White 1973: 70).

Education is also, of course, about far more than the acquisition of knowledge about particular subjects. One point stressed in *Towards a Compulsory Curriculum*, in addition to the issue of how one integrates knowledge across subjects, is that pupils 'should finish their education with an understanding of the many different ways of life which they and others may pursue' (White 1973: 43–4). Admitting that there is 'something unsatisfactory about laying down a list of the guiding principles embodied in ways of life' (p. 44), John goes on to present 'the following list as a rough attempt to outline some of these differences':

1 A way of life devoted to the pursuit of truth, in science, history, etc.
2 A way of life devoted to artistic creativity.
3 A way of life devoted to others' good: the altruistic way of life.
4 A way of life devoted to physical prowess or adventure.

5 A way of life devoted to physical pleasures more broadly understood, including those of food, drink and sex.
6 A religious way of life, premised on the belief that this life is only a preparation for an after-life.
7 A life devoted to the acquisition of goods.
8 A life devoted to the acquisition of power over others.
9 A way of life devoted to reflection on how one should live.
10 A way of life devoted to domesticity.
11 A way of life devoted to public affairs.
12 The ascetic way of life.
13 A way of life based on a Thoreauesque return to nature.
14 A way of life based on one's surrendering to someone else the decisions about what sort of life one should lead.

(White 1973: 44)

Now, it might be held that such a list is fraught with potential problems. I am unaware, for example, of any religion that holds that this life is only a preparation for an afterlife. More generally, are these ways of life mutually exclusive? (No, though there are limits to the number of one's devotions and bases.) Is there an implied hierarchy among them? (To some extent; for instance, 11 can be construed as a subset of 3. In any event, some are clearly easier to defend than others.) Is there an overarching moral framework in the background of this analysis? (Yes; by and large, one's life is better if one examines it on occasion, while lives differ in their effects on others.) The point that is being made here is surely a convincing one: too often, formal education fails to enable learners to reflect on why they do what they do or to consider who they want to be. Some such reflection and consideration, of course, can be achieved by each of us through our own efforts, helped by the influences of family and friends. But schools have a particular role to play here, a role that they too often abdicate.

A further argument advanced in *Towards a Compulsory Curriculum*, in a way that goes beyond the 'forms of knowledge' of Hirst (1965) and others, is that not all school subjects are of equal worth. This argument connects with the above question of whether all ways of life are of equal worth. In contradistinction to the assumptions of recent UK governments – motivated primarily by a naive set of beliefs about the importance of home-grown science, technology, engineering and mathematics talent for economic growth – John argues that 'The humanities have a more central role in the curriculum than the natural sciences ... because they alone enable one to weave together a human life' (White 1973: 63). In a way I find personally chastening, given that from the age of 14 at my secondary school I studied only physics, chemistry and mathematics, the point is pushed home forcefully:

> Suppose we take two secondary-age pupils who, after a broad primary education, specialize for a few years, one in physics, chemistry and mathematics,

> the other in literature, history and, later, philosophy. Suppose, too, that they never study anything except their specialisms. The humanist would be inadequately educated. He could well have a good appreciation of the larger bearings of life – of a variety of different ways of life open to him, of the moral considerations in these choices, of the need to integrate his life into a meaningful whole; he would also have some understanding of some particular activities he could pursue for intrinsic or extrinsic reasons; but he would lack an understanding of mathematics and physics and other activities dependent on these, and to this extent his options would be limited. But the scientist would not even be inadequately educated: he could scarcely be said to be educated at all. He would be a man without any general orientation to his life, apart from what he might pick up unreflectingly from his environment – at best, a specialist of genius but trapped within his discipline; at worst, a sophisticated serf.
>
> (White 1973: 63)

It would be relatively easy to critique this argument. Are not all of us trapped within our disciplines? Is it really the case that generations of students who have specialised in the sciences at secondary school can 'scarcely be said to be educated at all'? After all, in his famous Rede lecture, based on a sample size of some thirty to forty thousand interviews, C. P. Snow painted a picture of such individuals as far more likely to try to acquaint themselves with music and literature that their arts- and humanities-based equivalents were to try to acquaint themselves with mathematics and science. As Snow concluded, speaking of these non-scientists: 'But what about the other side? They are impoverished too – perhaps more seriously, because they are vainer about it' (Snow 1959). I am inclined to be generous to John in his use of the above argument. Feyerabend has always been my favourite philosopher of science, not least because of his intentional use of hyperbole as a powerful communications device.

The aims of the curriculum

As indicated above, the central premise that education should serve to benefit each learner was present in John's first published book. Fuller treatments as to the aims of education followed, including a 1996 booklet titled *The Aims of School Education*, published by the Institute for Public Policy Research (White 1996). In its 14 pages, possible national aims for the school curriculum are advanced and suggestions are made as to how the journey from aims to curriculum might be traversed.

A further development of what a school curriculum might look like if one were to begin with aims rather than subjects is presented in some of John's most recent writing, notably *An Aims-based Curriculum* (Reiss and White 2013). Here the argument begins with the premise that the aim of the school curriculum is twofold: to enable each learner to lead a life that is personally flourishing; and to help others to do so, too. (Reasons for this fundamental premise are explored in the section below on 'Well-being'.) Granted this assumption, a central aim of a school should therefore be to prepare students for a life of autonomous, whole-hearted and successful engagement in worthwhile relationships, activities and experiences. With many of these – cooperative work activity, friendships and enjoying literature, for instance – it makes good sense to see that students gain first-hand experience. For others – things like mountaineering, composing symphonies, choosing to live an unmarried life, running a multinational company – imagined rather than direct involvement is likely to be more appropriate, for a range of self-evident reasons. This aim also involves acquainting students with a wide range of possible options from which to choose. With their development towards autonomous adulthood in mind, schools should provide students with increasing opportunities to decide between the pursuits that best suit them. Young children are likely to need greater guidance from their teachers, just as they do from their parents. Part of the function of schooling, and indeed parenting, is to prepare children for the time when they will need to, and be able to, make decisions more independently.

We want children to want other people, as well as themselves, to lead fulfilling lives. Negatively, this means not hurting them, not lying to them, not breaking one's word or in other ways impeding them in this. Positively, it means helping them to reach their goals, respecting their autonomy and being fair, friendly and cooperative in one's dealings with them. Schools can reinforce and extend what parents and others in families do in developing morality in children. Schools can widen students' moral sensitivity beyond the domestic circle to those in other communities, locally, nationally and globally. They can also help them to think about moral conflicts in their own lives and in the wider spheres just mentioned. They can encourage students to reflect on the basis of morality, including whether this is religious or non-religious.

As part of their moral education, schools should help students to become informed and active citizens of a liberal democratic society. Dispositionally, this means encouraging them to take an interest in political affairs at local, national and global levels from the standpoint of a concern for the general good, and to do this with due regard to the values of a liberal democracy such as freedom, individual autonomy, equal consideration and cooperation. Young people also need to possess whatever sorts of understanding these dispositions entail, for example an understanding of the nature of liberal democracy in general, of divergences of opinion about it, and of its application to the circumstances of their own society.

As future citizens, the great majority of students will contribute to the general well-being, as well as to their own, through work. This will often be remunerated, though much of it, e.g. caring for children or elderly relatives, may not be. As autonomous beings, students will eventually have to make choices about what kind of work to engage in. Schools should be helping them in this by making them aware of a wide range of vocational possibilities and routes into them, as well as their advantages and disadvantages. This is a particularly important function of schools as this is something that few parents can provide for their children.

The rest of Reiss and White (2013) builds on this argument. In some places the conclusions may be considered somewhat radical; in others they seem quite conventional. For example, we conclude that, in the UK, school children should acquire some understanding of:

- the change from an agrarian to an industrial society, based first on steam and then on other sources of power;
- the rise and fall of the British Empire;
- the increase in population and rise of urbanisation;
- the change from monarchical/aristocratic to democratic government and the rise of liberalism;
- changes in the occupational and class structures and their reflection in political changes;
- changes in social welfare provision;
- international conflict and moves towards cooperation in Europe and globally;
- USA superpower status and the recent rise of newly powerful and rapidly developing economies;
- divisions between rich and poor countries;
- the spread of democratisation and challenges to this;
- the depletion of resources and issues of sustainability.

(Reiss and White 2013: 32)

This is not a very startling list of suggestions. However, it follows from first principles (the two fundamental aims of education) rather than simply deriving from existing history and citizenship curricula. Whether the conclusions are seen as far reaching or straightforward, the intention behind *An Aims-based Curriculum* is to provide a framework for the development of a coherent set of aims for the curriculum, some for implementation at national level, others at the level of each school.

Mathematics

In virtually all countries, two subjects enjoy especially privileged status in the school curriculum: the national language and mathematics. Few would argue against the high status accorded to a country's national language, but why is mathematics held in such universally high regard? In *Why Learn Mathematics?*, Steve Bramall and John White, along with the authors in this edited volume, attempt to answer this question. As one might expect, given John's earlier characterisation of the worth of an education with too great a focus on mathematics and the physical sciences, the editors do not pull their punches. However, again typically of John, balance is provided, with almost half the authors being mathematics educators, teachers or, in one case, an advanced level student then applying to universities to read a mathematics-related subject.

John's own position is most fully worked out in his own chapter in Bramall and White (2000). He asks whether the study of mathematics should be compulsory for all in schools until the age of 16 (at the time the school-leaving age). He begins by noting that parents, governors and employers all see mathematics and English as the two most important subjects in the curriculum. He goes on to identify two main groups of arguments for the study of school mathematics: one instrumental (i.e. the harnessing of mathematics to the demands of everyday life and the economy), the other non-instrumental (e.g. mathematics as intrinsically interesting).

John begins with the non-instrumental arguments and quotes Fred Clarke, a former director of the IOE, who wrote that 'the ultimate reason for teaching long division to little Jonny is that he is an immortal soul' (Clarke 1923: 2). However, John argues:

> Few of us living in a more secular age could go along with the religious assumptions in this. Yet many more of us are insensibly influenced by other aspects of the Platonic-Cartesian theory. Especially the notion that mathematical thinking is in some way superior to other forms of thinking – both academic forms like those of the historian or literary critic, and the practical reasoning on which we rely day-to-day in the planning of our personal and institutional lives.
>
> (White 2000: 72)

In the *Republic* the philosopher kings study mathematics for ten years to help equip them for their role. John, though, concludes that 'It is a myth, then, that if we want to develop young people's minds, one of the best ways of doing this is to give them a rigorous training in mathematics' (p. 73). (In passing, we can note that comparable arguments are sometimes offered for the teaching of certain other subjects including Latin and philosophy, and even chess.) Learning mathematics makes you better at mathematics and subjects that use mathematics, such as physics and economics, but there is no evidence that it makes you better at anything else. John is also unenthusiastic about the possibility that learning mathematics gives one, except in its role as a handmaiden to science, a key to understanding the fundamental realities of the universe.

John then turns to more successful non-instrumental reasons for studying mathematics and identifies three: the intrinsic delight in mathematical thinking that 'many' (John is generous here) have experienced in proving, for example, that the square root of 2 is irrational; the necessary role of mathematics within science, taken as intrinsically interesting apart from its technology implications; the place of mathematics as an achievement of human culture. However, these three reasons, even if granted, do not show that mathematics must be taught right up to the age at which one can leave school. John concludes:

> These considerations point towards a compulsory taster course in mathematics after the age of 11 rather than a compulsory five-year course. This would

> enable those who don't already have an inclination for it to see if one develops. If they find no hint of joy in it despite the taster course, it would be sensible to let them drop it. After all, there are plenty of alternatives among which they might find something more appealing. Beyond the taster courses, there would be voluntary courses, perhaps within some constrained option system, for those who like the subject. If teaching on the taster course has been sufficiently inspiring, one may expect many, perhaps most children to want to take the subject further, but it would be unrealistic to expect everyone to do so.
>
> (White 2000: 76)

Discussion then turns to the instrumental reasons. Three potentially sound ones are identified:

> 1 It is a commonplace that we all need some understanding of simple arithmetic to manage our personal finances, measure areas around the house, etc. How much we need, especially in the age of the calculator, is a further question. Even before calculators came on the scene, most adults had little cause to tap into their knowledge of long division or long multiplication or square roots.
> 2 We also need some mathematics from a civic point of view. We have to be able to think in terms of millions and billions in order to grasp anything of national housekeeping; we need to understand graphical and other representations of quantitative data on policy matters such as are found in the media; we need some insight into how such statistics can be misleadingly presented.
> 3 Mathematics is a *sine qua non* of very many jobs.
>
> (White 2000: 79)

With reference to these instrumental reasons, John again concludes that they do not furnish a good argument for compulsory mathematics up to age 16. Perhaps somewhat optimistically, he holds that the mathematics needed in respect of argument 1 should mostly be attained by the end of primary school. The mathematics to satisfy the requirements of argument 2 should be provided by a short, focused compulsory course at secondary level, preferably tied in with courses in education for citizenship. With respect to argument 3, 'Rather than thinking of pre-equipping students for vocational possibilities, we should ensure that they can take up voluntary courses in requisite subjects once their vocational preferences are clear' (p. 80).

Well-being

As we have seen, John has always put the interest of the learner at the heart of his curriculum philosophy. These ideas are brought together in the recent *Exploring Well-being in Schools* (White 2011a), where well-being is taken as being synonymous with fulfilment and flourishing. The book begins by looking at the recent upsurge of interest in well-being and then goes on to examine what precisely well-being entails. Here, the considerable diversity of possible answers is noted. For a start, there is the fundamental though rarely asked question of whether this life is all there is or whether there is also a life to come. The answer proposed – the correct one it seems to me – is that children 'should be encouraged to make up their own minds about the possibility of life after death' (p. 18). After a section on religious conceptions of well-being, we are taken through accounts of utilitarianism followed by needs satisfaction, the attainment of positional goods (such as fame and large amounts of money) and desire satisfaction. As an illustration of how enjoyable it can be to read John's writing, here is his exemplification of Mill's as opposed to Bentham's version of utilitarianism: 'If you think sipping a pina colada on a balcony in Tobago is what it is all about, you are plain wrong. You would do better going inside, opening up your laptop and starting your next critical article on Flaubert' (p. 21).

John concludes that:

> A flourishing life is one filled with successful and whole-hearted engagement in worthwhile activities and relationships. It has to be, on the whole, *successful*, since repeated failure in our projects and liaisons clearly detracts from our well-being. It has to be *whole-hearted* because, again, it is hard to see how dragging ourselves through even the most valuable pursuits in a tired, listless, merely dutiful or uncommitted way can make our life go well. What counts as *worthwhile* is partly dependent on our biology: we would not prize sexual intimacy if we reproduced, amoeba-like, by fission. But it is mainly a cultural matter ...
>
> Several misconceptions need defusing. A flourishing life is not to be identified with a pleasurable one, or with a life in which one succeeds in satisfying one's major informed desires. This casts doubt on links often made between well-being and wealth, celebrity or positional goods. Secondly, in order to flourish, we do not need to have our own flourishing as a goal.
>
> (pp. 113–14)

It is worth emphasising that John sees schooling as a natural extension of parenting. He presents a fictional account of a young girl called Willow, that begins with her envelopment in close, loving relationships as soon as she is born. Progressing through her parents' delight at her participation in early games such as peek-a-boo, she develops to the point where:

> Parents and carers help her to make sense of the world around her. They encourage her delight at frogs, furry caterpillars and other joys of the natural world. They play imaginative games with her, develop her nascent sense of humour. And all the time they are shaping the kind of person she is, getting her to be self-confident, self-reliant, patient and helpful to other people. They let her know that she cannot always get her way, keep her from too

> much inappropriate food or drink and do not make a fuss over little knocks and falls.
>
> (pp. 124–5)

Home and school alike are seen as helping children to live abundantly and helping others to do so too. Unsurprisingly, there is a call for less of a gap between teachers and parents, for class sizes to be smaller and for the development of dispositions to be given more weight in schools: 'The starting point is that she should have the positive qualities needed for a flourishing life. We would not want her to become brilliant at algebra and Latin, but also cripplingly anxious, or cynical, or a sadist' (p. 131).

Curriculum history

The year 2011 was particularly productive for John. In addition to the publication of *Exploring Well-being in Schools* (White 2011a), *The Invention of the Secondary Curriculum* (White 2011b) appeared. Many would not think of John as an academic historian but he has a history degree and *The Invention of the Secondary Curriculum* was awarded second prize by the Society for Educational Studies for the best book on education published that year. It provides a compelling narrative, attempting to explain how we have ended up with the curriculum we have in Britain and many other countries.

The origins of today's school curricula are seen in the second half of the sixteenth century when Petrus Ramus (aka Pierre de la Ramée) successfully argued that material to be taught in schools and universities should be universally true (thus excluding epistemologically dubious material as well as material requiring an aesthetic response), grouped together so as to avoid overlaps between subjects and presented from the most general definition through increasing levels of specificity. John admits that historical causation is complex but argues that Ramus' influence persists to this day. Ramus was also a great believer in hard work – his personal motto was *Labor omnia vincit* – and textbooks.

Ramus and his immediate successors did not have everything their own way with their anti-scholastic philosophy but they did have some major early successes, notably in Scotland where first Glasgow University and then the universities of St Andrews and Aberdeen and the town college of Edinburgh reordered their curriculum along the lines they proposed. For example, in 1641 King's College, Aberdeen had a year 1 curriculum that consisted mainly of Greek and Hebrew, a year 2 one of logic, rhetoric and mathematics, a year 3 one of ethics, politics and economics and a year 4 one of natural philosophy, which included astronomy, geography, optics and music.

A whole cast of influences led to further developments in the curricula of both schools and universities over the next two centuries. Of particular importance in England was the foundation of London University, later University College London (UCL), in 1826. London University was originally conceived as a

Dissenting University, given the exclusion, until the 1870s, of English dissenters from Oxford and Cambridge. Unlike Oxford and Cambridge, the new university's four-year general course was lecture-based and had considerable similarities with the Scottish curricula that had arisen two centuries earlier. Latin, Greek and mathematics were covered in years 1 and 2, logic, philosophy of mind, chemistry and natural philosophy in year 3, and jurisprudence, political economy, natural philosophy, moral philosophy and political philosophy in year 4.

London University's curricular pattern soon began to spread to younger age groups. In 1838 the London matriculation exam was introduced as a precondition of taking a London degree. The subjects were mathematics, natural philosophy, chemistry, Greek, Latin, English language, history, geography and natural history. This examination was soon used for other institutions such as Owens College, Manchester and other colleges with dissenting connections. Soon too it was being used not only for potential university entrants but more broadly.

By the end of the nineteenth century what can be termed a comprehensive curriculum based on a range of discrete subjects was becoming widely established in British secondary schools. Such a school curriculum also featured in an increasing number of other countries, particularly those where Protestantism was strong or where colonial links to such countries were close. A subject-based curriculum remained at the heart of the grammar school system that flourished after the 1945 introduction of the tripartite system of secondary education and such an arrangement was buttressed by the academic arguments about the nature of knowledge of Phenix (1964), Peters (1966) and, above all, Hirst (1965).

Furthermore, for all that the twentieth century showed great changes in school organisation and certain aspects of pedagogy (including the use of IT), remarkably few changes happened with regard to the curriculum. John had already pointed out (White 1990: 14) that Hitler or Stalin would not have objected to the solitary statement in England's 1988 National Curriculum as to its purpose, namely that it must be a balanced and broadly-based curriculum that: (a) promotes the spiritual, moral, cultural, mental and physical development of pupils at the school and of society; (b) prepares such pupils for the opportunities, responsibilities and experiences of adult life. Furthermore:

> ... speaking of Stalin, it is instructive to see what kind of national curriculum *he* had. Leaving out tiny inputs on the USSR Constitution, astronomy and psychology, it consisted of: language and literature, mathematics, history, geography, the sciences of biology, physics and chemistry, a foreign language, physical education, drawing, singing and practical work in agriculture or industry. The list is almost identical to Mr Baker's ten foundation subjects. Not only that, three of Stalin's items were classified as 'important subjects' – language, mathematics and science. Today we call these 'core subjects'. Detailed syllabuses for every subject mentioned, covering the ten years of compulsory education, were laid down rigidly from the centre.
>
> (Ibid.)

It might be argued that the considerable similarities between curricula worldwide – because these extend beyond England and the former USSR – suggest there is a validity in such collections of subjects. I think John's response would be that such aggregations are in large measure the result of an uncritical acceptance of historical legacies and that this is holding back schools from providing the better education that they could.

Conclusion

In his writings, John has consistently advocated that the curriculum be designed and implemented for the needs of learners. Indeed, the volume of his selected writings in the prestigious World Library of Educationalists series is titled *The Curriculum and the Child* (White 2005). Of course, there is more to education than the curriculum, but by maintaining a consistent approach to the question of why we have the curricula we have and how they might be better constructed, John has bought a conceptual rigour to curriculum studies, proceeding analytically but also engaging with normative issues, while writing in a way that connects with policy-makers and teachers too. I'll end with the paragraph with which he began his Introduction to *The Curriculum and the Child*:

> It must have been the lack of coherence in my own schooling that first prompted me to think about the aims of education. What were all those bits and pieces of learning supposed to be about? Those four languages and their grammars. The courting habits of the earthworm. The Second Crusade. Attempting and failing to jump over the buck. That sixth form essay for the headmaster on 'Eating Onions' (his choice of title) …

References

Bramall, S. and White, J. (eds) (2000) *Why Learn Maths?* London: Institute of Education, University of London.

Clarke, F. (1923) *Essays in the Politics of Education*. Oxford: Oxford University Press.

Crace, J. (2006) 'John White: what's the point of being bright as a button?', *Guardian*, 28 February. Available at: http://www.theguardian.com/education/2006/feb/28/academicexperts.highereducationprofile (accessed 4 January 2014).

Hirst, P. H. (1965) 'Liberal education and the nature of knowledge', in R. E. D. Archambault (ed.), *Philosophical Analysis and Education*. London: Routledge & Kegan Paul, pp. 113–38.

Peters, R. S. (1966) *Ethics and Education*. London: Allen & Unwin.

Phenix, P. H. (1964) *Realms of Meaning*. New York: McGraw-Hill.

Reiss, M. and White, J. (2009) 'Atheism needs to be studied in schools', *The Independent*, Education, 16 July, p. 4.

Reiss, M. and White, J. (2013) *An Aims-based Curriculum: The Significance of Human Flourishing for Schools*. London: IOE Press.

Snow, C. P. (1959) *The Rede Lecture*. Cambridge: Cambridge University Press. Available at: http://s-f-walker.org.uk/pubsebooks/2cultures/Rede-lecture-2-cultures.pdf (accessed 10 January 2014).

White, J. (1973) *Towards a Compulsory Curriculum*. London: Routledge & Kegan Paul.

White, J. (1990) *Education and the Good Life*. London: Kegan Paul.

White, J. (1996) *The Aims of School Education*. London: Institute for Public Policy Research.

White, J. (2000) 'Should mathematics be compulsory for all until the age of 16?', in S. Bramall and J. White (eds), *Why Learn Maths?* London: Institute of Education, University of London, pp. 71–84.

White, J. (2005) *The Curriculum and the Child: The Selected Works of John White*. London: Routledge.

White, J. (2011a) *Exploring Well-being in Schools: A Guide to Making Children's Lives More Fulfilling*. London: Routledge.

White, J. (2011b) *The Invention of the Secondary Curriculum*. New York: Palgrave Macmillan.

Chapter 4

Is good school leadership 'visionary'?

Janet Orchard

Attempts to capture the distinguishing qualities of very good schools and their leaders in terms of 'vision' and being 'visionary' are relatively common. For example, an advertisement for a head teacher's position might specify that the successful candidate will be 'creative and visionary' or have 'the ability to inspire through vision and leadership' (TES 2013). A leadership training provider might boast the opportunity to 'establish your vision and non-negotiables for school leadership' (SSAT 2012) on its courses. The Office for Standards in Education in England (Ofsted 2012b) identifies 'communicating the vision' as a key activity that is undertaken by leaders who are 'effective'.

Beyond signalling that it is a necessary aspect of high-quality leadership though, it is not clear exactly what having a 'vision' or being 'visionary' in each of these cases might mean. Nor is it agreed consistently that 'vision' is indeed necessary. When the National Standards for Headteachers in England (DfES 2004) were first published, they identified 'vision' as 'critical' to headship, suggesting that the head teacher's 'core function' is to provide 'vision, leadership and direction for the school and ensure that it is managed and organised to meet its aims and targets' (p. 3).[1] References made to 'vision' in the *Ofsted Inspection Framework for Schools in England* have come (Ofsted 2003) and gone (Ofsted 2009) and been reinstated again (Ofsted 2012). Inspectors consider the extent to which leaders and managers 'demonstrate an ambitious vision for the school and high expectations of all pupils and teachers' (p. 19).

The Pay and Conditions Document for Teachers in England and Wales, the basis on which contracts of employment for head teachers in maintained schools are determined, used to make no mention of 'vision' whatsoever (e.g. DCSF 2009). However, more recently the 'Professional responsibilities' identified for head teachers have included – within a section on 'Whole school organisation, strategy and development' – the stipulation (47.2) that they may be required to provide overall strategic leadership and, with others, lead, develop and support the school's strategic direction, vision, values and priorities (DfE 2013: 48).

This chapter considers three possible interpretations of 'vision', arguing that the association made between 'vision' and good leadership in ordinary language derives originally from the Book of Proverbs, from which at least three interpretations of 'vision' relevant to the context of leadership and schooling have passed into common usage. 'Vision' may be used to describe a privileged form of perception or mental seeing. Alternatively, 'vision' may be used to describe a capacity to think creatively in the sense in which John White explores the imagination in his book *The Child's Mind* (2002). 'Vision' may also be used to describe an ideal future state.

Once these possible conceptions of 'vision' are elucidated, it proves much easier to distinguish between helpful and unhelpful uses of the term related to the practice of leadership in education. Where it is conceived as a form of knowing characteristic of good leadership, it proves more helpful to interpret 'vision' as a form of imaginative perception that many people might cultivate rather than as an intuitive capacity to know the future good that is exclusive to certain, privileged individuals. Indeed, this latter interpretation should not be encouraged in schools located in democratic societies, where commitment to the principles of political liberty and equality entitle ordinary citizens to determine such matters for themselves; at a strategic level, if not in detail, as John White (1982) has long argued.

A clear sense of future direction and purpose may well be significant to the strategic development of a particular school. However, 'vision' in this sense need not originate consistently and predictably in the mind of a single individual leader. In this light, and with the rights and responsibilities of the democratic way of life in mind, the notion of 'shared vision', as an overlapping consensus of an ideal future state, reached through a process of fair and open deliberation, seems preferable.

There may be personal qualities that set very good school leaders apart, including interpretation and the ability to exercise sound professional judgment. In principle, these might legitimately be described in terms of 'vision', as 'vision' interpreted along these lines has been attributed to good leadership before in Judaeo-Christian tradition. Moreover, 'vision' in this sense lacks the connotations of personal aura and charisma which the term can attract and which prove problematic in democratic terms. Despite this potential, 'vision' in this sense has not yet been appropriated by Educational Leadership Management and Administration (ELMA) literature.

With so many interpretations of 'vision' possible, there is considerable scope for confusion, hence good reason why the discourse of 'vision' in this context should be examined critically. Given the biblical origins of the metaphor, the chapter begins by appropriating biblical hermeneutics to interrogate the meaning of 'vision'. Treated with care, the notion sheds light on qualities that may well promote improvement in schools. Concern with 'vision' highlights not only the need for imaginative and creative thinking when decisions are to be made, but also ambiguity, which can allow an unhelpful and undesirable account of autocratic school leadership to be promoted, so that an alternative and/or analogy to 'vision' may ultimately prove preferable.

The biblical origins of 'vision'

Where references are made to 'vision' in professional development literature that is aimed at school leaders, the phrase 'without vision, a people perish', is commonly alluded to. For example, in a Leading Edge Seminar for the National College for School Leadership in England, creative thinker in education Robert Fisher (2002) described it as one of several 'statements' that have come to influence his view of leadership. The origins of the phrase are biblical, to be found in Proverbs 29: 18, although if Fisher is aware of this – and it is not clear that he is – he plays down the association. Respected leadership writer, facilitator and consultant Professor John West-Burnham does acknowledge vision's provenance in the Christian Bible overtly. West-Burnham describes 'where there is no vision, the people perish' as an orthodoxy of modern theories of leadership and organisational effectiveness (http://www.is-toolkit.com/knowledge_library/kl_files/WhyVision_JohnWestBurnham.pdf (accessed 25 February 2014)). Vision, he goes on to suggest, is fundamental to effective leadership and forms of organisational activity.

The trap into which both Fisher and West-Burnham appear to fall is to assume that the meaning of 'without vision, a people perish' is self-evident, when it is not. It is a popular 'common-sense' saying, assimilated from scripture into spoken English at a time when familiarity with biblical imagery was relatively commonplace, and the phrase does have a deceptively authoritative air of wisdom about it. West-Burnham goes on to suggest that 'vision' provides a focus for all aspects of organisational life which characterises the organisation to others. Yet this observation fails to capture with any clarity what a 'vision' is, what the proverb is saying about 'vision' and what this might have to say to us which illuminates the nature of very good leadership. The significance of this omission is compounded by not one, but three possible interpretations of the passage, as revealed by the following brief exegesis.

'Vision' as a non-natural experience

The Book of Proverbs was written originally in Hebrew for a community of Messianic Jews. They believed literally that they were living in the last days, interpreting the radical social and political changes around them as signs that the 'eschaton' was imminent (Anderson 1978). Given the extraordinary nature of the times, it is perhaps not surprising to learn that this community believed there were prophets living among them. It is to this literal, overwhelmingly powerful, direct revelation of the word of God to which the Hebrew word 'hazon' refers.

> Hazon means a prophetic vision or oracle, in which the will and purpose of Yahweh are made known: it is given to the people. The reference is either to oracles of the prophets, or more probably, to the utterances of the sages, for which the same divine inspiration and authority is claimed.
>
> (Scott 1985: n18a)

Moreover, the 'people' to whom the 'vision' is given do not include humanity at large but God's chosen people, Israel. From the Hebrew, then, Proverbs 29: 18 translates 'without prophecy, the people of God will perish'. An interpretation of 'vision' along these lines is still widely understood among speakers of English. It may be defined as 'a supernatural or prophetic apparition' (*Oxford English Dictionary*), even if many people may doubt whether such experiences happen.

'Vision' as imaginative perception

The form of Proverbs 29: 18 used by Fisher comes from the Authorised Version. Like other modern translations, this draws on the Vulgate compiled by St Jerome in the fourth century so comes from Hebrew through Latin into English. The context in which the Vulgate was translated has an impact on the text too; the early Christian community for whom this text was prepared believed that the age of prophecy in its literal sense had ended. The Messiah had come in the person of Jesus, who had lived on Earth and died on the cross for the sins of the world. With his resurrection, they believed, came new hope; the fear of annihilation was over.

The notion of a 'vision' seen through this lens develops a figurative meaning, grounded in the expectation of a long and stable future: without *imaginative perception*, the people will never flourish (Scott 1985). Christianity in the fourth century had been adopted as the official religion of the Holy Roman Empire. The 'people' for whom the message was intended were no longer a small, specific and marginalised group of political and religious radicals but humanity as a whole, implying truth common to all people.

Modern English picks up on this interpretation of 'vision' too. The *Oxford English Dictionary* defines 'vision' as 'a thing or idea perceived vividly in the imagination'. Is this what West-Burnham understands the meaning of 'vision' to be, the quality which exercises such a positive influence on organisations, including schools?

'Vision' as interpretation

There is a third possible interpretation of the Proverbs 29: 18 text. The Septuagint translated the Hebrew Bible into Greek for Jews dispersed by Roman occupation (Anderson 1978) during the last century before the Common Era. This community no longer expected the literal prospect of prophecy among them either but were closer in time and culture to its possibility. The translation of the passage deliberately steers clear of any association with prophecy so that 'hazon' becomes translated as 'interpretation' or 'exegesis'.[2]

The emphasis on interpretation arises from the concern of a scattered community to retain a distinctive cultural and religious identity. The Law, or Torah, is what holds the Jewish people together. Proverbs 29: 18 translates into English from the Septuagint to mean: 'Where there is no interpretation, a nation acts contrary to the law'. Without accurate and consistent interpretation of the law, including its enforcement, by those in authority, the nation of Israel will fall apart.

There are possible connections between this interpretation of 'vision' and its use in modern English but these are more strained. The *Oxford English Dictionary* states that 'vision' can be used to describe a quality of 'statesmanlike foresight' or 'sagacity in planning' that may or may not connect with this reading of the text. 'Foresight', for example, could be linked just as easily with the notion of imaginative perception.

Without 'vision', would schools perish?

The ability to develop a distinctive 'vision' is widely regarded as a 'hallmark' of successful leadership. Yet as Bush and Glover acknowledge the term is 'highly problematic'(2003). 'Vision' is an important if complex idea that can be used to shed light on the nature of good school leadership, they suggest (Bush and Glover 2003) without demonstrating with sufficient clarity how 'vision' ought to be interpreted in this context. 'Vision' may well allude to something of genuine importance to leadership but without greater clarity of meaning its value must be qualified. Of particular concern, however, is that 'vision' is used without qualification to promote as best practice an overly directive approach to leadership in schools. Examples are taken next from policy and practice to illustrate how the three possible interpretations of 'vision' that have been identified may be used to distinguish conceptions that are consistent with democratic values from those that are more problematic.

'Vision' as a non-natural experience?

It seems far-fetched to connect 'vision', understood as 'a supernatural or prophetic apparition', with the more earthly and grounded professional knowledge required of good school leaders. Can this really be what researchers in the ELMA field have in mind when stressing the significance of 'vision' to best practice? Visual metaphors are used regularly in English to define non-natural sense experiences of various kinds, including 'enlightenment', 'illumination'. These words describe a form of internal 'seeing' leading to a feeling of deep comprehension which might happen in an intense burst as 'a flash of inspiration', or gradually as the 'light dawns' over time.

Richard Peters (1966) likens the experience to some kind of 'inner flash', an intuitive feeling of inner certainty that leads to an unusual degree of prescience about the future. Is this what a 'vision' should be taken to mean? Do the very best leaders 'know' the best possible future for the school they lead, if not literally in a dream, certainly independently and without consultation?

The appeal of this account to someone with a particular view of leadership, either as a leader or follower, is not difficult to understand. However, of all the possible interpretations of 'vision' discussed in this chapter, it is the least democratic.

The feeling of growing confidence and certainty a leader might experience when 'the penny drops' or the 'light dawns' needs to be held in check. A head teacher who claimed on the basis of intuition to know something about education would be confusing belief with fact.

Senge (1992) is right in one sense to associate the power of a 'vision' with the response that bright ideas generate rather than the idea itself. The National Standards for Headteachers in England (DfES 2004) suggest that a good leader is able to communicate 'vision' in a compelling fashion to 'inspire' and 'challenge'. Yet inspiration is a personal and subjective matter. A 'visionary' insight to one person might seem abhorrent to another.

Furthermore, in a democracy ordinary citizens hold differing conceptions of the good life. Where their values and preferences are founded on an intuitive sense of what is right or good, these cannot be challenged or verified by rational means. Reason offers a practical basis against which competing values can be assessed and decisions made. Reason cannot reconcile every disagreement in a pluralist society but it provides the rules of engagement and terms of reference upon which they can be discussed at least.

Intuitions, on the other hand, are private mental experiences that cannot be challenged or verified by argument or persuasion. Granted, a 'bright idea', a 'pipe dream', followed through by systematic reflection as to its feasibility could provide a helpful stimulus for change. Yet to act on impulse alone, to make decisions where the welfare of others could be at stake on the basis of a whim and without further thought, seems inconsiderate at best, at worst potentially reckless. With regard to vision and good school leadership it is hard to see how such a quality could be 'fundamental to effective leadership and forms of organisational activity' (see above).

The National Standards for Headteachers in England (DfES 2004) go on to suggest that head teachers should be committed to 'a collaborative school vision of excellence and equity that sets high standards for every pupil' (p. 6). By 'collaboration', it seems reasonable to infer that notions of excellence and equity have been discussed openly in the school and a consensus of opinion reached; this would reflect a positive state of affairs in a democratic context. Consistent with this idea of vision is the belief that while collective deliberation over aims and values might take longer, the quality of the deliberation is better than reflection in isolation.

However, if a 'vision' is a private mental event, exclusive to particular individuals, it cannot be 'shared' in any meaningful sense because it is by definition private and particular to that person.[3] The idea of a shared or collaborative 'vision' on this view becomes something that the head teacher imparts for her followers to implement. This is precisely the kind of emphasis on 'vision' with which Fullan feels uncomfortable.

> The current emphasis on vision in leadership can be misleading. Vision can blind leaders in a number of ways [...] The high-powered, charismatic principal who 'radically transforms the school' in four or five years can [...] be blinding and misleading as a role model ... Principals are blinded by their

> own vision when they feel they must manipulate the teachers and the school culture to conform to it.
>
> (1992: 19)

There are particular cases where people may expect individual leaders to make executive decisions. Imagine that tragedy struck in a school, so that a pupil was killed suddenly perhaps, or fire took hold of the school building: in such exceptional circumstances a good leader might articulate a clear plan of action which others chose to follow without debate. However, even in the face of such adversity the best responses would be likely to reflect improvisation on a careful, premeditated plan to deal with emergencies rather than intuitive brilliance at the time and on the spot.

One study has explored the kinds of 'vision' that are proposed by school leaders and found them to be 'neither surprising nor striking nor controversial' but very traditional, 'closely in line with what one might expect on the British system of education' (Bolam *et al.* 1993: 35). There is no suggestion, in the National Standards for Headteachers in England (DfES 2004) for example, that 'utopian' change might be desirable. The concept of a 'utopia' is far more straightforward than a 'vision', defined in the *Oxford English Dictionary* as 'an imagined perfect place or state of things'. However, the association in ordinary language between utopian thinking and the ideals of the political left (which isn't assumed here) may be too strong in practice to find widespread favour.

There are two final further difficulties with this view of 'vision'. First, if it could be demonstrated that the future good for a school could be known with precision by a particularly insightful individual, this information would only be very useful if it could also be 'known' how the goal could be reached. Such a strategy would rely on direct and reliable causal links between identified inputs and the desired results or outputs. However, there is very little evidence that such precise relationships exist in practice and rather more evidence, on the contrary, of too many variable possibilities and circumstances to translate knowledge of an ideal future state into reality.

Nor is it clear that the value of a 'vision' lies in 'knowing' what a school ought to be like. It may lie in the process or the quality of the experience of conceiving future possibilities imaginatively and creatively instead. This is not to dismiss the value of meeting targets entirely, although once met there are always new targets; rather it is to highlight the importance of the means by which something is achieved, not the achievement. If the value of 'vision' does lie in the process, good schools should distribute opportunities for creative thought widely, not keep them as the preserve of one or two people.

'Vision' as imaginative perception?

Some form of 'imaginative perception' seems far closer to the meaning of 'vision' intended in the National Standards for Headteachers. One of the key areas of headship identified there is the role of 'Shaping the Future' of the school. Head teachers are expected not to dictate but to create a *shared* vision and strategic plan which 'inspires and motivates' members of the school community. At least one element of the professional knowledge required to meet this challenge is the capacity to know about 'leading change, creativity and innovation' (DFES 2004: 6). There are close and obvious connections here between 'vision', creativity and imaginative thought.

However, the imagination is a complex philosophical theme, as John White demonstrates in *The Child's Mind*. Understanding 'vision' or 'visionary thinking', even in this particular sense, is not straightforward. Is 'vision' the capacity to perceive imaginatively or that which is perceived through the imagination?

Imaginative perception is a similarly abstract and philosophically complex concept, requiring further analysis if this interpretation of 'vision' is to help us understand leadership qualities better. Some theories of the imagination, for example, would argue that only certain people who are unusually clever, sophisticated or intelligent would be capable of imaginative thinking (Kenny 1989). Anthony Kenny suggests that imagination is bound up with the ability to create original ideas, a mental capacity not every person possesses to equal degree. Is 'vision' as imaginative perception, like intuitive insight, a special and exclusive gift?

John White has demonstrated other ways in which the imagination is described in common speech which do not derive from a privileged form of intellectual insight (2002). One form of imaginative perception, seeing 'in the mind's eye' (White 2002), has been highlighted already as a form of thinking which involves no particularly unusual or sophisticated mental skill. A head teacher might attempt to illustrate, with practical examples, what the school in her charge could be like in five years' time to try to enthuse and motivate members of staff. Those listening would be required to imagine 'in their minds eye' as much as the head teacher. It is not clear that such a conventional image qualifies, however, as a 'vision'.

Imagination can also be understood to mean the capacity to 'suppose', or to think 'beyond actuality into the sphere of the possible' (White 2002: 121). People suppose when they 'speculate', for example, or 'entertain alternative scenarios' of what could be the case (White 2002: 123). These connotations of imaginative perception connect very clearly with the mental skills and dispositions that might be needed to discharge school leadership well. Those with ample opportunity to practise thinking of this kind may well prove more adept at it than others over time.

Head teachers are often required to think in ways that combine conventional images of known objects in order to make something new. Kate Griffin, for example, illustrates her capacity to 'foster creativity' as a head teacher by adapting a conventional model of care for employees from industry to the context of a school staffroom in an original way.

> A few years ago I employed somebody to serve coffee in the staff room before school and at break time. This encouraged a much higher proportion of staff to gather there and the opportunities for conversation, the development of ideas and the exchange of information that this created have been invaluable. Certainly the return has far exceeded the investment.
>
> (2001: 24)

Head teachers suppose when they generate new ideas based on systems or practices that exist already, translating them to other, acceptable purposes (White 2002). For example, the toilet facilities available to pupils in English schools are often terrible; this is a problem for which no standard, adequate response is currently available. One creative head teacher decided to overcome the difficulty in his primary school by involving pupils from the school council.

While many schools have student councils, few use this mechanism as an active force for institutional change. In this case, however, the head teacher included the pupils actively in decisions regarding refurbishment and design, and gave them a budget and access to the building contractors. When the work was complete, he listened to suggestions pupils made to keep the facilities pleasant and fresh once they were finished.[4] His imagination and the confidence he showed in the pupils were rewarded.

Kenny is right in one sense to emphasise the sense of originality inherent to being 'imaginative'. Head teacher John Cain, for example, is able to suppose beyond the actual to the possible to describe his idea of a possible future state without painting a mental picture that seems strikingly creative. He emphasises the importance of achieving realistic targets related to the school roll and improved examination results.

> Broadly the vision running around in my mind was to increase the intake, raise standards, and to have the students behaving well in good facilities. By the year 2001 there would be 850 students, achieving a GCSE pass rate at above the national average in a school which would value and respect all its members.
>
> (1999: 100)

If what distinguishes imaginative thinking is the capacity to entertain alternative scenarios and think beyond standard conventional responses, it is not clear from this 'vision' how far Cain in this particular instance meets those criteria.

At the same time, John White points out, genuinely creative ideas must still remain 'within the bounds of what is appropriate in the context' even if they transcend conventional expectations. Very rude or mad people can transcend convention with ease, White continues, but that does not make them imaginative (2002: 124). A head teacher of a small primary school decides to spend a year's school capitation on balsa wood because she wants every child to have an opportunity to make something. Her 'vision' is most certainly original but a swift intervention from a teacher's union is needed to limit the havoc wreaked by her eccentricity.

It is not clear from the examples given here that to attribute creative genius to these practically minded head teachers would describe a quality 'core' to the purpose of a head teacher in the way 'vision' has been identified. Nor, if the imaginative perception required of head teachers is closer to the quality of 'supposition' described by John White, is it clear in a democracy why/that the quality of 'vision' should be confined to the head teacher. Other people are capable of supposition. The head teacher who addressed the difficulties with the school toilets imaginatively did so by allowing the pupils in his school the opportunity to think imaginatively too.

The 'Standards' state:

> Critical to the role of headship is working with the governing body and others to create a *shared vision* and strategic plan which inspires and motivates pupils, staff and all other members of the school community. This *vision* should express core educational values and moral purpose and be inclusive of all stakeholders' values and beliefs. The strategic planning process is critical to sustaining school improvement and ensuring that the school moves forward for the benefit of its pupils.
>
> (DfES 2004: 6)

If a 'vision' is to be shared, all members of the school community deserve an opportunity to be imaginative. If vision is an expression of educational values there can be no expert knowledge of the best possible future for the school, only opinions, so by opening this subject up for discussion the 'vision' that is agreed cannot in one sense be 'wrong'. Expertise on the other hand would be needed to coordinate the process well, to structure the debate so that it is constructive, consistent with democratic values and ultimately conclusive.

So 'vision', a mental image of the possible future state of a school culminating from a process of consultation through which imaginative suggestions and ideas are shared, may be important to 'shaping the future' of a school but says nothing in particular about the head teacher. A head teacher who did not feel they personally were particularly imaginative might be very successful in creating a shared vision if confident creative thinkers were appointed to other positions of responsibility in a senior management team. A 'vision' may be the product of imaginative perception; however, *the* 'vision' and being imaginative do not mean the same thing.

The responsibility distinctive to the head teacher lies, as the Teachers' Pay and Conditions Document (DfES 2005) implies, in ensuring that the aims and objectives of the school and policies for their implementation are formulated. The 'Standards' (DfES 2004) suggest this ought to be done in a way that includes members of the school community. 'Vision' could be critical in this sense to the flourishing of a school in a liberal democracy but not critical to the role of a head teacher. Other personal qualities and attitudes would be needed for this to happen which might be critical to the best school leadership which are not about the imagination but something else instead.

'Vision' as interpretation?

A final, unexpected complication may be introduced to the analysis at this point. 'Vision' can be taken to imply the capacity of good leaders to understand the rights and responsibilities of the community they lead, such that they successfully and consistently distinguish legitimate actions and beliefs from the illegitimate. Furthermore, 'interpretation' of this kind may be a widely recognised quality of good leaders. However, the way in which vision and interpretation are interconnected in this third reading of the Proverbs passage is a dimension of vision in leadership omitted from accounts in the existing ELMA literature.

Thomas Greenfield has identified 'vision' with the idea of a 'moral imagination' (1993). The best leaders, he suggests, are those able to perceive accurately how things could be in the future and where the discrepancies might lie between this and the state of things as they now are. There are obvious links between this notion of the imagination and the capacity for supposition discussed by John White.

The *moral* dimension to imaginative thinking of this kind, Greenfield suggests, lies in the capacity to bring clear personal and organisational values to the role of educational leadership (1993). This view is supported by Bush and Glover, who argue that good leaders are informed by and communicate clear sets of personal and educational values representing their sense of '"moral purpose" for the school' (2003), as well as by Gold *et al.* (2003). This point needs to be qualified: a skilled, successfully corrupt head teacher could be 'good' at what she did and her actions could infuse a school with 'moral purpose' of a particularly unpleasant kind (Wright 2003). Nonetheless, priority is regularly afforded to the quality of ethical decision-making that individuals demonstrate in accounts of good school leadership in the ELMA literature.

Rarely, if ever, though, does that literature insist that the moral purpose of school leadership be considered within the wider political context in which it is situated. In many cases, given its widespread acceptance across the world, this will require the leader to bring personal and organisational values to their role that are appropriate to a democracy. Following John White's lead, it has been argued already (see above) that genuinely creative ideas will remain within the bounds of what is contextually appropriate, even if they transcend conventional expectations. In democracy's case, contextually appropriate values rest characteristically on a dual commitment to political liberty and political equality (Wolff 1996: 85).

Hence, local schools, individuals engaged in educational practice who are being true to the notion of vision in this third sense of interpretation appropriate to the context, will need to be able to demonstrate a form of moral purpose which is acceptable within these bounds. This is not to argue that where schools are located in a democratic context they need to act as though they were a democracy. Schools lack the constitution of a political constituency and many of the members of school communities are under age.

However, as John White has argued in *The Aims of Education Restated* (1982), in a democracy the purpose and content of state education is a political matter to be decided through a democratic political process. School leaders, as educational professionals, are no more privileged in this process than other citizens. As they are not privy to privileged knowledge of right and wrong in relation to education and the good life, they should not be in a position to dictate a school's moral purpose.

The value of autonomy should be promoted too by educational leaders in a democratic society. This places particular pressure on the traditional model of the head teacher as the 'lynch pin' (White 1983) of the school. Values will be transmitted through the means by which head teachers execute their professional responsibilities: the Standards stress the responsibility of head teachers to 'model the values and vision of the school' (DfES 2004: 6). If state maintained schools are required to promote democratic values, including autonomy, that power to decide autonomously cannot be limited to the head teacher.

However, the 'Standards' also make it clear that vision should be shared across a school, albeit that head teachers are responsible for ensuring this happens. A newly constituted section on 'Strengthening Community', moreover, requires head teachers to involve parents and the community too in 'supporting the learning of children and in defining and realising the school vision' (DFES 2004: 11). The values underpinning the curriculum can and should be promoted through the way schools are organised.

Currently head teachers with 'vision', in the sense that they 'transcend the bounds of convention', have developed models of institutional change that are consistent, not at odds, with democratic values in this way. Moreover, efficiency is not grounds for denying people in schools an opportunity to be consulted in matters directly concerning their well-being. An influential study in the ELMA literature (Gold *et al.* 2003) found that schools flourished when led in ways informed by democratic values, and studies focused on children and young people and their achievement in schools (e.g. Dutson-Steinfeld 2005; Flutter and Rudduck 2004; Morgan and Streb 2002) show how they may take on an active and constructive responsibility for decision-making in ways that do not detract from other kinds of educational attainment.

John MacBeath has encouraged schools for a long time to 'speak for themselves' (1999) through largely democratic means. This does not reflect normal or expected practice, however. The 'Standards' now state that head teachers should find ways to 'build, communicate and implement a shared vision' (DfES 2004: 6) but do not indicate clearly how this might be realised.

While head teachers might be innovative thinkers, I have argued that it is confusing to see this quality as essential to their role. The idea of 'vision' is strongly associated with being creative and hard therefore to distance from a personal capacity to initiate radical social change. People who enjoy thinking creatively are valuable members of liberal democratic society and may contribute ideas that lead to radical change but need not hold official positions of formal responsibility or leadership.

People who do take on formal positions of leadership, on the other hand, need to know and interpret the bounds within which radical change might be possible. These bounds are informed by the values appropriate to a particular context. Leaders need also to act in ways informed by these same values.

These qualities can legitimately be described as 'vision' too. In the *Oxford English Dictionary* 'vision' is also defined as 'statesmanlike foresight' or 'sagacity in planning'; both relate to the skill of interpreting values in context. Statesmen at their best are diplomatic and politically astute: their concern, to hold the social order together with references to the principles by which it stands. A sage develops great wisdom over time through lived experience. These ideals of leadership appear at first glance to relate well to the role of the head teacher but move away from the qualities that appear to be identified with 'vision' in the existing policy and research literature.

Conclusion

If 'vision' is to be referred to in school leadership policy documents at all, its meaning needs to be clear, coherent and consistent. This is not the case at present; three related but distinct interpretations – a privileged form of perception, a mental image of an ideal future state and an ability to judge the best – are analysed in detail here. Two meanings of 'vision' in particular contribute to very different ideals of the school leader. One is inconsistent with liberal democratic values: this should be made clearer. Some people will continue to believe leadership should be 'visionary' in a charismatic sense but this is not a view that should be enshrined or sanctioned in policy.

The use of 'vision' in the most recently revised National Standards for Headteachers in England can be interpreted in ways that are more consistent with liberal democratic values. 'Vision' is used to highlight the importance of imaginative thinking in the life of a school community, the place of regular and structured discussion of aims and values, goals and aspirations for the future. This account locates 'vision' as a function of human reason rather than unusually gifted or perceptive awareness. 'Vision' in this sense need not come from the head teacher.

Distinctive to the formal authority of the head teacher is the capacity to interpret legal and statutory requirements made of a school according to the particular context in which the school is situated. This quality could legitimately be described as 'vision' too, although it is a less familiar sense of the word; distancing it from less desirable connotations in a democratic context of personal, charismatic authority is difficult, however. 'Vision' in this sense is extremely important to good school leadership: the ability to interpret what to do in the right place, right time and in the right way.

Notes

1 The National Standards for Headteachers provided an official framework for the role in schools in England from 2004 to 2010. After this, they were archived on the Department for Education website and remain available for reference use, without being considered to reflect current policy or guidance. As they have not been replaced, however, they remain useful as a reflection of influential ideas about vision in the dominant school leadership discourse.
2 I am most grateful to Revd Dr Darryl Hannah who was kind enough to guide me through all these interpretations of Proverbs 29: 18.
3 I am very grateful to John White for making this observation in correspondence.
4 The positive impact of his initiative was reported in the *Times Educational Supplement* in March 2003.

References

Anderson, B. (1978) *The Living World of the Old Testament.* Harlow: Longman.
Bolam, R. *et al.* (1993) *Effective Management in Schools.* London: HMSO.
Bush, T. and Glover, D. (2003) *School Leadership: Concepts and Evidence.* Nottingham: NCSL.
Cain, J. (1999) 'The process of vision creation – intuition and accountability', in H. Tomlinson, H. Gunter and P. Smith (eds), *Living Headship Voices, Values and Vision.* London: Paul Chapman.
DCSF (2009) *School Teachers' Pay and Conditions Document 2009 and Guidance on School Teachers' Pay and Conditions.* London: Department for Children, Schools and Families.
DfE (2013) *School Teachers' Pay and Conditions Document 2013 and Guidance on School Teachers' Pay and Conditions.* London: Department for Education.
DfES (2004) *National Standards for Headteachers* (revised). Nottingham: DfES Publications.
DfES (2005) *School Teachers' Pay and Conditions Document 2005 and Guidance on School Teachers' Pay and Conditions.* Norwich: The Stationery Office.
Dutson-Steinfeld, A. (2005) *Student Voice: No Longer an Optional Novelty.* London: Specialist Schools and Academies Trust.
Fisher, R. (2002) *Creating a Thinking School.* Leading Edge Seminar, National College for School Leadership.
Flutter, J. and Rudduck, J. (2004) *Consulting Pupils: What's in It for Schools?* London: RoutledgeFalmer.
Fullan, M. (1992) 'Visions that blind', *Educational Leadership*, 49 (5): 19–20.
Gold, A. *et al.* (2003) 'Principled principals? Values-driven leadership: evidence from ten case studies of "outstanding" school leader', *Educational Management and Administration*, 3 (2): 127–38.
Greenfield, T. (1993) 'The decline and fall of science in educational administration', in T. Greenfield and P. Ribbins (eds), *Greenfield on Educational Administration: Towards a Humane Science.* London: Routledge.
Griffin, K. (2001) *Building the Capacity for Change: The Creativity of School Leadership.* Leicester: SHA.
Kenny, A. (1989) *The Metaphysics of Mind.* Oxford: Oxford University Press.

MacBeath, J. (1999) *Schools Must Speak For Themselves: The Case for School Self-Evaluation*. London: Routledge/National Union of Teachers.

Morgan, W. and Streb, M. (2002) 'Building citizenship: how student voice in service-learning develops civic values', *Social Science Quarterly*, 82: 154–69.

Ofsted (2003) *Inspecting Schools: Framework for Inspecting Schools*. London: Ofsted.

Ofsted (2009) *The Framework for School Inspection*. Manchester: Ofsted.

Ofsted (2012a) *Getting to Good*. Available at: http://www.slideshare.net/Ofstednews/getting-to-good (last accessed 23 November 2013).

Ofsted (2012b) *The Framework for School Inspection*. Manchester: Ofsted (last revised December 2013 and last accessed 6 January 2014)

Peters, R. S. (1966) *Ethics and Education*. London: George Allen & Unwin.

Scott, R. B. Y. (1985) *The Anchor Bible*. Garden City, NY: Doubleday & Compass.

Senge, P. (1992) *The Fifth Discipline: The Art and Practice of the Learning Organization*. London: Century.

SSAT (The Schools Network) (2012) *Aspirant Headteachers Programme*. Available at: http://www.ssatuk.co.uk/ssat/support/leadership/aspirant-headteachers-programme/ (last accessed 6 January 2014).

TES (Times Educational Supplement) (2013) Available at: http://www.tes.co.uk/job/head-teacher-178074 (accessed 23 November 2013).

West-Burnham, J. (n.d.) 'Why Vision'. Available at: http://www.is-toolkit.com/knowledge_library/kl_files/WhyVision_JohnWestBurnham.pdf (last accessed 25 February 2014).

White, J. (1982) *The Aims of Education Restated*. London: Routledge & Kegan Paul.

White, J. (2002) *The Child's Mind*. London: RoutledgeFalmer.

White, P. (1983) *Beyond Domination: An Essay in the Political Philosophy of Education*. London: Routledge & Kegan Paul.

Wolff, J. (1996) *An Introduction to Political Philosophy*. Oxford: Oxford University Press.

Wright, N. (2003) 'Principled "bastard" leadership?', *Educational Management and Administration*, 31 (2): 139–43.

Chapter 5

Democratic fellowship and the practice of human possibility

Michael Fielding

Introduction

I have admired John White's work for over 40 years. In 1970, as a young teacher, I was won to the cause and the narrative of an ascendant philosophy of education through the clarity of his argument, the courage of his stance (in this particular instance against the diminishing determinism of Hans Eysenck's view of intelligence – see White 1969, 1970), the inclusiveness of his values and what has turned out to be his continuing commitment to the wider responsibilities of philosophers as public intellectuals. He has, for me, always been someone whose commitment to the social and political underpinnings of education invited allegiance to a generously conceived account of philosophy's aspirations.

That generosity of conception and tenacity of grounded engagement also reflect an inclination to see education in its broadest and deepest sense as the foundational project in which all of us should be engaged, not just as philosophers of education but as citizens and persons. Taken in combination, John White's exemplary commitments to the emancipatory possibilities of philosophy, his enduring attention to systemic as well as particular presumptions of those involved in education, and his willingness to open up areas of enquiry that receive less philosophical attention than they deserve are not only a testament to the wisdom and humanity of his spirit and the importance of his philosophical *oeuvre*, they provide us with a remarkable legacy to both cherish and emulate.

These foundational, holistic orientations and their inclination to challenge the educational status quo in the name, not just of a democratic polity, but also of a generously conceived view of human flourishing (see, for example, Reiss and White 2013; White 2007, 2009) provide an inspiration for and link to the philosophical and practical aspirations of this chapter.

Despite its anthropological, political and educational importance, the particular focus of my reflections is at once difficult to name and philosophically problematic. More in vogue from the mid-nineteenth to the mid-twentieth centuries its immediate hinterland is a cluster of related notions that includes community, fellowship, fraternity and solidarity. Although I will engage with fraternity, the invariably neglected, third imperative of the French Revolution, I have chosen to pursue its typically English formulation as 'fellowship', or as I shall later call it, 'democratic fellowship'. Difficult to name with accuracy or in ways which invite allegiance or appropriate recognition, its existential and philosophical hinterland are, nonetheless, foundationally important in both the narrative and the actuality of what John Dewey calls an 'inclusive human order' (Dewey 1941: 134), in democracy as a way of life.

Indeed, it is in good part the growing crises of liberal democracy that have guided the direction and the specific focus of my contribution. Three powerful examples spring to mind – (1) the vulnerability of democratic systems of government to the predatory ambitions and moral indifference of transnational capitalism; (2) the combined presumptions of privilege and greed that have for some years disfigured the workings of the UK parliamentary democracy; and (3) the emergence of nascent democracies in countries whose recent histories have either been riven with deep division or suppressed by dictatorial rule. These developments have not only highlighted very different understandings of and approaches to democracy, they have also invited a renewed focus on the foundational conditions which democracy requires.

One of the key issues which attention to foundational aspirations of democracy seeks to address has often to do, not just with the mutually conditioning relationship between liberty and equality, but also with ways in which those two emancipatory values are grounded in the realities of human encounter. Just as importantly, and equally elusively, the argument is that the interdependence of freedom and equality requires us to attend both to the preconditions of democratic politics and the purposes it espouses. This third dimension, this third principle – variously called fraternity, community or fellowship – is, in one sense, more important than either of its better known companions for it asks us to attend with more than a passing nod to fundamental issues of political anthropology and political purpose. It asks us how democratic conversations might begin in earnest and to what ends they aspire. It reminds us that politics is a means towards particular kinds of human flourishing.

Fraternity and fellowship: excavating democracy's forgotten foundations

Prompted by these foundational questions of means and ends and their appropriate interrelationship within democracy as a way of life, not merely a mechanism for making collective decisions and holding each other to account, the nature and role of centripetal imperatives like fraternity and fellowship begin to acquire a greater significance.

How are we to locate these much neglected, frustratingly elusive notions, neither of which has been philosophically well served in the latter half of the twentieth century? Much of the relatively sparse theoretical work on these overlapping concepts allies them, if not within the precise formulation of the *liberté, egalité, fraternité trinôme*, then certainly within a nexus of democratic aspirations within which liberty and equality play a guiding role. Of course, notions of fraternity and fellowship predate the French Revolution by many centuries. Nonetheless, their interrelated, declamatory articulation in the events and ambitions of 1789 still retains an emblematic significance for many of us today, and what attention they have subsequently received invariably locates them within that democratic framework.

Fraternity and its discontents

More commonly encountered in writing on political theory aimed at a broad readership – see, for example, Bernard Crick (1978), Eric Hobsbawm (1975) and Ferdinand Mount (1976) – academic, philosophical engagement with fraternity is relatively rare. Certainly, it pales into insignificance when set alongside the substantial corpus of work on its companion notions of liberty and equality. There are, of course, exceptions. For example, the US philosopher, Carl Cohen, argues that

> Democracy's need for (fraternity) is on the deepest level of all, because it provides the context within which equality can be established and freedom can be protected. Of the three ideals, therefore, fraternity must be given temporal and logical priority. There can be no self-government where there is no community recognizing itself as an entity within which self-government might be proposed or realized. Fraternity institutes the democratic community, as equality characterizes it, and liberty safeguards it. These ideals are not in need of defense. To the extent that each is embedded in a democracy – as condition, justification and presupposition – the realization of them and their intrinsic values go hand in hand with the realization of democracy … Where community consciousness, fraternity, has not developed, democracy cannot even begin.
>
> (Cohen 1973: 274, 284)

Likewise, the great Plato scholar, Gregory Vlastos, in a powerful pair of papers (Vlastos 1942a, 1942b) published at the beginning of the Second World War insists on the need to connect 'personal dignity, the root idea in both equality and liberty, with fraternal living' (Vlastos 1942a: 1–2). Expanding and underscoring the point he suggests:

> It is not too much to say that the very survival of democracy in our time depends on the capacity to realise this connection in practice as well as in theory. It requires the transformation of a predominantly differential society into one which is predominantly fraternal … [W]ithout fraternity neither liberty nor equality finds massive fulfilment. Without fraternity liberty stands in contradiction to equality, and each in contradiction with itself. Liberty without fraternity is parasitic liberty. Equality without fraternity is powerless to oppose inequalities.
>
> (Ibid.: 2)

These two contributions notwithstanding, work of this kind is rare rather than customary and when it does exist (e.g. Kainz 1984) fraternity tends not to be the primary focus of the larger work in which it is located.

Fortuitously, there have been recent signs of renewed political interest in fraternity – as, for example, in the work of Conservative writers like Jesse Norman (Norman *et al.* 2007) and Danny Kruger (Kruger 2007) arguing for a 'compassionate conservatism', and on the left from Jon Cruddas and Jonathan Rutherford (Rutherford 2008) arguing for what Jon Cruddas in his Introduction to the Labour Party's *One Nation Labour* has called 'the politics of being together' (Cruddas 2013: 6). It will be interesting to see if this burgeoning literature directs philosophical attention more concertedly in similar directions.

In the field of philosophy of education fraternity has been subject to similarly intermittent, if eminent, attention. The 1960s to the 1980s saw seminal work from Richard Peters (1966) and Patricia White (1983) but, to the best of my knowledge, no major contributions then followed in their wake. More recently, under Patricia White's creative aegis, the last decade has seen the development of insightful and timely work by Judith Suissa (2006) and Mary Healy (2013). My hope is that the crises of democracy to which I alluded earlier prompt further work in our field.

Fellowship – 'the spirit of democracy'

If the situation is uncertain with regard to fraternity, it is even more so with regard to its companion notion of fellowship. So far as I am aware, Caroline McCulloch's exploration of its role in the work of Peter Kropotkin and William Morris (McCulloch 1984) is the only academic contribution to the field in many decades. While now rarely used in a political context, it is worth reminding ourselves that fellowship has not only been central to the writings of communitarian anarchists like Kropotkin and libertarian socialists like Morris. It was central, too, to the next generation of socialist intellectuals like G. D. H. Cole and R. F. Tawney and to similarly inclined academic philosophers like John Macmurray, all very significant public intellectuals whose work continues to arouse interest and further study in their various fields. Given the increasing resonance of Cole's commitment to non-state forms of socialism and Tawney's coruscating moral and political critique of 'acquisitive society' it is worth briefly drawing attention to the central place of fellowship in their work. Likewise with Macmurray, whose philosophical work on the centrality of fellowship in human flourishing provides the theoretical basis and inspiration of much of my own advocacy. I begin with Tawney, perhaps the best known of the three for his advocacy of fellowship as a centrally important socialist value. I then look in a little more detail at the writings of Cole for whom fellowship provided an equally compelling lodestar. It is his notion of 'democratic fellowship' for which I argue later in the chapter. Lastly, I turn to Macmurray's account of fellowship and his sophisticated and extended examination of its importance as both the precursor to and fulfilment of creative human flourishing.

Interestingly, given the centrality of fellowship in the work of Tawney and Cole, the foundational strength of their advocacy was not matched by an equivalent analytic rigour. In Tawney's case, one writer has suggested that keeping the idea loose may have been deliberate because the kind of fellowship Tawney wished to promote was open-ended (Terrill 1974: 219). In Cole's case, it has been suggested that while 'Democracy, fellowship, community [were] the central tenets in Cole's socialist vocabulary, [c]haracteristically, they were given no clear definition, nor were they separated in any satisfactory way' (Wright 1979: 271). The loose, open-textured nature of the writing on fellowship from both of its best-known twentieth-century British protagonists thus poses problems for philosophers who are not steeped in the range and depth of their work. While exploring the notion of fellowship through engagement with some of the key texts of both writers, I thus rely more heavily than usual on the studies of leading scholars in the field. These include Tony Wright who has authored compelling, often beautifully written, books on both Tawney (Wright 1987) and Cole (Wright 1979) and Ross Terrill whose fine *R. H. Tawney and His Times: Socialism as Fellowship* (Terrill 1974) has much to say that is insightful and thought-provoking on this most elusive of notions.

Socialism as fellowship: Tawney and Cole on the foundational values of democracy

Tawney's ontology – 'the fact fellowship'

Tony Wright suggests that

> what is significant about Tawney's position is the *combined* nature of his argument for moral health and social health. On the one hand, fellowship is a moral expression describing proper valuation of human beings. On the other hand it is a description of the quality of social relationships to be found in a society built upon that evaluation. The important point is that for Tawney it was *both* of these things.
>
> (Wright 1987: 79 italics in the original)

For Tawney fellowship had an ontological significance connected to the profound existential, noumenal equality of all persons qua persons routed in his Christian belief in the fatherhood of God. Hence, in his reflections on the merits or otherwise of equal pay he insists that

> What is repulsive is not that one man should earn more than others … It is that some classes should be excluded from the heritage of civilization which others enjoy, and that the fact of human fellowship, which is ultimate and profound, should be obscured by economic contrasts, which are trivial and superficial.
>
> (Tawney 1964: 113)

Fellowship is certainly a moral notion in both an immanent and a socially normative sense, but it is more than that. It is the fact that it is 'ultimate and profound' that gives it its enduring significance. The absolute priority of fellowship in Tawney's work lies both in its presumption of a deep and immutable equality and, just as importantly, in its enabling and transformative capacity. Fellowship presumes and supports the normative requirements of equality. More importantly, it transcends and transforms those requirements to make equality real in fully human terms. As Ross Terrill remarks, 'Fellowship was ... an end in itself for Tawney. It was the right condition of life for human beings. Its value was independent of its results, whether in production of goods or in the strength and grandeur of the state' (Terrill 1974: 170).

There is one other observation of Terrill's I wish to highlight and that concerns what one might call the agentic powers of fellowship, its capacity not just to characterise a just, creative and humanly fulfilling society, but to intervene in or enable its creation. This goes to the heart of the debate about the nature and importance of fellowship. It is at once tantalisingly difficult and fundamentally important, hence my quoting the passage at some length. Terrill argues that for Tawney:

> Fellowship would be *made possible.* It would not actually be *made.* Some organizationists propose to organize fellowship. Some vitalists propose to whip it up. Tawney went no further than to facilitate and encourage it. The power arrangements of society would not require fellowship; that way lay totalitarianism. Power arrangements were not neglected. But their importance was more for what they prevented than for what they guaranteed ... [W]ith Tawney's fellowship ... domination of one man by another was prevented. But communion was not compulsory. The citizens would simply be *within reach of each other.*
>
> (Ibid.: 217–18, italics in the original)

Here one of the key issues with regard to fellowship, to which I shall return again and again because it is at once so central and so difficult, has to do with its location on a continuum which at one end embraces the enabling subtleties of invitation and at the other the non-negotiable resolve of requirement. It touches, in effect, on the preconditions, purposes and limits of democratic politics.

Cole on fellowship – 'socialism's first principle'

Despite the fact that Wright reminds us that fellowship was given no clear definition in Cole's *oeuvre* it is, nonetheless, possible to feel our way towards the kind of impulses that underpinned his advocacy and to say some potentially helpful things about their consequences for the form of participatory democracy he espoused.

Wright himself is helpful in suggesting that in Cole's triumvirate of socialist aspirations

> 'fellowship' described the socialist form of social relationships; that 'democracy' described the nature of exercise and distribution of social power necessary for fellowship; and that 'community' described both the character of the whole conception and denoted the tradition of social thought to which it belonged.
>
> (p. 271)

He is also helpful in suggesting the foundational nature of fellowship. For Cole fellowship was

> the key socialist principle, from which other principles were derived. Hence it was different from and superior to, the practical principle of social justice, which was ultimately far too quantitative ... to serve as the socialist essence. Fellowship *implied* social justice (and the other socialist principles), but the order of derivation was crucial.
>
> (p. 271, italics in the original)

In my own reading of Cole's advocacy of fellowship I have found three texts particularly helpful. They are 'Why I Am a Socialist' (Cole 1932), 'Democracy Face to Face with Hugeness' (Cole 1941a) and 'The Essentials of Democracy' (Cole 1941b).

In the first of these he sees fellowship as not only 'vital to the Socialist idea' (Cole 1932: 322), but its 'first principle' (ibid.: 323). For Cole:

> Social justice is not of the essence of Socialism. For justice seems to imply the meting out to each of something quantitative and limited, whereas Socialism itself implies a real living in and for one another. A mother is not content to be just to her child; nor can a Socialist be content to seek justice for the human race.
>
> (Ibid.)

Two points are worth drawing out here that link fellowship, equality and individuality and apply to both Tawney and Cole. In making remarks about an overly quantitative reading of social justice and equality, Cole was not denying the importance of equality. Rather he was seeking to affirm the priority of fellowship in the nexus of socialist ideals. Fellowship and, indeed, Cole's fundamental notion of democracy are irrevocably tied in to a prior, more elemental imperative, to the need for encounter between people as persons, not just as citizens.

Equality is important because if fellowship is to be both inclusive and real its demands must 'stop any one man being treated merely or mainly as a means to some other man's ends' (ibid.: 326). Equality is thus 'the political and social expression of the idea of fellowship' (ibid.).

With regard to individuality, he acknowledges 'each to count as one and none as for more than one' as, 'for many purposes, an admirable political and social maxim' (ibid.: 323), but, in the end, he rejects it as 'far too quantitative to be more than a very imperfect way of expressing the ideal' (ibid.). While acknowledging the necessarily communal nature of individuality, Cole also underscores its inviolability: '[F]ellowship does not count heads; or, if it does it counts everyone as more than one – in fact, as infinite' (ibid.).

Cole's searing attacks on atomistic forms of democracy, and particularly on what he saw as its betrayal in its parliamentary forms, rest ultimately on his belief that situated encounters which enable and enhance a profound, existential connectedness is what human beings need to flourish and what democracy is about. In 'Democracy Face to Face with Hugeness' he insists this requires 'groups small enough to express the spirit of neighbourhood and personal acquaintance' (Cole 1941a: 95). So strongly does he feel about this that he goes so far as to say: 'It is worthwhile to be bombed or invaded, if only blitz or invasion can teach us this lesson' (ibid.: 95). In some respects it is an unsettling essay to read. Imagery of loneliness and bewilderment – the consequences of democracy's internal betrayal as much as fascism's external confrontation – punctuates the narrative, as it does in all three pieces under consideration.

These lines of thinking are developed further in the third, companion essay, 'The Essentials of Democracy' (Cole 1941b). Here equality and justice as the necessary, formal requirements of democracy are situated, transformed and transcended through the fellowship of encounter. In a passage that sums up much of what is central to Cole's life and work he insists that his notion of democracy

> involves a sense of comradeship, friendliness, brotherhood – call it what you like. I mean a warm sense – not a mere recognition, cold as fish. I mean that democracy means loving your neighbours, or at any rate being able to love them when you do not happen to dislike them too much – and even then, when they are in trouble, and come to you looking for help and sympathy. A democrat is someone who has a physical glow of sympathy and love for anyone who comes to him honestly, looking for help or sympathy: a man is not a democrat, however justly he might try to behave towards his fellow man, unless he feels like that. But – and here is the point – you cannot feel that glow about people – individual people, with capacities for doing and suffering – unless and until you get to know them personally. And you cannot know, personally, more than quite a small number of people.
>
> That is why real democracies have either to be small, or to be broken up into small, human groups in which men and women can know and love each other.
>
> (Ibid.: 98–9)

While quite properly acknowledging that 'knowing your neighbours as real persons is not of itself democracy', Cole, nonetheless, insists that 'this sort of knowing is part of the material out of which democracy is to be built. You cannot build democracy without it' (ibid.).

John Macmurray – fellowship and the conditions of freedom

A life-long socialist like Tawney and Cole, Macmurray not only saw fellowship as foundational to human being and becoming, he also shared their commitment to deep equality, to the primacy of agency and to the interconnected capacity of both to contribute to just, creative and fulfilling relations between persons. What Macmurray's philosophical background enables him to do, perhaps more acutely than either Tawney or Cole, is help us reflect more deeply and more searchingly on both the precondition and the purposes of politics, on its limitations and constraints as well as its possibilities, and on the place of fellowship in the mosaic of social, political and communal life.

One of the most convenient sources of Macmurray's writing on fellowship is *Conditions of Freedom* (Macmurray 1950) which develops an account of human relations that enables him to explore how and to what extent aspirations to freedom in the contemporary world can be appropriately served by political action. In effect, it is a short exploration of fellowship and its relation to the possibilities and limitations of politics as an enabler of human flourishing.

A key Macmurrayan distinction concerns the differences between personal and political freedom, between relations of fellowship typical of community and relations of cooperation typical of society. Personal relations of fellowship, quintessentially exemplified by friendship, are non-instrumental. We enter into these kinds of relationship, not with any end in view or ulterior motive, but simply because it is in and through these kinds of encounter, characterised by their constitutive principles of freedom and equality, that we can be and become most fully ourselves. Furthermore:

> Since we can only be ourselves in fellowship, in mutual caring for one another, it follows that the intention to enter into fellowship is implicit in every human being and in every human activity. This is indeed what makes us human ... The ground of fellowship is common humanity ... the natural tendency of any two human beings who meet one another is to enter into fellowship.
>
> (Ibid.: 84)

Here what might have earlier felt like the rather quirky grounds of Cole's insistence on the foundational necessity of fellowship's role in democratic ways of life receives a fuller philosophical justification.

In contrast to personal relations of fellowship, functional relations of society are instrumental in origin and thus aspectival and partial in the degree to which we reveal our personhood. Defined by their purposes and tasks, indifferent to the claims of personal equality, their freedoms circumscribed and shaped by their focus on outcomes, functional relations enable us to achieve our intentions through cooperating with others.

While both kinds of relationship are important and interdependent, they are not of equal importance: the functional is for the sake of the personal (see Fielding 2007 for further exploration and critique). Not only are the functional relations typical of the political realm for the sake of the personal relations of community, the key point here is that they cannot achieve their purposes unless there is a sufficiently well established, inclusive human basis on which its work can begin. In Macmurray's view, 'the extent and quality of such political freedom as we can achieve depends in the last resort upon the extent and quality of the fellowship which is available to sustain it' (Macmurray 1950: 69). Furthermore, not only does fellowship determine the conditional possibilities of successful politics, it also provides the most important grounds for its justification: 'the unity of co-operation, which is the care of politics, has significance only through the human fellowship which it makes possible; and by its validity and its success must be judged'(ibid.: 69–70).

If Macmurray is right here, what then are the wider consequences, the strategic implications behind his championing of fellowship as both the precondition and the ultimate preoccupation of democratic politics? What kinds of action should we now take if the fellowship for which he argues is to become an increasingly insistent reality in our ways of life?

These are not easy questions to answer: indeed, their importance is commensurate with their level of difficultly. For Macmurray, while it is true that 'The democratic slogan – liberty, equality, fraternity – embodies correctly the principles of human fellowship' (ibid.: 75), he also insists we should not assume, as so many have done in the past, that this is primarily a political project. To do so was, in Macmurray's view, a serious error which entailed 'the confusion of community with organized society, and implicitly set territorial limits to human fellowship' (ibid.). He does acknowledge that 'the organized co-operation of human beings is for the sake of fellowship of the common life, and in this sense the freedom and equality of brotherhood is the end to which the state is a means' (ibid.). However, he goes on to say 'it is an indirect end. The State, as such, being a centre of organization within territorial limits, can only provide at best the material conditions in which fellowship can flourish and through which it can manifest itself' (ibid.).

Well, perhaps. But there are a number of important riders, firstly, to do with the democratic imperatives of equality; secondly, to do with the interdependence between the functional life and the personal life; and, thirdly, to do with what, later in the book, Macmurray calls 'the State (as an) instrument of fellowship' (ibid.: 101), with how fellowship is made, maintained and extended.

The first of my supplementary observations links strongly with Tawney and Cole's conjoint egalitarian insistence on the range and depth of fellowship's empirical actuality. Providing 'the material conditions' which robustly enable the freedom and equality of *all* members of society, not just some, is a not insignificant task.

Secondly, in Macmurray's analysis, not only is the functional life for the sake of the personal life and the personal life through the functional life, the actuality of their interrelation has day-to-day consequences. As he said in his prefigurative 1941 BBC radio talks:

> It is not possible to keep the two lives separate. The kind of working life a man has to live decides the kind of personal life he can have ... The personal life needs cultivation, and that means time and resources.
>
> (Macmurray 1941: 822)

Echoing Terrill's judgment that for Tawney fellowship could and should be *made possible*, but not actually be *made*, my third supplementary points to Macmurray's similar position in which he insists that 'the State [can be an] instrument of fellowship; the means to the expression, in common activities, of a true community' (Macmurray 1950: 101). My activist reading of Macmurray argues that it has a positive obligation to do so. Why? Because 'it is only insofar as the State is an expression of fellowship that it can be an instrument of justice, and of freedom through justice ... [T]he law is not necessarily justice' (ibid.). Within a democratic polity there is thus, in my own view, if not in Macmurray's, a substantive need, not only to identify and celebrate ways in which human fellowship weaves its way through the fabric of our daily lives, but also to actively extend that fellowship.

There is much in Macmurray's writing that suggests coordination and celebration are as far as functional organisations could or should go in the development of fellowship:

> Freedom is the product of fellowship, and the laws of friendship are its conditions. These conditions are spiritual, moral, religious: that is to say, they depend upon the motives that animate men in their personal relations with one another. The struggle for freedom is the struggle for the transformation of human motives, for the triumph of friendship over mistrust, of love over fear.
>
> (Ibid.: 104).

I understand both the ontological and the political weight of his argument and yet my hunch is that there is more to be said and more we can do to problematise and take seriously the urgent necessity of 'extending fellowship as co-operation extends' (ibid.: 102).

Since I can only gesture at these matters here, a single point will have to suffice. It is that, accepting and welcoming the legitimacy and resonance of Macmurray's foundational insistence that 'the functional is for the sake of the personal and the personal through the functional', our task is to develop it in ways which extend and deepen the interdependence of the functional and the personal, while all the while retaining the primacy of the personal. Here my suggestion is that the functional is not only for the sake of the personal, but *expressive* of it in a conscious and developmental sense. Under the aegis of such an approach not only would an organisation's structures be human scale and person friendly, its deep culture would be committed to what Macmurray calls 'the maintenance and re-enforcement of the consciousness of fellowship' (ibid.: 86).

We do, of course, need to be wary of the increasingly rampant contemporary perversion of the personal-functional nexus in which the personal is co-opted as an agent of the functional and thereby profoundly betrayed (see Fielding 2006). Clothed in the language of pseudo-emotion, of 'passionate commitment' to 'making a difference', we are now wearily familiar with the unguent inflections of hyperbolic discourse thinly veiling the voracious, bottom-line imperatives of contemporary capitalism. This should not, however, dissuade us from the legitimacy of the challenge set for us by writers like Tawney, Cole and Macmurray, who, in their different ways, insisted on fellowship as both means and end of human flourishing. It is in naming and understanding the interdependence of the cultural norms and structural architecture of organisations and their equivalent manifestations within the wider context of democratic society that we can, once again, renew our understanding of fellowship as both fact and aspiration, exemplification and inspiration.

Naming necessity: democratic fellowship and the practice of human possibility

I suggested earlier that one among the many reasons fellowship deserves further consideration is its propensity to invite renewed engagement with the preconditions, purposes and limits of democratic politics. The difficulties it poses, specifically for philosophers and more generally for others considering its potential deployment in the context of contemporary debate, have often to do with its frustrating propensity to entice and elude in equal measure, its potential to identify an important crossroads in human endeavour yet remain ambivalent about the direction of travel.

In some ways more worrying still are the contingencies of history that make language vulnerable to the vicissitudes of time and circumstance, vulnerabilities which, perhaps ironically, John Macmurray points out in typically forthright terms:

> However significant an old philosophy may be, it can never be adequate to the demands of the present. Its spirit may still be alive, but the body of the ideas and the words in which it is expressed itself grows old and weak and ineffective. Words and ideas must continually be recreated, or they soon cease to express the significance that lies behind them, and conceal or destroy it instead.
>
> (Macmurray 1932: 73)

Writing half a century later, these sentiments were rearticulated elegantly and insistently by the Canadian philosopher Michael Ignatieff:

> Words like fraternity, belonging and community are so soaked with nostalgia and utopianism that they are nearly useless as guides to the real possibilities of solidarity within modern society. Modern life has changed the possibilities of civic solidarity, and our language stumbles behind like an overburdened porter with a mountain of old cases.
>
> (Ignatieff 1984: 138)

In affirming what he sees as our human need for justice, liberty and solidarity he also insists:

> [We] ... need as much as anything else, language adequate to the times in which we live. We need to see how we live now and we can only see with words and images which leave us no escape into nostalgia for some other time and place.
>
> (Ibid.: 141)

Cognisant of these difficulties of language and of Macmurray's insistence on the need to understand and respect the boundaries as well as the intersections of personal and political domains, it is with some trepidation that I end by championing a Colean marriage of democracy and fellowship. Whatever its difficulties and uncertainties my sense is that 'democratic fellowship' names priorities and partnerships that are not only legitimate but necessary in our struggle to create ways of being and becoming more fully human as we step cautiously into the twenty-first century.

'Democracy' reminds us of the inviolability of emancipatory values that insist on the inclusive presumptions of equality and the universal aspirations of both positive and negative liberty. 'Fellowship' reminds us of the existential foundations of human being, of an invitational impulse that seeks, if not to undermine or disrupt the functional, then to supplement it in ways which reaffirm the non-negotiable legitimacy of personhood. 'Democratic fellowship' is at its heart an internally transgressive notion insisting on the inevitable interdependence of the personal and the political. It affirms the insufficiency of politics by reminding us of its interpersonal derivations and the absolute necessity of its widely conceived human obligations. It affirms the necessity of politics by reminding us of the double fact of our enduring vulnerability and the subsequent inevitability of our human interdependence.

I draw my chapter to a close with an observation that invites us back to the heart of Macmurray's philosophical anthropology. As I write, I hear, once again, of bewildering acts of neglect, indifference, even cruelty, in the health service and other caring professions. How can this be so? How can those whose primary task and wider commitment is to the well-being and care of vulnerable human beings behave routinely and unseeingly in ways which deny the primacy of their purpose and the integrity of their calling? How is it that we can receive the most advanced medical treatment, recorded with exemplary efficiency and sophistication, but never receive a smile of recognition or the warmth of even fleeting human encounter which fellowship invites and the prospect of our recovery requires?

We live in an era that largely reverses Macmurray's priorities and in so doing destroys the very possibility of human flourishing. The functional has not only marginalised the personal: in the neo-liberal totalitarianism of the market the personal now has significance only insofar as it serves functional ends. Schooling has betrayed the education of persons. We need, now more than ever, John White's long-standing insistence both on the public clarity and enacted priority of educational aims and, in the resonant language of one of his most recent publications, we must reaffirm 'the significance of human flourishing for schools' (Reiss and White 2013). Our significance as learners and teachers has become casually and routinely derivative; we are only as important as our most recent test results. The casuistry of calibration blinds us not only to the necessary priority of purpose and principle, but to the deeper ontology of human being and becoming.

Democratic fellowship names, simultaneously and interdependently, our needs as persons and the companion, enacted entitlement of political recognition. In the future it may be that the unity and integrity of human priorities and emancipatory purposes will be articulated in other ways in tune with different times. My hope is that 'democratic fellowship' will do us for the time being and that the words of William Morris will continue to inspire, just as they did Tawney, Cole and Macmurray before us:

> Fellowship is life and lack of fellowship is death: and the deeds that ye do upon the earth, it is for fellowship's sake that ye do them.
>
> (Morris 1968: 51)

Acknowledgments

My thanks to Frank Kirkpatrick and John Costello for their scholarship, their patience and their good fellowship.

References

Cohen, C. (1973) *Democracy*. New York: Free Press.

Cole, G. D. H. (1932) 'Why I am a Socialist', in G. D. H. Cole, *Economic Tracts for the Times*. London: Macmillan, pp. 321–7.

Cole, G. D. H. (1941a) 'Democracy face to face with hugeness', *Supplement to the Christian Newsletter*. Revised and reprinted in G. D. H. Cole (1950) *Essays in Social Theory*. London: Macmillan, pp. 91–6.

Cole, G. D. H. (1941b) 'The essentials of democracy,' in *Europe, Russia and the Future*. Revised and reprinted in G. D. H. Cole (1950) *Essays in Social Theory*. London: Macmillan, pp. 97–112.

Crick, B. (1978) 'Fraternity: the forgotten value', *Higher Education Quarterly*, 32 (2): 145–56.

Cruddas, J. (2013) 'Introduction', in J. Cruddas (ed.), *One Nation Labour: Debating the Future*. London: Labour List, pp. 4–7.

Dewey, J. (1941) 'For a new education', *New Era*, 22 (6): 134–5.

Fielding, M. (2006) 'Leadership, personalization and high performance schooling: naming the new totalitarianism', *School Leadership and Management*, 26 (4): 347–69.

Fielding, M. (2007) 'The human cost and intellectual poverty of high performance schooling: radical philosophy, John Macmurray and the remaking of person-centred education', *Journal of Education Policy*, 22 (4): 383–409.

Healy, M. (2013) *Philosophical Perspectives on Social Cohesion: New Directions for Education Policy*. London: Bloomsbury.

Hobsbawm, E. (1975) 'Fraternity', *New Society*, 27 November, pp. 471–3.

Ignatieff, M. (1984) *The Needs of Strangers*. London: Chatto & Windus.

Kainz, H. P. (1984) *Democracy, East and West: A Philosophical Overview*. London: Macmillan.

Kruger, D. (2007) *On Fraternity: Politics Beyond Liberty and Equality*. London: Civitas.

McCulloch, C. (1984) 'The problem of fellowship in communitarian theory: William Morris and Peter Kropotkin', *Political Studies*, XXXII: 437–50.

Macmurray, J. (1932) *Freedom in the Modern World*. London: Faber.

Macmurray, J. (1941) 'Two lives in one', *The Listener*, 36 (675), 18 December, p. 822.

Macmurray, J. (1950) *Conditions of Freedom*. London: Faber.

Morris, W. (1968) [1886/87] 'The Dream of John Ball', in *Three Works by William Morris*. London: Lawrence & Wishart, pp. 33–113.

Mount, F. (1976) 'The dilution of fraternity: brothers and others in utopia', *Encounter*, October, pp. 17–32.

Norman, J., Ussher, K. and Alexander, D. (2007) *From Here to Fraternity: Perspectives on Social Responsibility*. London: CentreForum.

Peters, R. S. (1966) *Ethics and Education*. London: Allen & Unwin.

Reiss, M. and White, J. (2013) *An Aims-based Curriculum: The Significance of Human Flourishing for Schools*. London: Institute of Education Press.

Rutherford, J. (2008) 'Fraternity without equality and other Conservative ideals', *Soundings*, 39: 98–107.

Suissa, J. (2006) *Anarchism and Education: A Philosophical Perspective*. London: Routledge.

Tawney, R. H. (1964) *Equality*. London: Unwin Books.

Terrill, R. (1974) *R. H. Tawney and His Times: Socialism as Fellowship*. London: André Deutsch.

Vlastos, G. (1942a) 'Religious foundations of democracy: fraternity and liberty', *Journal of Religion*, XXII (1), January, pp. 1–19.

Vlastos, G. (1942b) 'Religious foundations of democracy: fraternity and equality', *Journal of Religion*, XXII (2), April, pp. 137–55.

White, J. (1969) 'Intelligence – the new Puritanism', *Times Educational Supplement*, 24 October.

White, J. (1970) 'Eysenck on intelligence: a reply', *Times Educational Supplement*, 16 January.

White, J. (2007) 'Education for well-being', *Education Review*, 19 (1): 28–33.

White, J. (2009) 'Education and a meaningful life', *Oxford Review of Education*, 35 (4): 423–35.
White, P. (1983) *Beyond Domination*. London: Routledge & Kegan Paul.
Wright, A. W. (1979) *G. D. H. Cole and Socialist Democracy*. Oxford: Clarendon Press.
Wright, A. W. (1987) *R. H. Tawney*. Manchester: Manchester University Press.

Chapter 6

On intelligence

Carrie Winstanley

Coming to philosophy of education from educational psychology I found working with John White invigorating and freeing. I was permitted to ask the kinds of questions that had been bothering me about education, children, thinking and learning. At times it was slightly daunting to realise anew that I was having these discussions with someone of John White's stature and experience, but it was a privilege to undertake my studies with him. When he retired I worked additionally with Professor Harry Brighouse and it was remarkable to experience them both discussing my ideas. Since then I have worked with John White through the Philosophy of Education Society of Great Britain for more than a decade and I remain impressed with his energy, breadth of interests, output and convictions. It has been an honour to work on this collection.

Introduction

In White's 2002 publication *The Child's Mind*, he asks 'Who needs intelligence?' (Chapter 5, pp. 78–97). In this chapter, I will argue that the concept is a useful one, despite scant attention from philosophers, manifold difficulties within both psychology and education and some serious ongoing controversies. White argues:

> It is doubtful whether a century of psychologising about intelligence has advanced our knowledge beyond what was already grasped by Aristotle. It has certainly given us ideologies, unjustified claims and confusions aplenty, but that will be no comfort to parents and teachers looking for clarity and enlightenment.
>
> (White 2002: 95)

We can partly examine this postulation through reviewing a summary covering a key 65-year period in the study of intelligence as presented by Sternberg (2000: 8). He examines exactly what has been learnt. Two special editions of the *Journal of Educational Psychology* (1921 and then 1986) focus on contemporary experts' definitions of intelligence and its measurement and make interesting comparative reading. Further developments have since taken place but the main points remain relevant. Common themes persist, as do some continuing concerns:

> Attributes such as adaptation to the environment, basic mental processes, and higher order thinking (e.g. reasoning, problem solving, decision making) were prominent in both listings.
>
> (Ibid.: 8)

It is possible to show how some of these issues do link to everyday usage of the concept of intelligence and that they can be useful to those parents and teachers about whom White is worrying. Defining intelligence is far from straightforward, however, and Sternberg outlines the two issues that crop up repeatedly without consensus or resolution:

> Is intelligence one thing, or is it manifold? [...] some panellists defined intelligence quite narrowly in terms of biological or cognitive elements, whereas others included a broader array of elements, including motivation and personality. The issue of breadth, like that of the one versus many, remains unresolved.
>
> (Ibid.: 8)

I will consider these issues in more detail and I do agree with White's analysis that the psychological investigation of intelligence has become more complex, possibly thereby increasing confusion by adding further dimensions over the years and yet still failing to resolve some of the thornier questions. However, the additional elements also show an enriching of our concept of intelligence and this can add to its usefulness in education. Shifting conceptions show an acceptance of new understandings. For example, Sternberg reports:

> Despite similarities in views of the 65 years, some salient differences could also be found. [...] The later panellists showed considerable emphasis on the role of context, and particularly of culture, in defining intelligence, whereas such emphasis was absent in the earlier symposium.
>
> (Ibid.: 9)

It is worth noting that the psychological discussions concerned both definitions and measurement of intelligence. It is very difficult to discuss one aspect without the other since they are closely intertwined. Much of the controversy in the field stems from the use and misuse of measurements of intelligence and so this needs to be considered when examining the usefulness of the concept (Gould 1984). This chapter reviews how we talk about and understand intelligence and considers some of the persistent problems and how they impact on education.

In philosophy, issues around animal intelligence and artificial intelligence are found with more frequency than discussions of human intelligence.[1] Hand notes that 'analyses of the ordinary concept of intelligence are few and far between in philosophical literature' (2007: 35). White had previously also observed this point, listing the allied areas that are more frequently tackled:

> Intelligence is a topic more written about by psychologists than philosophers. In philosophical works we can find discussions of consciousness, perception, thought action, memory, emotion, and imagination, but rarely anything on intelligence.
>
> (White 2002: 78)

It is certain that many of the words allied to intelligence are contested concepts and would benefit from conceptual clarity. Perhaps it is fairly unsurprising that the concept of intelligence is not much studied in philosophy considering the overlap with the topics that *are* discussed. These aspects link to some of the persistent psychological components of definitions of intelligence already noted – thinking, reasoning, adapting and the like. What is more surprising is that the notion of intelligence is tackled infrequently within the specific domain of philosophy of education, since talk of intelligence is common in schools and in people's homes when considering how best to help children learn. Teachers talk of mixed-ability classes, of cognition and metacognition, of thinking and problem-solving, while parents discuss the differences between how they and their children learn and consider their relative strengths and their intelligence.

To muddy the waters further one can consider the psychometric ideas of intelligence, those aspects that psychologists believe can be reliably measured. Psychological tests and measures have influenced how people think and talk about intelligence. Some of these controversies have been extreme and some of the researchers unjustly vilified (for example, Howe reports that Jensen was a victim of 'over-hasty conclusions' (1997: 13)). Howe also notes:

> By and large, [however], investigators have not been intentionally misleading. Numerous errors have been made, typically as a result of faulty inferences or reliance on inadequate evidence, but honest scientists do make mistakes.
>
> (Howe 1997: 12)

Difficulties arise due to the sensitive and fundamental nature of intelligence. Howe, again:

> In the face of findings that seemed to have alarming social implications, there has been a tendency to politicize the debate on intelligence, or even to regard certain issues as being taboo. These reactions have impeded objective assessment.
>
> (Howe 1997: 13)

Understandably, teachers link ideas about the nature of intelligence with its measurement. Even given the criticism and controversy around testing and the uses of testing, the concept of intelligence as measurable continues to have currency. For example, in the field of 'gifted education' Eyre reports of teachers that:

> They continue to believe that it is possible to define a children's level of ability by the use of a test and to give it a numerical score.
>
> (Eyre 1997: 3)

The confusion over the status of intelligence 'scores' is problematic and the actual purpose (diagnostic) is often lost, with the score reduced to a label.

Ordinary usage

How is the word 'intelligence' used in common parlance? 'He is very intelligent'; 'She is quite intelligent'; 'He isn't very intelligent'. These are all acceptable uses of the word in general everyday talk. Here people are understanding intelligence as a kind of capacity or internal mental strength. It is also frequently understood that this capacity can be utilised effectively or ineffectively. We might say, 'She is an intelligent girl, but she doesn't really apply herself', or 'He is not very intelligent, but he is diligent and makes the most of what he has'. This distinguishes between someone's capacity and their performance, but still holds that some kind of central mental power exists.

Hand has no problem with this notion, describing intelligence as 'a quality of mind possessed to different degrees by different people' (2007: 40). White does not allow for such individual differences in intelligence. All typically developing people have a capacity to 'acquire abilities or capacities' and so all are equally intelligent in this sense (2002: 86–8). White prefers to use the phrase, 'flexible adaptation of means to ends (intelligence)' (2002: 87), implying a propensity not a capacity.

The value of intelligence to society is betrayed by its common usage. The metaphors and imagery are telling. Most people would prefer to be 'bright' or 'sparky' rather than 'dull' or 'dim'. To be intelligent is to be 'switched on' and 'alert', not 'slow' or 'limited'. White notes that it is an 'ethically neutral capacity' and cautions educationalists against 'placing intelligence on the pedestal it has so often occupied these last hundred years' (2002: 86). He notes that intelligence has been considered a positive quality despite its separation from a richer idea of practical wisdom, leaving a more impoverished notion of intelligence. I would agree that intelligence is often considered to be a favourable quality, but only up to a certain point. The words soon have a negative ring if the person in question is considered too intelligent to be 'normal'. These people are 'nerds', 'swots', 'precocious' or 'boffins', and while the words can sometimes be used in an endearing or flippant way, they are also terms used in a bullying fashion.[2]

Winch distinguishes between ordinary use of the term and that of psychologists. He rejects the notion of intelligence as a unitary property of the mind, suggesting that different types of domain-specific behaviours can be described variously as more or less intelligent. He therefore cites adjectival uses of 'intelligence':

> We have no difficulty with such expressions such as 'He is an intelligent footballer' or 'She handled that parent in an intelligent manner', which suggest a disposition of the footballer or the head teacher to behave in certain ways highly appropriate to the activities in which they are engaging.
>
> (1990: 7)

In 2004, I tried to show how I found this to be an unhelpful use of the term 'intelligent' in trying to clarify what most people mean when they use the word.[3] I agreed that we infer dispositional characteristics from such uses, linking intelligence to specific activities and behaviour. However, this example is more a description of proficiency and the result of experience than a description of what people routinely mean by the word intelligence. When people talk of an 'intelligent footballer' the context usually determines what they mean by the word 'intelligence' and how it relates to the person in question. It could mean that the person is both 'intelligent *and* a footballer', which could still imply the central processing or capacity model that people often understand by intelligence. The alternative interpretation would be that the footballer 'plays intelligently' and in this case the word 'intelligence' should be replaced by the word 'skilfully'. The skills involved in football involve concept application (strategy and tactics) and the flexible adaptation of means to ends in addition to physical skills, but this is not what we normally mean when we use the word 'intelligent'.

We more commonly say that someone '*is* intelligent' and possibly use this as an explanation for being good at *x* or *y*, not that they are 'intelligent *at*' *x* or *y*. The confusion arises over how 'intelligence' is sometimes synonymous with 'intellectual capacity' and sometimes synonymous with 'skilful'. Both uses are found in everyday language and nuances of speech or writing often indicate which particular meaning is being used. Just because we are comfortable saying 'she handled that parent in an intelligent manner', this does not mean that we do not also have a conception of 'intelligence' as a noun, representing the capacity understood as the psychologists' central processing model, or indeed some other model. In one of these instances, the intelligence described is general and a property of the mind and in the other it is about performance and application. For clarity, words such as 'skills', 'talents', 'abilities', etc. 'need to be distinguished from one another and from the term 'intelligence'.

Having previously taken issue with Ryle's use of the phrase to be 'intelligent at' something, Hand reviews the same passage from Winch's work presented above. He says: 'As a description of ordinary usage, it is spectacularly wide of the mark' (2007: 38). He provides two possible interpretations but concludes that neither is satisfactory, and rejects the notion that there is a type of intelligence that could be considered specific to a domain.

The use of intelligence as a description of behaviour is commonplace but problems arise when people seek to explain behaviour through discussing intelligence. In trying to explain, we are left with a circular argument such as: 'He is a talented flautist because he plays the flute well. He plays the flute well because he is a talented flautist.' It tells us nothing helpful in this instance. As Howe puts it:

> Although the level of someone's intelligence is frequently put forward as being a possible reason for that person's success or failure at intellectual tasks, intelligence level is in reality only a descriptive measure, not an explanatory concept [...] invoking someone's high measured intelligence in order to explain a person's success is no more meaningful than putting forward productivity as the explanation of a factory's level of output.
>
> (Howe 1988: 349–50)

Certainly, intelligence levels cannot constitute the entire explanation of someone's performance. Howe considers that a 'person's level of tested intelligence provides rather little information about that individual, and considerably less than many writers who use the term in psychological literature appear to believe' (ibid.: 358). This may be so, but does not mean that the concept has no uses.

It is right that philosophers discussing terms should be striving for conceptual clarity, but it is also the case that for casual, everyday use most people would not worry about these fine distinctions. So, who does need a good definition of intelligence and can there be one that meets everyone's professional needs as well as reflecting general use? Psychologists, teachers, medical staff, social workers and employers need coherent working definitions to discuss the abilities, needs, development and learning of the people for whom they are responsible. All can use the word 'intelligent' in different ways, but this need not matter if there is a shared understanding within the context in question. What does matter is that any information or conjecture held about someone's perceived intelligence is employed responsibly, in the best interests of that person. The information must also be well-grounded, accurate, fair and as infallible as possible. The professionalism of the 'caretaker' should be the guarantee of these standards and since it seems unlikely that the concept of intelligence is about to disappear from public and professional life, it merits further examination, with particular reference to debunking underlying mistakes about the concept of intelligence. Poor use of information about intelligence can disadvantage vulnerable people. Howe argues:

> I think there are strong factual grounds for questioning a number of those assumptions about human ability that many people see as self-evidently true, or 'obviously' correct or just common sense. [...] even those assumptions that almost everyone takes for granted may actually be mistaken. That is a serious matter because the ways in which we adults think about abilities have practical consequences that affect the lives and fortunes of numerous

> children. If the beliefs that guide our decisions and actions are faulty, it is entirely possible that we could be denying children opportunities that would help them to thrive, by putting them off from valuable learning experiences and effectively slamming doors in their faces.
>
> (Howe 1990: 28)

So it is worthwhile considering some of these assumptions and commonly held views that can be detrimental to children. They are ideas that have been so powerful in psychology that they have impacted on laypeople and can be seen across most of Western culture.[4] White (2006) argues that many of the ideas have roots in the sixteenth-century Protestant Reformation and that the ideas are almost too resilient and ubiquitous to be noticed. How have the ideas come about?

How have we come to understand 'intelligence' as we do?

Myriad books have been written on the history of intelligence and there is no way to do the complex developments justice in this chapter. However, some of the key players need to be mentioned within this discussion of the concept and I want to highlight a few specific points through looking at the development of testing intelligence in psychology, since that is where the major work on the concept has been undertaken.[5]

Biometrics was born in the nineteenth century as scientists attempted to quantify everything in the natural world, a relatively new approach used famously by Francis Galton who considered intelligence to be hereditary, fixed and measurable. Through studies of eminent families and their achievements, together with measurements of the physique, calculations of reaction times and evaluation of sensory perception, he established a measure of intelligence that he claimed could explain differing abilities. His first publications (1865) were used to 'explain' the dominance of his race over others. From the outset this field has been beset by controversy over methods, conclusions and use of data.

One of Galton's contemporary detractors was Alfred Binet who was 'astonished by the considerable place reserved to the sensations and simple processes in Galton's work' (1896, cited in Brody 2000: 17). Binet (with Henri and later Simon) proposed far more complex tests based on cognitive processing, with elements of digit span, simple arithmetic, writing and sentence completion. These were designed to help diagnose children with learning and behavioural difficulties in order to improve their life opportunities through a suitable education. Over the years, increasingly sophisticated measures such as the testing of reasoning, judgment and understanding of abstract ideas were included, and comprehensive diagnostic tests were developed. It is important to emphasise that the impetus for Binet to creative the quantitative index of abilities that correlate with academic work was the need to improve the educational experience of children, in particular those deemed uneducable. Binet never used factor analysis or converted mental age scores into a simple Intelligence Quotient (IQ was developed by Stern in 1912), and he was rightly concerned that his tests would be misused.

Binet was never a supporter of the eugenics movement so infamously created by Galton and others. White acknowledges that Binet believed that measured intelligence could be improved and notes that he has a 'different cast of mind' from most theorists of intelligence (White 2006:). White's focus is the development of the Galtonian project and so he does not concentrate further on the possible relevance of Binet's conceptions. Instead, he considers the work of Burt in the UK as this is also relevant to his second theme, that of the development of the curriculum. He does, however, look at the reach of Galton's work across the Atlantic through H. H. Goddard and Lewis Terman. Both of these controversial figures moved the eugenics movement forward in the United States.

It is not feasible to cover all the relevant theorists in any depth but I would like to mention Leta Hollingworth in relation to the more well-known Terman. She made some interesting contributions to the debate on intelligence and her work demonstrates that not all the assumptions that are ascribed to intelligence theorists are as straightforward as they are sometimes presented. As with many other female scientists, she is often overlooked in discussions of her field. In the 1900s she undertook work with women on perceptual, cognitive and motor activities and was able to demonstrate that they were not incapacitated during menstruation, as was held to be true at the time. She also demonstrated that women were as capable as men of holding a wide range of abilities. It was thought that women had lower ceilings of ability and potential achievement than their male counterparts and Hollingworth was able to show this proposition to be false. Her work with young children and adolescents is more frequently cited than that on gender; like Terman she worked with 'gifted children' but unlike him she established a school and attempted to find the best way to encourage them to learn. She did agree with many of Terman's ideas and was also involved with the eugenics movement, to a lesser degree. She strongly felt, however, that as well as inheritance, environmental factors and education could significantly impact on intelligence and achievement.

Hollingworth is only one of a series of people working in psychology and intelligence whose ideas are often ignored in discussion of the key central concepts, giving the impression that there has been more consensus than perhaps exists. Focusing on the difference in views also helps to show up the more marked similarities. White is correct, I think, to emphasise the 'resilience of the Galtonian perspective, its ability to survive for over a century despite what seem gross flaws' (2006: 25). Additionally, however, it would also be interesting to examine more of Galton's detractors (like Binet, Theodore Simon and Hollingworth) and those who also undermined the biometric approach (such as Clark Wissler). Such studies might help dismantle some of the negative and dominant themes in intelligence theory.

This early work in psychology set the stage for all that followed. As already noted, the same problems keep rearing up in both the testing of intelligence and the use of the test scores. These are well-rehearsed issues: '[...] everyone will know about the controversies over the IQ that have preoccupied psychologists for most of the twentieth century' (White 2002: 78). I will then turn to the impact of the recurring themes on children in education, since this is where the concept of intelligence could do some good, or could be used for ill.

Persistent problems in intelligence

In addition to issues mentioned earlier in Sternberg's 1986 paper, other concerns are apparent in discussions about the concept of intelligence. These include worries about the ceilings and limits to intelligence and to intelligence tests, questions of whether intelligence is largely innate or more a result of environmental influences, apparent similarities and differences in intelligence between different genders and races, among others. How these questions impact on education is of interest here.

Ideas about the origins and limits of intelligence are closely connected. With theorists who feel that intelligence is innate, inherited and genetic, it generally follows that they understand both that differences between individuals' intelligence exist and that limits to their abilities are also fixed. White discusses both Galton and Burt's assumptions of these notions (White 2006: 15–17), wondering how they came to these conclusions. One explanation is found in the analogies they draw between physical strength and intelligence, a notion criticised by Ryle (1949). White finds their claims unverifiable and unfalsifiable and so inappropriate for empirical science (White 2002: 90, 2006: 16), but also shows how this link between mental and physical differences was forged as part of the eugenics project and that this derived from Puritan beliefs. The eugenics movement that has so overshadowed work about intelligence is predicated on the notion that hereditary characteristics are dominant and can be controlled by tactical and severe limits on how people are educated and brought up, and in some cases how they are treated, to the point of being prevented from reproducing.

For the practical action of teaching, this idea might seem rather distant and irrelevant; after all, teachers do not stop to wonder how or why children came to be the way they are before teaching each new idea or setting up each activity. They are more properly concerned with helping them develop in suitable ways, whatever the origin of their current levels of intelligence and competence. When a problem arises they might delve into the background and history of the child's learning or current influences, but are not likely to ponder the notions of ceilings or innateness. It might be true that for the teacher in the classroom, the origin of the child's abilities are of no consequence; after all, they normally have to teach whoever is in their class no matter what their personality, background, interests, behaviour and abilities. Hand asserts that the issue of innateness is open, and he considers that 'the position one happens to take in the nature-nurture debate has no bearing at all on one's ability to distinguish intelligent people from unintelligent ones' (Hand 1997: 40). While people may be able to distinguish effectively between different levels of intelligence, their views on the origin of ability may in fact be prejudicial. It is possible that teachers may have views about all sorts of aspects concerning the pupils in their care and their views about the children's intelligence could impinge on how they work with them in the classroom. Subconscious assumptions about the presumed intelligence of children of different genders, ethnicities or other factors in their background could impact on their expectations of the children's abilities, aspirations and potential achievements.

The idea of innateness of intelligence is embedded in many people's ordinary understanding of the concept and is something that is not necessarily routinely questioned. The notion that intelligence is inherited, together with the idea of individual ceilings on ability, has had an enormous impact on social policy and educational structures in the UK, particularly from the 1940s up until the introduction of comprehensive schooling in the 1960s. So, these ideas impact on teachers by being assumptions that many unquestioningly hold, while also shaping the system in which they are working.

There is another highly contested issue that is often raised, examined, debunked but yet revived, and that is to do with difference in intelligence across gender and racial groups. Well-known controversies around work by Jensen and by Herrnstein and Murray are shown by White to have links back to Galtonian ideas (White 2006: 140). Such is the ingrained nature of these ideas about intelligence that psychologists reporting findings (inevitably based around test scores) have to warn against their misuse. In explaining how differences across occupational, racial, urban-rural and gender groups are negligible, Loehlin counsels:

> Stereotyping, the assumption that the members of such categories are much more homogenous than they are, is simply a mark of ignorance regarding the facts. [...] a grasp of the facts can clarify the problem and focus attention on the critical issues to be resolved.
>
> (Loehlin, cited in Sternberg 2000: 191)

Let us return to a notion raised earlier, the concept of intelligence as a single entity or as manifold. In relation to education, the Multiple Intelligences (MI) work of Gardner has been prominent relatively recently (1983). The idea that intelligence is multi-faceted goes back much earlier though, to psychologists Guilford, Carroll and Thurstone, for example (see Sternberg 2000). White has criticised Gardner's ideas roundly, saying he has 'fundamental misgivings about the truth of MI theory' (White 2006: 140). He does, however, support the notion that intelligence can take many forms, citing Ryle's notion that 'the boxer, the surgeon, the poet and the salesman apply their special criteria in the performance of their special tasks' (Ryle 1949: 48). Hand, as mentioned above, takes issue with this 'equation of intelligence with competence' (2007: 37) and focuses his definition of intelligence on having an 'aptitude for theorizing' (ibid.: 41).

Since MI theory has been the mainstay of many a professional development course since the late 1980s, it is well known by teachers and has served to unsettle the idea of a singular entity concept of intelligence. Since in our common usage of terms, we do not subject all our utterances to careful scrutiny, it is highly possible to hold both that there is a singular idea of intelligence and that there are multiple factors also at play, in that one can have both a general level of ability and then additional specialised abilities. This may not be a logical position, but I have certainly found it to be quite common among teachers.[6] It seems that MI has, in some cases, been added to notions of a single unitary concept of intelligence rather than replacing the idea.

Contemporary challenges to traditional ideas

The arguments around MI have also extended to include different aspects of personality, such as motivation, attention and self-regulation (Sternberg 2000). Sternberg also suggests that we could potentially embrace a notion in which there is no prototype for intelligence and that we would have mental exemplars of people who exhibit different types of intelligent behaviour and through these could keep hold of an idea of intelligence (2000: 9).

The notion that intelligence is a fixed capacity is also being challenged with people increasingly accepting the possibilities of changing levels of intelligence across generations as well as within individuals, such as through the Flynn effect (Loehlin 2000: 180). Also, due to the well-publicised difficulties and fallibilities of intelligence tests, people are fortunately more open to the notion that these scores provide only a snapshot of abilities at a specific point in time and that this is not the entire story of that person's limits or possibilities, as Binet tried to assert back in the 1900s.

Dweck's ideas about people's attitudes to the idea of intelligence being fixed or malleable have also shown that it is generally unhelpful to consider the concept as immutable (Dweck 2006). She does not herself provide a definition of intelligence but does demonstrate that attitudes to learning and to self-understanding can have a direct and significant effect on performance. Through her ideas of a 'growth mindset' and a contrasting 'fixed mindset', her work is influencing education by encouraging teachers to use language that does not reinforce a concept of intelligence as being fixed, as having a ceiling, nor as innate. She aims to give people control over their sense of their own intelligence and to help them consider that it is worthwhile investing effort in the tasks they undertake.

Work in molecular genetics, neuroscience and neuroimaging is also shifting the way in which ideas of intelligence are understood as well as showing us increasing detail about how people think and the individual differences and similarities in brain function, efficiency and neuroplasticity (Posner and Rothbart 2006).[7] How far these developments will take our concepts of intelligence is unknown, but they are providing a challenge to perceived views.

New ideas are also being seen in testing. The usual tests designed for diagnosis of learning pathologies and to identify areas in need of remediation are not very useful for the majority of children, i.e. those without specific difficulties or exceptionalities. In these cases, testing performance in detail may be more useful than testing aptitude; this would mean analysing how someone approaches a task rather than simply evaluating the final quality of their response. Similarly, a kind of portfolio assessment would also be helpful in that it could allow teachers to incorporate a range of tasks undertaken at different times and in varying contexts to build a fuller picture of a child's abilities.

So, as White asks, 'Who needs intelligence?'

In education, despite persistent problems with the concept of intelligence, it has some merit. Some of these uses are discussed by Hand (2007: 44–5) and include its usefulness in helping teachers 'plan and pace their teaching' (ibid.: 44) and establishing 'expectations about [pupils'] normal rate of learning in theoretical areas' (ibid.: 45). For those working with children who are not developing typically, there could be other diagnostic uses for holding a concept of intelligence.

White is concerned that the concepts of intelligence are divisive, requiring that resources are directed at providing a good life for the minority. This kind of thinking will prevent the creation of a flourishing life for all:

> It devises ideological structures, partly to do with the innateness of intelligence and a sacrosanct traditional curriculum, to reinforce the power of the more privileged.
>
> (2006: 156–7)

This is partly due to the narrow conceptions of intelligence that dominate the narrative, as we have seen. However, not all definitions of intelligence are entirely impoverished. Sternberg, for example, has written on the role of wisdom or practical intelligence in his triarchic theory (1997). He talks of 'goal-directed adaptive behaviour' and considers practical and creative factors as well as analytic intelligence. Some of this is pretty close to White's preferred definition of flexible adaptation of means to ends.

As discussed above, the history of the concept of intelligence is complex and controversial and the endurance of some deeply divisive and negative uses of test scores haunt any use of the ideas today. White highlights the 'spell of past thinking' (2006: 156) and exhorts us to free ourselves from any unjust conventional perspectives. What is needed is an understanding of intelligence that is rounded and that allows for the complexities of social and psychological human development. As a psychologist who has devoted his working life to the concept, Sternberg urges something similar:

> Intelligence and wisdom are closely related, with wisdom a special part of intelligence. With a world in turmoil, perhaps we need to turn our attention in schools not only to the development of knowledge base, or even of intelligence, narrowly or broadly defined. Perhaps we need to turn our attention to the development of wisdom. We ignore wisdom at our peril.
>
> (2000: 646)

Conceptions of intelligence that take a broader view such as this could help us break away from the Galtonian ideas and their negative legacies and perhaps, echoing Aristotle, with wisdom as a key factor in psychological models, philosophers may be more inclined to join in the discussion.

Notes

1 See, for example, Dennett (1983), cited in Zentall (2000) and Schank and Towle (2000).
2 See, for example, Wallace *et al.* (2009).
3 Unpublished doctoral thesis.
4 Other cultural conceptions of intelligence do challenge commonly held understandings – see Sternberg (2000: 5–7).
5 More details about all the ideas raised in this section and for the history of intelligence and testing can be found in Brody (2000).
6 From discussions delivering continuing professional development programmes to practising teachers both in the UK and abroad between 2000 and 2014.
7 See also the American Psychological Association (APA) for a wide range of sources on developments in psychology, intelligence, genetics and neuroscience, and for a few articles on the application of these findings to education.

References

American Psychological Association (n.d.) http://www.apa.org/about/index.aspx (accessed January 2014).

Bartholomew, D. J. (2004) *Measuring Intelligence: Facts and Fallacies.* Cambridge: Cambridge University Press.

Brody, N. (2000) 'History of theories in measurement of intelligence', in R. J. Sternberg (ed.), *Handbook of Intelligence.* Cambridge: Cambridge University Press, pp. 16–33.

Dweck, C. (2006) *Mindset: The Psychology of Success.* London: Random House.

Eyre, D. (1997) *Able Children in Ordinary Schools.* London: David Fulton.

Fine, C. (2010) *Delusions of Gender: How Our Minds, Society, and Neurosexism Create Difference.* London: W. W. Norton.

Gardner, H. (1983) *Frames of Mind: The Theory of Multiple Intelligences.* New York: Basic Books.

Gould, S. J. (1984) *The Mismeasure of Man.* New York: Norton.

Hand, M. (2007) 'The concept of intelligence', *London Review of Education*, 5 (1): 35–46.

Howe, M. J. A. (1990) 'Children's differing capabilities: doubts about common sense explanations', *Gifted and Talented*, 1: 28–31.
Howe, M. J. A. (1997) *IQ in Question: The Truth About Intelligence.* London: Sage.
Loehlin, J. C. (2000) 'Group differences in intelligence', in R. J. Sternberg (ed.), *Handbook of Intelligence.* Cambridge: Cambridge University Press, pp. 176–93.
Posner, M. I. and Rothbart, M. K. (2006) *Educating the Human Brain.* Washington, DC: APA Books.
Ryle, G. (1949) *The Concept of Mind.* Harmondsworth: Penguin.
Schank, R. C. and Towle, B. (2000) 'Artificial intelligence', in R. J. Sternberg (ed.), *Handbook of Intelligence.* Cambridge: Cambridge University Press, pp. 341–58.
Sternberg, R. J. (ed.) (2000) *Handbook of Intelligence.* Cambridge: Cambridge University Press.
Wallace, B., Leyden, S., Montgomery, D., Winstanley, C., Pomerantz, M. and Fitton, S. (2009) *Raising the Achievement of All Pupils Within an Inclusive Setting: Practical Strategies for Developing Best Practice.* London: Routledge.
White, J. (2002) *The Child's Mind.* London: Routledge.
White, J. (2006) *Intelligence, Destiny and Education: The Ideological Roots of Intelligence Testing.* London: Routledge.
Winch, C. (2010) 'Vocational education, knowing how and intelligence concepts', *Journal of Philosophy of Education*, 44 (4): 551–67.
Zentall, T. R. (2000) 'Animal intelligence', in R. J. Sternberg (ed.), *Handbook of Intelligence.* Cambridge: Cambridge University Press, pp. 197–215.

Chapter 7

Well-being and education[1]

Doret de Ruyter

To me, one of John White's most significant contributions to our discipline and educational practice is his work on well-being. It is remarkable that he is still highly dedicated to this cause – though he is fortunately able to spend time on other worthwhile activities and with his family and friends too (see for examples White 2011). As a relative outsider I would say he is flourishing and I think that when asked he would say that he has had a happy life so far and hopes that it will continue for many years. Thus John White is a fine example of what a life of well-being means.

Introduction

Well-being and education are intimately related. Usually, parents and teachers hope that children will do well in life and they want to contribute to children's ability to lead a life of well-being when they are adults. In other words, well-being is perceived to be an aim of education. They also have a responsibility for the well-being of children while they are growing up, which means that well-being lies not only in the future as something to be realised, but also in the present. Both present and future well-being are important. Parents who focus on the future of their child and aim to ensure that their child has all the possibilities that will give him or her the best chances to live a flourishing life may be too preoccupied with the future to consider the present too. White compares this to orthodox religious views that give more weight to the afterlife and see life on earth as less important – although it is important to live life in such a way that entrance to heaven is possible (2011: 18). Why enjoy a life of sin for about 75 years if one can enjoy eternal well-being? Analogously, why not invest about 18 years for the benefit of the next 60 years? While it is clear that childhood is predominantly a period of development, exploration and learning – children have to learn many things in order to be able to live an independent life and in childhood human beings are best attuned to learning – well-being is not only an end-state. Childhood can (or has to) also be a happy period and, as White has it, learning is a worthwhile activity that allows in principle (not always in practice) for children's flourishing in their development too (2011: 17, 18).

Thus parents and teachers normally pursue two aims in educating c
child's future well-being, i.e. being a flourishing adult, and his or
flourishing. For clarity's sake, I will refer to the first as the aim of educatio..
the second as present well-being. The concept 'well-being' seems, however, to have a different meaning in these two different contexts. In this contribution I want to clarify these two interpretations. However, before I begin with the elucidation of the concept, I first need to say a bit more about well-being as an aim of education, because this idea is not beyond contention.

Well-being as an aim of education

Is well-being an aim of education? Of course, will be the first answer from most people. They might add that it is not or should not be the only aim of education, that it is also important for children to develop into moral persons and citizens who contribute to the welfare of society, but that parents normally pursue their children's well-being and that one also expects teachers to contribute to the possibility that pupils will be able to lead a flourishing life. This answer presupposes a distinction between a person's own well-being and that of others. The philosophical discussion about whether or not a person's well-being includes moral dispositions or whether it refers just to prudence and self-interest, which can but may not necessarily involve altruism, is age old (see also White 1990). I will not resolve it in this chapter, but it is possible to distinguish at least three different positions that affirm or counter the distinction. Firstly, one might say that *the* aim of education is living a good life, which includes not only one's own good, but also that of others (see, for instance, Haybron 2008). Secondly, as White (2011) notes, suggesting that well-being is an aim of education refers not just to the well being of an individual child, but also to that of other human beings surrounding him or her (sentient beings) close by or farther away. This means that well-being as an aim of education includes the development of both prudent and moral behaviour. Finally, one can suggest that people are social beings who need and normally want to have good relationships with others and that altruism is therefore part and parcel of their own well-being (see, for instance, White 1990).

In line with the position that education aims for living a good life, a second response might be that well-being can be, but should not be, the aim of education. While this answer does not imply that parents and teachers ignore the well-being of children now and in the future, it is not perceived as the aim of education. This answer hinges on the interpretation of well-being. Take, for instance, Peters' conception of the educated person as the aim of education. In his description and justification of this idea, the person's well-being does not feature explicitly. However, this depends on what one believes constitutes well-being. The conception of the educated person can imply a theory of well-being, possibly by invoking a particular interpretation of flourishing. So while people who give this response do not say that well-being is an aim of education, the aim that they are defending might be interpreted in such terms without doing injustice to their position. It should be noted that this is not true in general. Barrow, for instance, states that '[M]any would perhaps accept that schools should have a responsibility for developing the physical health and the mental health (encompassing such things as confidence) of individuals as well as socializing them. But such concerns seems to be distinct from the business of educating them' (1999: 17).

Thirdly, it might be argued that well-being cannot be an aim of education because well-being is not something that can be achieved as a goal. It refers to a state of being or a state of feeling that is a by-product of one's activities or the realisation of one's plans (see, for instance, Elster 1981). So instead of well-being, the aim of education should be described as the acquisition or personalisation of knowledge, skills and dispositions with which children are able to discover which activities or engagements will contribute to their well-being. Moreover, parents and teachers cannot pursue this for children; this is something that children have to realise themselves. Educators can only provide the tools with which children are able to lead a life that we can describe as a life of well-being. I agree with both these claims. I take it that well-being refers to a state that comes with particular engagements – what these are, and how they are achieved, will be dealt with below. Furthermore, only a person him or herself can make themselves flourish (see, for instance, Rasmussen 1999), which is not to deny that he or she needs others too. However, well-being could still be regarded as an aim, depending on how one defines an 'aim of education'. If it refers to the final answer in the justification of why one educates children and why education has the content it has, then well-being can be regarded as an aim of education.[2] The acquisition of knowledge, capacities and dispositions are indeed what parents and teachers pursue, but if they are asked why, they can say that they do so to further children's well-being.

Finally, some people may want to make a distinction between the aims of parental upbringing and school education. They may say that parents will (or should) have the well-being of their children at heart and will (or should) raise their children in the way they believe will best enhance the (future) well-being of their children. They are also able to do so because they have an intimate relationship with their children and can therefore discover what constitutes well-being for their children and what they need. Schools or teachers on the other hand cannot pursue the well-being of each and every individual child that enters the classroom because they are not able to form such an intimate relationship with them. And they should not, because teachers have to pursue different aims in educating children. There are two possible responses to this point. Firstly, in many countries, the well-being of pupils is perceived as an aim of school education and in the UK, for instance, the National Curriculum includes the subject Personal, Social, Health and Economic education. Thus one might say that this is a rather conservative or ill-conceived idea about school education (see, for instance, White 2011). Secondly, one might say that this position is based on a particular interpretation of well-being that is rather confined and highly subjective, and that it represents a misunderstanding of the way in which people pursue well-being. One can also argue that well-being requires the development of knowledge, capacities and dispositions too. And this is what schools aim for.

John White has defended the promotion of pupils' well-being in his entire *oeuvre*. It did not feature as much in his earliest work, but since *The Aims of Education Restated* (1982) and more extensively in his *Education and the Good Life*, which he says constitutes an important improvement on *The Aims of Education Restated* (1990: 11), his work deals with what constitutes well-being and how educators can promote it.[3] With White, I take it that well-being can be conceived of as an aim of education, that it is one of the final justifications of the aspirations of parents and teachers. But what do we mean by well-being?

Well-being, flourishing and happiness explored

Making sense of the wealth of theories

Writing about well-being as an aim of education and doing justice to all the shoulders on which one stands is a difficult task because of the overwhelming number of books and articles written about the subject in the past decades. Philosophers, psychologists and sociologists have embraced this concept, a development in which the reintroduction of virtue ethics within philosophy and the emergence of positive psychology have played an important role. There are three dominant terms in the literature: in addition to 'well-being', the terms 'flourishing' and 'happiness' are used. The difficulty in explicating the meaning of the concepts is not only that there are different concepts and conceptions in the literature, but also that the three terms are used for the same concepts. Some authors, like John White, use the terms well-being and flourishing interchangeably, while others suggest that happiness and flourishing have the same meaning. This means that an investigation of what might be an appropriate theory of well-being should not exclude works on flourishing and happiness. In this section I will give a concise overview, ending with a description of John White's theory, with which I will compare my own views.

Well-being

Like White, I interpret well-being as an umbrella term under which various theories reside, which can be called theories of flourishing or happiness (see also Haybron 2008). As well-being cannot be used as an adjective – one cannot say that one lives a well-being life – one needs one of these two other terms as an adjective. And by using either flourishing or happiness, it is possible to indicate that one is defending a particular theory of well-being. The most commonly encountered distinction in theories of well-being is that between objective theories and subjective theories. According to objective theories, which I will discuss more extensively below, persons live a life of well-being if they realise goods that are deemed to be objectively good for all people (Arneson 1999) or if they develop or have developed their natural capacities (Aristotle). In contrast, subjective theories claim that persons' well-being refers to the positive evaluation by persons themselves: they have fulfilled their (informed) desires and they are satisfied with the way their life is going; they are happy.

In our daily language we tend to use 'well-being' in both an objective and subjective sense. When Alice answers our query as to how she is doing by saying that she is fine, she is using well-being in a subjective sense, just as we are – we interpret her answer as meaning that she is satisfied with her life at that moment or that she is happy. And such is the answer we hope to get, for we wish people to have a life that is filled with satisfaction.[4] It can also refer to a description of personal attainment. When Brian says to Catherine that Derek is doing really well because Derek is successful in his job, he is financially well off and he just got married to a beautiful and intelligent woman, he is using well-being in an objective sense – referring to the fulfilment of states that are good for human beings. Brian does not mention what Derek thinks or feels about all this. He might well be rather miserable and be hiding this from outsiders. These two meanings of the term are not necessarily related to the distinction between a first and third person perspective. Brian may also tell Catherine that Derek phoned him yesterday with the happy news that he has been promoted to the position that he had always dreamt of, that he and his wife are expecting a baby that they had been looking forward to for years and that they have bought the house that they wanted. He could not be a happier man. These two senses refer to different ideas about what constitutes well-being. Based on our common language and, importantly, the fact that we attach value to both of them, I suggest that a theory of well-being should combine these two interpretations. Such a mixed theory, as it is called, defends the idea that well-being should be used in cases where persons not only fulfil (give meaningful content to) objective goods or develop their capacities, i.e. that they flourish, but also when persons are satisfied with the way in which they are doing so.

For clarity's sake, in the remainder of this chapter I will use the term 'well-being' as an overarching term, 'flourishing' for an objective or inter-subjective theory of well-being and 'happiness' for subjective theories of well-being (see also De Ruyter 2007). I believe that White uses flourishing as the predominant adjective with reason and will demonstrate that he does indeed defend a version of a non-subjective theory of well-being. It is a particular version of a desire-fulfilment theory (2011: 92), in which the values on which well-being rests are inter-subjective. Thus it might be perceived of as a third possibility next to objective and subjective theories – though one that is closer to objective than to subjective theories of well-being.

Flourishing

While all authors who develop a theory of flourishing refer to Aristotle, who first used the term, there are various theories of flourishing that are more or less closely related to Aristotle's *eudaimonia*.[5] Yet there are several common characteristics that can be said to be necessary for saying that a theory is a theory of flourishing.[6]

Firstly, central to these theories is the idea of optimal functioning or the pursuit of excellence or the best in oneself (see, for instance, Kraut 1979; Rasmussen 1999; Huta 2013), which qualifies what can be called well-being in a non-subjective sense. This can be interpreted naturalistically or biologically, but as we will see, this is not necessarily the case. Secondly, characteristic of theories about flourishing is the notion of achievement or what White calls success. A person can be said to flourish only if she does something successfully.

I defend the view that flourishing as success in the pursuit of excellence, i.e. achieving excellence, is a necessary condition for well-being, but with two qualifications. Firstly, we have to make a distinction between different conceptions of flourishing. I regard theories that define flourishing as the complete realisation of one's capacities or the complete fulfilment of worthwhile goods as theories of ideal flourishing. This is a perfect, or ideal, conception of flourishing. An ideal conception of flourishing can be distinguished from both an actual and a realistic conception. The actual conception concerns an evaluation of the person's present state and uses less demanding (realistic) standards. While it still refers to achievement, or as White would have it success, it does not require a person to have successfully and perfectly achieved all aspects of his or her potential flourishing. Thus one can say that a person is flourishing even though he or she does not meet the ideal of flourishing, just as we can say that we live in a democracy even though it does not meet the ideal of a democracy. The realistic conception has particular relevance in relation to flourishing as an aim of education. While one can pursue the ideal of flourishing, this perfect state is unrealisable. If one takes into account what people can achieve given their circumstances and abilities, one is working with a realistic conception of flourishing[7] (see also Rasmussen 1999).

Secondly, I think it important to interpret flourishing in an agent-dependent manner. (Complete) fulfilment can be conceptualised in agent-neutral terms and in agent-dependent or individualised as well as agent-relative terms[8] (see Rasmussen 1999). This distinction is not the same as that between subjective and objective accounts of well-being. Subjective theories are necessarily agent-dependent (although the definition is agent-neutral), but agent-dependent theories are not necessarily subjective, for agent-dependent theories can still insist that there are better or worse lives for a person, and claim that a person is living a worse life than he or she could (and is therefore not flourishing). Agent-dependency still presumes that there are objective or inter-subjective goods, but acknowledges that there are diverse ways in which these can be fulfilled. People have different qualities and live in different circumstances and therefore the ways in which they flourish will be diverse. Nor is this distinction similar to that between ideal flourishing, actual flourishing and realistic flourishing. Actual flourishing can also be based on agent-neutral and agent-dependent interpretations of flourishing. One might conclude that a person is not actually flourishing if he or she does not meet certain agent-neutral criteria; in other words, one can have a realistic view of what a person may come to achieve, but nevertheless define this in agent-neutral terms. However, as I have implicitly suggested in the description of actual flourishing and realistic expectations, in my view these two do take into account the particularities of individuals.

Happiness

As I said in the introduction to this section, 'happiness' is also used interchangeably with 'flourishing', which goes back to the discussion of how *eudaimonia* is best translated. However, I find it more helpful to use 'happiness' for subjective evaluations and subjective states rather than non-subjective ones. Among the plethora of books on happiness by philosophers and psychologists published since the turn of the century, I believe that Haybron's provides the best overview and evaluation of theories of happiness.[9] He defines happiness as 'for one's emotional condition to be broadly positive – involving stances of attunement, engagement, and endorsement – with negative central affective states and mood propensities only to a minor extent' (2008: 147). This positive emotion is not a mere psychological state. It is a person's positive evaluation based on his or her own standards and aims (see Kraut 1979: 178). This does not mean that one cannot evaluate the source of a person's happiness and advise him or her to find it somewhere else, or that parents should refrain from presenting valuable sources, influencing their children's standards of happiness and steering them away from instant gratification and feelings of happiness. Theories of happiness, except for (simplistic) hedonism, both within philosophy (for example, the informed-desire theory defended by Griffin) and psychology (for instance, subjective well-being theory as developed by Diener or Seligman and Peterson's positive psychological theories), stress that happiness is the dominance of positive emotions over negative ones with regard to those aspects of one's life regarded as meaningful by the person him or herself. However, the more one believes that these sources and standards can be objectively assessed as better or worse, the less subjective the theory becomes and the more it becomes what is called a mixed theory.

Mixed theories

John White's theory of well-being (or flourishing) is an example of an agent-dependent but non-subjective theory; it is an inter-subjective theory. For an account of his ideas I refer to his book *Exploring Well-Being in Schools* (White 2011) and several recent articles.

White defines well-being or a flourishing life as 'a life spent in whole-hearted and successful engagement in worthwhile relationships and activities' (e.g. 2002, 2005: 30, 2007: 18, 2011: 124), which is very similar to Raz's definition (2004), as quoted in note 1, and which clearly influenced White's position. White's theory consists of three central elements: (a) wholeheartedness; (b) success; and (c) 'worthwhileness'.

Wholeheartedness

Flourishing requires that the person is able to undertake activities that he or she enjoys. This brings in an agent-dependent and a subjective aspect. According to White, a person, at least in liberal democratic societies, will flourish if he or she can engage with those relationships and those activities that he or she has autonomously chosen. While in his earlier work (e.g. 1982, 1990) White argued that this requires a person's critical reflection on available options, he now defends a more minimal interpretation of autonomy which presumes that the person's engagements are those which are self-chosen and which he or she can wholeheartedly endorse. This of course requires reflection on the part of the person, but not necessarily critical reflection about his or herself or his or her options. The options in question are ones that he or she can live from the inside, as Harry Brighouse (2006) puts it.

Success

White does not describe precisely what he means by being successful, but he seems to mean something like fulfilling worthwhile activities in the way in which they are intended. For instance, playing soccer successfully means, among other things, kicking the ball rather than throwing it, contributing as a team player, trying to win by scoring as many goals as possible and playing fairly. Note that this does not mean that one is only successful if one actually wins. However, there is also a subjective element in White's objective interpretation. Doing things successfully, be it work or hobbies, and having successful relationships with family and friends leads to fulfilment. And fulfilment is, in White's view, a necessary condition for well-being.

I agree with this account and have defended the view (e.g. 2004, 2007) that to attribute well-being to a person requires that he or she be able to confirm that they are flourishing; his or her feelings have to be in tune with what he or she does. And this should be true for all the domains that constitute his or her well-being (I will return to this point below) – activities and engagements in these domains should, at a minimum, not be detrimental to or undermine his or her well-being. People value and rank activities and engagements differently, so the fulfilment of pursuits in one domain can carry more weight than in another. Consider, for example, the work that people do, a subject about which White has written extensively (e.g. White 1997), and compare Anne and Joyce who both work on a factory assembly line. Their jobs do not contribute to their well-being, for they would both prefer different, more inspiring jobs. However, while Anne suffers because she detests her job, work for Joyce is a means to earn money to pay for the holidays she loves.

Finally, it is important to note that people can be highly successful in worthwhile activities and even be very satisfied but nevertheless not have a life of well-being. For instance, while one can say, with Brighouse (2006), that Van Gogh was flourishing, albeit only in the sense that he developed fully in one area of his life and did something utterly worthwhile (which he also considered worthwhile and with which he identified), his was not a life of well-being given the (at times extreme) psychological distress he suffered. This is a matter of degree, obviously, as it is possible to say that people experience well-being at many periods in their life or that they have a high level of well-being at certain periods and a lower level at others.[10]

'Worthwhileness'

The idea that well-being is a state in which a person is satisfied because he or she is successful in the activities and engagements that are important to them is in White's view necessary but not sufficient.

White rejects the informed-desire theory of well-being on the basis that people may be mistaken in their beliefs of what they should desire. Even if people fulfil desires that may be wholeheartedly felt, autonomously chosen and reflected upon on the basis of the relevant information, and feel happy, they still may not live flourishing lives. To explain 'worthwhileness', White draws on Joseph Raz's theory of values. Raz defends a social dependence thesis, which consists of two (sub-)theses: 'The special social dependence thesis claims that some values exist only if there are (or were) social practices sustaining them. The (general) social dependence thesis claims that, with some exceptions, all values depend on social practices either by being subject to the special thesis or through their dependence on values that are subject to the special thesis' (2003: 19).

Raz sees the relation between value and practice as on the one hand a necessary relation, i.e. a value will only come into existence within a social practice, but on the other hand a contingent one, as he claims that values do not depend on the original practice to remain of value; practices are necessary for the origin of values, but not for their continuity, and practices can change without the associated values necessarily disappearing. In line with this theory, White suggests that well-being depends on the satisfaction of desires that are deemed to be valuable by a collection of people who form – in a loose way – a social practice (he sometimes uses the terms 'culture' or 'tradition'). What is valuable or worthwhile is what this collection of people believes to be of value and what they desire (2002: 452), the origins of which extend into the past.

My conception of well-being has many similarities to White's. I suggest that a person lives a life of well-being if she is able to give meaningful content to the goods that are important to human beings and if she is able to make the most of her qualities. These will allow her to live her life to the full. The meaningful content and optimal development are agent-dependent. What is agent-neutral is that there are certain goods that can be said to be good for all human beings and that optimal development is something that human people should aspire towards. When they do so they will flourish, but in the course of their development they will also flourish if they can successfully do the things that not only matter in themselves but also contribute to their development.

Whose goods, whose values?

I take it as a universal feature of mankind that human beings want to live a flourishing life. Characteristic of all living species is that they have an instinct to survive. Humans (and maybe other animals too) also have the ability to think about what they do with their lives; normally they want to make the most of their lives and hope that they will be blessed with good fortune.

I think that White and I share a similar view on the way objective goods should be interpreted as being necessary for human flourishing. What I mean by 'objective' is that the goods can be established to be important for human beings irrespective of a person's endorsement of these goods. The goods I believe to be objectively good are few and they include substantive goods as well as the need for autonomy, which I here interpret in a rather minimal way much in line with White. Similar to the capabilities that Nussbaum, among others, argues to be 'central requirements of a life with dignity' (2006: 75), objective goods comprise basic needs[11] like food, shelter, safety and health and goods that are related to what I call existential needs, social relations,[12] intellectual, creative/aesthetic and physical pursuits, and autonomy. While the list is short, there are many ways in which these goods can be given content or meaning. These objective goods require an agent-dependent content.

I think White and I also share the view that both basic and existential needs are related to human nature. That they are met and that people can fulfil the objective goods are necessary conditions of flourishing – which is thus also related to human nature. However, the way in which they are fulfilled or how humans develop is not inherent to human nature or an individual's human character in a teleological sense – they are not predetermined. In his earlier work (e.g. 1982), White is more explicit on the relation between the goods of human flourishing and human nature than in his later work, where he seems to focus more particularly on the way in which human beings fulfil these goods (2002, 2007, 2011), which then become things that groups of people (that may be smaller or larger, sometimes he refers to cultures) see as valuable goods, as goods that make their life meaningful or worth their while (2002, 2007). It is 'an accumulated wisdom …' (2002: 454). This wisdom is that which 'is passed on within traditions and reflected upon and changed by people of wider experience and greater reflectiveness' (2002: 454). Although I agree with White that the values that we use to giving meaningful content to these goods reflect inter-subjective judgments, I want to emphasise the universality of the objective goods more than White does (again, particularly in his later work). Even though human nature is diverse, as human beings differ, for instance, because of their gender, temperament and capacities or talents, they also have much in common. I believe it is important to acknowledge that fulfilling these objective goods is a central part of what Nussbaum refers to as our common humanity, which is independent of culture or tradition.

The meaning and use of well-being in education

I argued above that well-being as an aim of education seems to refer to a different interpretation of well-being than children's well-being in the present. Now that I have clarified the term and have described the mixed theory, I can address this issue more precisely. I suggest that when we reflect on well-being as an aim of education we have an ideal conception of flourishing in mind and we stress the objective aspect while not losing sight of the subjective aspect, whereas in the case of children's present well-being we look at their actual flourishing and zoom in on the subjective aspect (see also Kraut 1979).[13]

When parents say that they hope that their newborn will live a flourishing life or a life of well-being, they mean that they hope he or she will lead a worthwhile life or a successful life, to which they will likely, but not necessarily, add that he or she be satisfied with what they do. The same goes for our expressed wishes for other people's children. Think, for instance, of the following scenario. Nancy is at a baby shower and says to the (expecting) mother: 'I hope that Johnny will do OK.' Unless we know more about Nancy (for instance her temperament), about the circumstances in which Johnny is being born (maybe Nancy knows that Johnny has a hereditary disease and doing OK will be the best one can hope for him), we will think this is a rather bleak wish. We expect children's well-wishers to think of their future well-being in terms of higher levels. This is different from evaluating Johnny's life at a particular point during his adolescence or adulthood, when we would take into account what he has been able to achieve given his circumstances and abilities, as well as his level of satisfaction with his life.[14]

As an aim of education, well-being is used in an ideal sense. This is a descriptive observation, but I also want to make the normative claim that it is important that well-being as an aim of education be conceptualised in an ideal sense. When parents and teachers invoke an ideal conception of flourishing as an aim of education, they are committed to the realisation of the ideal well-being of children: they have the will to regulate their action in light of the relevant standard of excellence or perfection (compare Emmet 1994 or Frankfurt 1999). This does not mean that they will all pursue the same aim or do so in the same manner. The ways in which parents and teachers pursue this ideal will differ, not only because of the agent-dependent interpretation of flourishing, but also because they will have different views about the way they can best contribute to the likelihood that the children in question will flourish. In pursuing this aim they should also bear in mind the subjective well-being of children, which means that they realise that the ideal conception is too demanding as an aim to be achieved. The realistic conception has to inform their expectation of what children can actually achieve.[15]

Finally, both the ideal of flourishing as an aim of education and the present well-being of children requires reflection on the conditions in which children live and are being educated and can indicate to us how far the actual situation is removed from the ideal: what can (or should) educators do to optimise conditions in light of an ideal conception of flourishing? In other words, the ideal gives educators (or adults in general) a moral impetus to enable children to flourish (see, for instance, Raz 2004; Suissa 2008; White 2011). And this brings me to a distinction introduced by Lawrence (1993).

Lawrence distinguishes the ideal that 'we want in our lives to do what is best in whatever the circumstances and situations that arise' (p. 7) from what can be regarded as the ideal circumstances in which one could live, i.e. circumstances that could not be better for us as human beings.[16] Concern with the first ideal leads to a focus on the qualities of persons that can be seen as comprising their flourishing, while the second ideal focuses on the best environment for persons or the best activities for them to engage in, in order to flourish. This distinction is, I believe, insightful with regard to adults' responsibilities to pursue both well-being as an aim of education and children's present well-being. Adults need to focus not only on developing children's qualities, but also on the situation in which they are developing. As Lawrence has it:

> The ideally circumstanced ideal is one of our major practical concerns as rational agents. We should as individuals, as parents, and as citizens be concerned with the procurement of such circumstances, such situational-environments, as are optimal for humans (for ourselves, our families, our societies), that is, those that provide opportunities for the activities that are ideally the best.
>
> (p. 10)

In conclusion

Clarifying 'well-being' is a theoretical task in which one abstracts from daily life and the uniqueness of situations in which children grow up. This at least is the way in which I do philosophy of education. This does not mean that it lacks practical bearing – on the contrary; but any such bearing is indirect. The precise translation into educational practice I leave to experts. The work of philosophers of education is, however, important for them in addressing urgent educational and social questions, for instance about social media, the consequences of the economic crises on children's future, or the overwhelming number of options and choices still available in our society. Sound educational policies and interventions depend not only on rigorous empirical analysis, but also on the analysis of the central concepts, terms and justification of educational practices involved. It matters which conception of well-being is pursued in schools and by parents and used as a justification for educational practices. And to this, as I wrote in the first sentence, John White has made a significant contribution.

Notes

1 I thank Anders Schinkel and the editors for their comments on the first version of this chapter.
2 In contrast Raz believes that there is no 'independent force to care about people's well-being. Given that well-being consists in successful pursuit of *valuable* goals and relationships there is an obvious reason to pursue whatever it consists in, i.e. those valuable goals and relationships. But I could not think of a general reason for pursuing well-being, one's own or that of others, beyond that' (2004: 292). If one defines well-being in these terms and agrees with Raz that this is what constitutes well-being, as White does, it is possible to claim that well-being is not an additional aim that one has to pursue on top of teaching children the successful pursuit of valuable goals and relationships. However, one might also suggest that it is convenient to use the term well-being as a short-hand term.
3 Interestingly, it is only in 2011 that he published a book with the word 'well-being' in the title and only since his (halfhearted) retirement that he uses it in the titles of his works.
4 Although what 'we' believe is a good reason for feeling satisfied differs, as we will see.
5 Authors (White too) do not tend to accept Aristotle's teleological anthropology (or ontology in general). Although no one will deny that children are born with certain capacities and capabilities, these can be developed in a variety of ways (think, for instance, of intelligence, which can be developed and expressed in diverse jobs and hobbies).
6 Huta mentions nine common themes in conceptions of *eudaimonia* as a way of acting: excellence, authenticity/autonomy, development, full functioning, broad scope of concern, engagement, autotelism, contemplation and acceptance, while she has found seven common themes in conceptions of *eudaimonia* as a form of well-being: meaning, elevation, awe, connection, aliveness, fulfilment and competence (2013: 6, 7).
7 This might still be called ideal, because it is excellent that people achieve such; it is what I have called a common ideal – it is an ideal that is achievable (see, for example, De Ruyter 2007), but for clarity's sake I call it a realistic conception of flourishing.
8 Rasmussen makes a distinction between individualised (people flourish in different manners) and agent-relative aspects. The latter refers to the view that flourishing 'arises within and obtains only *in relationship to* some person's life' (1999: 6)
9 This does not mean that I agree with all of his claims.
10 Some, like Aristotle, claim that well-being and flourishing refer to a whole life (that one can only say of a person that he or she has had a flourishing life or well-being at the end of their life). However, most philosophers and psychologists suggest that well-being, flourishing or happiness can refer to particular periods (one can say that one flourishes or flourished in particular periods of time, but not in others) and some, the hedonists in particular, argue that happiness can apply to short periods of elation. I side with the majority and think that the second is the most plausible given the way in which we use the concepts, and that when we judge a person's life overall we take into account these periods. We do not have to wait until a person dies to say that they are flourishing although we do have to do so if we want to judge whether they had a flourishing life.
11 I want to add that the domains to which they belong or the objective goods that they are (health, food, shelter, relationship) in my view are not merely conditions, but are also domains that people can give a particular content.
12 This is both a basic need and an existential need.
13 Kraut states it somewhat differently. He suggests that we are objective in our early hopes and subjective in our later judgment.

14 Kraut claims that we have to turn to a subjective standard in our evaluation of the lives of adults, because there is no detailed and plausible theory (as yet) that describes 'what deviations from the ideal are compatible with happiness [or well-being, added by author]' (1979: 190). While I acknowledge that there is a grey area in which we are not certain we can appropriately use the term 'well-being' in evaluating a person's life, I do not think we need a detailed theory or precise standards to measure divergence from a golden standard.

15 Parents also have to take their own well-being into account and should be realistic in their expectations of their own abilities. This aspect is important, but cannot be dealt with within this article.

16 He calls these the 'however circumstanced ideal' and the 'ideally circumstanced ideal'.

References

Aristotle (1985) *Nicomachean Ethics*, trans. T. Irwin. Indianapolis, IN: Hackett.

Arneson, R. J. (1999) 'Human flourishing versus desire satisfaction', in E. Frankel Paul, F. D. Miller Jr and J. Paul (eds), *Human Flourishing*. Cambridge: Cambridge University Press, pp. 113–42.

Barrow, R. (1999) '"Or what's a heaven for?" The importance of aims in education', in R. Marples (ed.), *The Aims of Education*. London: Routledge, pp. 14–22.

Brighouse, H. (2006) *On Education*. London: Routledge.

de Ruyter, D. J. (2004) 'Pottering in the garden? On human flourishing and education', *British Journal of Educational Studies*, 52 (4): 377–89.

de Ruyter, D. J. (2007) 'Ideals, education and happy flourishing', *Educational Theory*, 57 (1): 23–35.

de Ruyter, D. J. (2012) 'On optimal development and becoming an optimiser', *Journal of Philosophy of Education*, 46 (1): 25–41.

Elster, J. (1981) 'States that are essentially by-products', *Social Science Information*, 20 (3): 431–73.

Emmet, D. (1994) *The Role of the Unrealisable. A Study in Regulative Ideals*. New York: St. Martin's Press.

Frankfurt, H. G. (1999) *Necessity, Volition and Love*. Cambridge: Cambridge University Press.

Haybron, D. M. (2008) *The Pursuit of Unhappiness. The Elusive Psychology of Well-being*. Oxford: Oxford University Press.

Huta, V. (2013) 'Eudaimonia', in S. David, I. Boniwell and A. C. Ayers (eds), *Oxford Handbook of Happiness*. Oxford: Oxford University Press, pp. 201–13.

Kraut, R. (1979) 'Two conceptions of happiness', *Philosophical Review*, 88 (2): 167–97.

Lawrence, G. (1993) 'Aristotle and the ideal life', *Philosophical Review*, 102 (1): 1–34.

Nussbaum, M. C. (2006) *Frontiers of Justice*. Cambridge: Belknap Press.

Rasmussen, D. B. (1999) 'Human flourishing and the appeal to human nature', in E. Frankel Paul, F. D. Miller Jr and J. Paul (eds), *Human Flourishing*. Cambridge: Cambridge University Press, pp. 1–43.

Raz, J. (2003) *The Practice of Value*. Oxford: Clarendon Press.

Raz, J. (2004) 'The role of well-being', *Psychological Perspectives*, 18 (1): 269–94.

Suissa, J. (2008) 'Lessons from a new science? On teaching happiness in schools', *Journal of Philosophy of Education*, 42 (3–4): 575–90.

White, J. (1982) *The Aims of Education Restated*. London: Routledge & Kegan Paul.
White, J. (1990) *Education and the Good Life: Beyond the National Curriculum*. London: Kogan Page.
White, J. (1997) 'Education, work and well-being', *Journal of Philosophy of Education*, 31 (2): 233–48.
White, J. (2002) 'Education, the market and the nature of personal well-being', *British Journal of Educational Studies*, 50 (4): 442–56.
White, J. (2005) 'Education for well-being', *Education Review*, 19: 1.
White, J. (2006) 'Autonomy, human flourishing and the curriculum', *Journal of Philosophy of Education*, 40 (3): 381–90.
White, J. (2007) 'Wellbeing and education: issues of culture and authority', *Journal of Philosophy of Education*, 41 (1): 18–28.
White, J. (2011) *Exploring Well-being in Schools: A Guide to Making Children's Lives More Fulfilling*. London: Routledge.

Chapter 8

Beyond moral education?

Michael Hand

I joined the London Institute of Education, fresh from my doctoral studies, in 2001, a year after John White's retirement as Professor of Philosophy of Education. Fortunately for me, retirement had little impact on John's involvement in either the intellectual life of the Institute or the field of philosophy of education. Over the last dozen years, John has continued to publish prolifically, to make major contributions to meetings, seminars and conferences at the Institute, and to be an unusually active Honorary Vice-President of the Philosophy of Education Society of Great Britain. He was even persuaded to come out of retirement for a short spell to lead the Institute's Philosophy Section during an interregnum between the incumbencies of Harry Brighouse and Terry McLaughlin. During this period I have come to know John well, to consider him a touchstone for my philosophical thinking, and to count him as a friend. It is a privilege to be able to contribute to this *Festschrift* in his honour.

In Chapter 3 of his landmark book *Education and the Good Life*, John White makes a radical proposal. He recommends that we abandon moral education in favour of 'education in altruism' (White 1990: 49). He advances a series of arguments intended to show that there are serious objections to moral education as traditionally understood, and that the legitimate purposes moral education is intended to serve are, in fact, better served by the cultivation of altruistic dispositions.

I think White is wrong about this. His mistake lies not in the conviction that schools should cultivate altruistic dispositions: undoubtedly they should. Rather it lies in the suggestion that education in altruism should *replace* moral education. While it is true that these two kinds of education aim to give children different sorts of motive for some similar sorts of conduct, it does not follow that we must choose between them. On the contrary, it seems to me clear that children should be educated in such a way that they are routinely moved to act, or to refrain from acting, *both* by concern and sympathy for others *and* by a sense of moral right and wrong.

I shall, then, defend a *complementarity thesis* against White's *supersession thesis.* I shall try to show, first, that the objections to moral education White raises can be satisfactorily answered and, second, that steps taken to enlarge children's sympathies, no matter how effective, will not eliminate the need for subscription to moral standards. Moral education is therefore both possible and a necessary complement to education in altruism. Before I turn to these tasks, though, let me say something about the distinction White is marking by the terms 'morality' and 'altruism'.

Morality and altruism

Morality, as White understands it, conforms to the model of law: a moral person is one who recognises the authority of a set of moral rules and regulates his or her conduct accordingly. Moral philosophy, correlatively, is the attempt to determine which, if any, moral rules are justified. White puts it like this:

> Central to traditional ways of conceiving morality has been the concept of law. We began our discussion of why morality has been taken to be important by referring to the social necessity of a 'moral framework'. This, as we have seen, is partly embodied in laws against murder, stealing, bodily harm and so on, and partly not so embodied. Where it has gone beyond the legal system, it has still traditionally taken a legalistic form: moral injunctions have been seen as *rules* to be obeyed, as belonging to a moral *code*. Critical moral philosophy has by and large conceived its task as trying to provide criteria to determine which conventionally accepted moral rules are reflectively acceptable, or as showing that such criteria are impossible in principle.
>
> (White 1990: 40)

Altruism, by contrast, has nothing to do with following rules or recognising authority. People with altruistic dispositions or virtues are naturally inclined to help and cooperate with others. They are motivated not by the requirements of morality but by sympathy, care and compassion:

> The Greeks, as can be seen in Plato and Aristotle, did not make laws, rules and principles the heart of ethical life. When Socrates asked 'How should we live?' or Aristotle wrote about the 'moral virtues', their frame of reference was personal well-being as a whole. Intrinsic to that well-being is, as befits the social animals that we are, a lively concern for the well-being of other people with whom we live, work and form communities. Our altruistic inclinations are woven, as elements of our own well-being, into settled dispositions of character, or virtues.
>
> (p. 41)

Fundamentally, then, the distinction White draws is between two kinds of motivation for other-regarding conduct. We may refrain from hitting, lying to or stealing from others because we take these things to be prohibited by rules we regard as authoritative; or we may so refrain because our 'lively concern for the well-being of other people' disinclines us to cause them harm or distress.

What White's radical proposal amounts to is the claim that, insofar as educators are concerned to encourage other-regarding conduct in children and young people, they should concentrate their efforts on the latter kind of motivation rather than the former. They should actively foster the dispositions of 'being attached to those close to one', 'having warm relationships with those with whom one comes into frequent contact', 'being well-disposed to strangers with whom one has face-to-face contact', and 'being disposed to protect others' well-being in general' (p. 47). This sort of sympathy-cultivating education is, he thinks, a considerable improvement on bringing children up 'to believe that ineluctable duties are laid on them to do or refrain from doing this or that' and 'to feel guilt and remorse when they fail to live up to their obligations' (p. 53).

The obvious reply to White's proposal is: why not both? Graham Haydon raises exactly this question in his lucid defence of rule-based moral education (Haydon 1999). Haydon readily concedes to White that something would be awry if people were *only* motivated to consider and assist others by a sense of moral duty, but doubts that this amounts to an argument against moral motivation per se. He asks: 'Is it desirable that this sort of motivation is available as one among the possible kinds of motivation that can move people to take account of the interests of others?' (p. 105); and he takes the answer to be a resounding 'yes'.

Why, then, is White so opposed to education in morality?

White's objections to moral education

The objections to morality and moral education White advances are of two basic kinds. Some pertain to what he sees as unavoidable uncertainty about which moral standards should be taught and what reasons children should be given for subscribing to them. Others pertain to what he sees as the 'unloveliness' of moral motivation. I shall call these his 'uncertainty objections' and 'unloveliness objections' respectively.

First, the uncertainty objections. A basic problem for moral education, White thinks, is that critical moral philosophy has failed to vindicate an agreed moral code. There is deep disagreement among rational people about both the content and the justification of morality. The only reasonable verdict on the range of moral theories currently available is that 'not one of them, either positive or negative, is without serious logical defects, patently evident to all but the most rigid-minded of their partisans' (p. 39). And the absence of a rational consensus, either in the academy or in society at large, on which moral rules we should follow and why makes it very difficult to give a credible account of moral education:

> It is not surprising that many of us are confused about how, or why, we should lead a moral life, or about how as teachers we can set about devising moral education programmes in school. The confusion in ourselves is an internalization of the fissures in our culture.
>
> (p. 45)

One possibility, of course, is for schools just to plump for a moral code and inculcate it in a way that discourages questioning or reflection. But this is hardly consistent with an education for autonomy and is patently open to abuse: White worries that uncritical moral education is an invitation to powerful religious and socio-economic groups to mould children in whatever image serves their interests. Moral education, as opposed to moral indoctrination, must surely be a matter of teaching the *right* moral standards and giving children *good reasons* to subscribe to them: but this is precisely what we are unable to do if White's diagnosis of the state of critical moral philosophy is correct.

Interestingly, White thinks we are in a happier position when it comes to the cultivation of altruistic virtues. Whereas 'conceptions of morality vary widely', he says, this is not true of conceptions of altruism: 'what altruistic dispositions are is not, by and large, mysterious' and 'we can agree on what it would be in general to be attentive to others' well-being' (p. 49). This is interesting because it represents an inversion of what is perhaps the conventional view about where we might hope to find consensus in the ethical sphere. It is not infrequently suggested that, while we can all agree on some basic moral rules (that it is wrong to kill, steal and lie, for example), we are unlikely to agree any time soon on which virtues are required for well-being or what exactly those virtues involve. The conventional view may well exaggerate the level of public disagreement about well-being and virtues, but it is bold to claim that education in altruism is more firmly rooted than moral education in ethical consensus.

An uncertainty objection to which White gives particular attention is the difficulty of explaining how moral reasons for action are possible. The authority of moral reasons is usually assumed to be independent of our desires and preferences: the requirements of duty do not cease to be requirements when we have no desire to comply with them. And yet it looks like a necessary condition of my having a reason to do something that my doing it would contribute to the satisfaction of some desire I have. Having a reason for action implies, as Bernard Williams puts it, 'a relativity of the reason statement to the agent's subjective motivational set' (Williams 1981: 102). Moral reasons are by nature external, yet external reasons seem to be impossible:

> A crucial question here is whether all one's reasons for actions must be 'internal' reasons, i.e. dependent on one's desires, or whether one can also have 'external' reasons, which are independent of them. If all reasons must be internal and I have no desire to do what morality demands of me where this clashes with self-interest, then moral reasons cannot weigh with me. The onus is on [defenders of morality] to show that some reasons can be external ... But no convincing argument has been put forward, to my knowledge, to support the possibility of external reasons.
>
> (p. 56)

White's uncertainty objections to moral education seem to me to rest on an unwarranted pessimism about the availability of shared, rationally justified moral standards. It is, first, difficult to dispute that there are some basic moral prohibitions (on stealing, cheating, causing harm, etc.) and prescriptions (to treat others fairly, help those in need, keep one's promises, etc.) upon which there is a very broad consensus in society. And, second, there is a familiar rational justification for these ordinary moral standards that appears to suffer from none of the 'serious logical defects' White finds so ubiquitous in moral theory. The justification I have in mind is the one advanced by H. L. A. Hart (1961), G. J. Warnock (1971) and J. L. Mackie (1977), and more recently by David Copp (2009). It is, briefly, that moral standards are justified when their currency in society serves to ameliorate what Copp calls the 'problem of sociality', the ever-present risk in human social groups of breakdowns in cooperation and outbreaks of conflict. This risk is ever-present because of certain contingent but permanent features of the human condition: namely, our vulnerability to one another, our limited capacity for sympathy, and a limited supply of needed or wanted resources. If we were invulnerable to attack, or capable of infinite altruism, or if supplies of the things we want were unlimited, it may well be that morality would be unnecessary; but in the world in which we find ourselves, none of these conditions is satisfied. We each want more than we would have if the resources available were shared out equally. We are each vulnerable to attempts by others to deprive us of the resources in our possession, or to eliminate us from the competition for resources as yet unclaimed. And we are each capable of much but not unlimited concern for the welfare of others: when push comes to shove we tend to prioritise our own interests and the interests of our loved ones. These three facts together give social groups an inherent instability; no matter how great and how widely recognised the advantages of social cooperation, the threat of conflict is an inescapable feature of communal life.

An effective strategy human beings have developed to avert this threat is that of formulating and enforcing public standards of conduct. These standards, as Mackie puts it, are 'ones whose central task is to protect the interests of persons other than the agent and which present themselves to an agent as checks on his natural inclinations or spontaneous tendencies to act' (Mackie 1977: 106). One mechanism for formulating and enforcing public standards of this kind is the law: in this case the rules are specified with precision and the machinery of the state is deployed to police them. Another mechanism, though, is morality. Here the rules are more loosely formulated and the sanctions for breaching them take the softer forms of guilt, shame and the disapproval of others. Failure to conform to moral standards is characteristically punishable both internally, by pangs of conscience, and externally, by 'many different forms of hostile social reaction, ranging from relatively informal expressions of contempt to severance of social relations or ostracism' (Hart 1961: 180).

Insofar as the moral standards current in a society serve to ameliorate the endemic human problem of sociality, members of that society have a sound justification for subscribing to those standards. We all have an interest in averting breakdowns of cooperation and outbreaks of conflict, so we all have an interest in holding ourselves and each other to rules of conduct that sustain cooperation and peace. And it is very plausible that many of the basic moral standards on which there is broad consensus in society do, in fact, serve to ameliorate this problem.

Two features of this account of moral justification are worth emphasising. First, it is not a blanket justification for the prevailing moral code. The moral standards widely accepted in a society may include some that do nothing at all to sustain cooperation and peace. They may include, for example, rules prohibiting certain non-harmful sexual practices, such as masturbation and fornication. So the mere fact that rules have found their way into the prevailing moral code of a society does not imply that they should be regarded as rationally justified.

Second, the problem-of-sociality justification leaves open the possibility of there being other legitimate forms of moral justification. Moral standards are not here *defined* as standards the function of which is to avert the threat of conflict. The claim is rather that averting the threat of conflict is a function of moral standards that serves to justify them. Perhaps they have other functions too, and perhaps some of these other functions have justificatory force. Or perhaps there are forms of justification for moral standards that make no reference to their function. Openness to these possibilities, or indeed a firm conviction that some other justificatory strategy is successful, is entirely compatible with the recognition that there is, at least, a sound functional justification for conflict-averting and cooperation-sustaining moral standards.

Notwithstanding some profound disagreements about the content and justification of morality in critical moral philosophy, then, White overstates the difficulty of identifying a set of basic moral standards that are both widely accepted and robustly justified. There is a familiar range of moral prohibitions and prescriptions general compliance with which is necessary to protect us against 'the built-in tendencies of things to go wrong' (Warnock 1971: 26). These moral standards, along with the rational justification for them, can and should be taught to children. For one thing, children's lives will go better if they know, see the point of, and comply with basic moral rules. For another, it is in the interests of everyone to ensure that each new generation submits to the authority of morality.

White is, of course, well aware of the account of moral justification I have sketched, and even rehearses it briefly at the outset of his discussion in *Education and the Good Life*:

> A framework of basic moral rules, with or without legal backing, is necessary in a society for its members to achieve personal well-being. If we lived every day in danger of being killed, injured, robbed, deceived and coerced, things would be far worse for us than if there were widely accepted prohibitions against them.
>
> (White 1990: 37)

But, having noted the argument, he seems quickly to set it aside in pursuit of his larger thesis about the absence of consensus in post-Enlightenment moral theory.

Later in the chapter he makes a half-hearted attempt to subsume adherence to basic moral rules under the heading of the altruistic disposition 'to protect others' well-being in general' (p. 47). He suggests that 'in acquiring dispositions of this sort, children acquire at the same time a sense of the bedrock significance of these prohibitions to our personal and social life', and this involves their coming to see '*why* lying and so on undermine personal well-being', as opposed to having these rules 'stamped in, for instance, by a system of sanctions' (p. 51). But here White unhelpfully blurs his own basic distinction between obedience to the authority of moral rules and action motivated by altruistic concern. Acquiring a sense of the 'bedrock significance' of moral prohibitions is surely a matter of coming to see them as authoritative, which is precisely the business of moral education rather than education in altruism. And while we may agree that giving children reasons to subscribe to moral standards is preferable to merely stamping them in, this is a preference for critical over uncritical forms of moral education, not a preference for cultivating virtues over teaching moral rules.

What of White's particular worry about the nature of moral reasons? His objection, recall, is that moral reasons are external and external reasons are impossible. The answer to this objection is that external reasons are not nearly as mysterious as White suggests. The existence of rationally justified public moral standards gives me a reason to comply with them that is quite independent of the content of my subjective motivational set. The same is true of the existence of epistemic norms, rules of grammar and principles of etiquette. Many perfectly ordinary reasons for action derive their authority from public normative systems and are therefore external to individual agents. Williams' scepticism about the possibility of external reasons arises from his curious insistence on there being a necessary connection between grasping an external reason and acquiring the motivation to act on it: 'the agent should acquire the motivation *because* he comes to believe the reason statement' (Williams 1981: 108–9). But there is no need to go along with the idea that external reasons must be intrinsically motivating. We can instead acknowledge that there is often a disconnect between reasons and motives: knowing what one ought to do is not the same thing as being motivated to do it. It follows that any adequate programme of moral education will advance on two fronts: it will *both* equip children with an understanding of what they have moral reason to do *and* cultivate in them the motivation to do it. Once the authority of reasons is logically uncoupled from the motivation to act on them, there ceases to be anything very troubling about external reasons.

I turn now to the second group of criticisms White levels against moral education, to what I am calling his unloveliness objections. The core complaint here is that morality rests on a 'stern conception of human life' (p. 42), on an unappealing picture of human beings as hemmed in on all sides by rules, as living always under threat of punishment for violations, as required to concern themselves 'with the Right, not with the Good' (p. 41). Because we are forever falling short of the standards imposed on us, our lives come to be dominated by guilt and shame in relation to our own transgressions, and by blame and disapproval in relation to the transgressions of others:

> Children are brought up to believe that ineluctable duties are laid on them to do or refrain from this or that, the content varying according to the moral system in question. They also learn, as part of this same scheme of thought, to feel guilt and remorse when they fail to live up to their obligations. They come to blame themselves for their shortcomings. And not only themselves. They are trained to see other people, too, through the same reductive spectacles, as abiders by, or deviants from, their moral duties. The combination of rigid adherence to favoured values, unwillingness to compromise, and the pervasive tendency to blame oneself and others for moral defects is a familiar feature of our contemporary ethical landscape, not least perhaps in Britain. But our ethical life does not *have* to be as unlovely as this.
>
> (p. 52)

White acknowledges that some moral codes are more demanding than others. Some are 'minimalist', in the sense that their content is restricted to 'prohibitions plus immediate relief of disaster in the here-and-now'; others are 'maximalist', in that they insist on 'unlimited responsibility on the part of individuals and/or governments to help provide the necessary conditions of personal well-being to everybody everywhere' (p. 38). Unfortunately, both minimally and maximally moral lives are unlovely in their own ways.

The problem with maximalism is that it 'moralizes the whole of one's life' (p. 43). It makes every decision a matter of working out what morality requires. No matter what the circumstances, no matter how trivial the choice with which we are confronted, there is always something that is morally required of us and it is always wrong to do anything else. Here moral standards are not just 'checks' on certain 'natural inclinations or spontaneous tendencies'; they are the only considerations with a legitimate bearing on action. There is no escape from the demands of duty, or from the guilt, shame, blame and disapproval that characteristically accompany them.

Minimalist morality leaves plenty of room for non-moral considerations in practical deliberation, but is detrimental to our well-being in a different way. It encourages a bifurcation in our practical reasoning between pleasing ourselves and meeting our obligations to others. We come to think of ourselves as 'constrained maximisers' (Gauthier 1986): we divide our time between pursuing our own interests ('maximising our utility') and constraining our pursuit of self-interest in accordance with the requirements of morality. And because the requirements of morality are minimal, it is possible 'to lead a morally upright life and devote virtually all one's attention to one's personal ambitions and enjoyments' (p. 44). Minimalist morality is unlovely because it promotes minimal attention to the interests and well-being of others.

In a later publication White cautions moral educators against the tendency to make 'a wall of steel in our lives between our moral duties and our inclinations', and speculates about the origins of this tendency:

> A difficulty has been that the religious tradition has bequeathed us no real picture of what a personally fulfilled life could be like except in terms of devotion to God and one's moral duties. Apart from this there are only the pleasures and temptations of our animal nature – held to be a common but false picture of a happy life, from which Duty alone can rescue us. As the religious view has waned over the twentieth century, not surprisingly the pagan conception of a happy life which it rejected has come into prominence.
>
> (White 1997: 24–5)

The thought, then, is that the religious worldview we have inherited offers us a choice between two impoverished accounts of human flourishing: we may devote our lives to satisfying either the inclinations of the flesh or the requirements of duty. Minimalist morality simply puts the two impoverished accounts together and invites us to strike a balance between them.

White's unloveliness objections are less than compelling. I have three points to make in reply to them. First, it should be clear that morality in the form I have defended it (that is, subscription to conflict-averting and cooperation-sustaining moral standards) cannot be said to burden moral agents with unlimited responsibility for others, or to moralise their whole lives, or to hem them in with rules. It just requires them to go about their business in ways that avoid causing harm and meet basic standards of fairness and charity. Most of us learn to operate within these constraints without undue difficulty and with only occasional lapses. While our own and others' moral infractions certainly, and properly, elicit in us feelings of guilt, shame and disapproval, they do not, in the ordinary run of things, occur frequently enough for such feelings to set the tone of our emotional lives or to crowd out more pleasing affective states and dispositions.

Second, we should not be too squeamish about feelings of guilt, shame, disapproval and disgust – what psychologists call the 'self-conscious' and 'other-condemning' moral emotions (Haidt 2003). They are unlovely, to be sure, but the forms of conduct it is their function to prevent are unlovelier still. Violence, theft, deception, cruelty and injustice blight human lives much more profoundly than the moral emotions. If by cultivating the latter we can significantly reduce incidence of the former, the price seems a small one to pay.

And third, while the conception of life as a balancing act between inclinations of the flesh and requirements of duty is indeed an impoverished one, responsibility for this conception can hardly be laid at the door of morality. I do not know how many people see themselves as constrained maximisers: perhaps White is right that contemporary practical reasoning is dominated by moral obligation on the one hand and pursuit of 'the *dolce vita* of physical comforts and pleasures' on the other (White 1997: 25); or perhaps the rich tradition of eudaimonic thinking White so persuasively champions continues to make available to us a wider range of practical considerations and ideals. But even if we are all constrained maximisers now, it is surely clear that the problem lies not in our recognition of constraints on conduct but in our narrow concern with maximising our own utility. To solve the problem we need to rediscover and reinvent ends and activities capable of giving our lives meaning beyond the self-interested pursuit of pleasure. We need to rid ourselves of the idea that, once our moral obligations are discharged, there is nothing left for us to do except feather our nests and recline in them. No doubt the way to start is by reminding ourselves of what the Greeks had to say about well-being and virtue. But no useful purpose is served in this endeavour by downplaying or doing away with morality. Whether our practical interests are restricted or expansive, whether we care only about 'sex, suntan and Sangria' (p. 25) or fill our lives with a panoply of worthwhile activities, we still need to operate within moral constraints. Our fundamental interest in sustaining cooperation and averting conflict by holding ourselves and each other to public standards of conduct is unaffected by the breadth and depth of our conceptions of the good. White's attempt to taint morality with the unloveliness of the utility maximiser must therefore be deemed unsuccessful.

The need for moral education

I have tried to show that White's uncertainty and unloveliness objections to moral education fail to find their mark. Contrary to the uncertainty objections, it is possible to identify a set of basic moral standards that are both widely accepted and robustly justified; and contrary to the unloveliness objections, subscription to these standards is neither unduly burdensome nor somehow implicated in shallow hedonism. We have been given no good reason to suppose that the enterprise of moral education is beset with insurmountable difficulties, or that it is incompatible with or contrary to the spirit of education in altruism.

Still, even if his objections are unsuccessful, it might be thought that White has weakened the case for moral education in schools in another way. By setting out an attractive and plausible account of education in altruism, and suggesting that care for others is the proper motivation for other-regarding conduct, White raises the possibility that moral education is simply redundant. If my arguments in the previous section are sound, we should not refrain from morally educating the young for fear that morality lacks a rational justification or makes life miserable; but perhaps we *should* refrain from doing so on the grounds that, insofar as we are cultivating in children an appropriate range of altruistic dispositions, persuading them to subscribe to moral standards as well is superfluous. If I am sufficiently well-disposed to others, I will be naturally inclined to treat them with consideration and there will be no need for me to think in terms of moral duty.

I think this argument for the redundancy of moral education is misconceived. Let me explain why.

Suppose we were to concede that a person with a full set of fully developed altruistic dispositions would act and refrain from acting in all the ways required by justified moral standards without having to subscribe to those standards. It would hardly follow from this concession that moral education is redundant. For what possible grounds could we have for thinking that programmes of education in altruism will be so successful that every child will acquire a full set of fully developed altruistic dispositions? We have no examples of educational programmes with a 100 per cent success rate and no reason to think that altruism is easier to teach than algebra, allegory or anatomy. Given the knowledge that at least some children will reach adulthood without having reached the intended level of altruism, the case for supplementing education in altruism with moral education is compelling. Of course, we cannot expect programmes of moral education to be entirely successful either, but that just reinforces the argument for tackling the problem on more than one front. The predictably uneven outcomes of educational efforts leave little room for doubt that teaching two kinds of motivation for other-regarding conduct is better than teaching one.

This belt-and-braces reply to the redundancy argument is enough to show that the complementarity thesis has more to commend it than the supersession thesis. But there is a deeper reason for insisting on the importance of moral education. We ought *not* to concede, as we did a moment ago, that a person with a full set of fully developed altruistic dispositions would act and refrain from acting in all the ways required by justified moral standards without having to subscribe to those standards. Education in altruism will not suffice because the problem morality serves to ameliorate is not restricted to societies whose members lack virtue: in order to avert conflict and sustain cooperation, even people with a deep and genuine concern for one another's well-being must hold themselves and each other to public standards of conduct.

Recall the terms of the problem of sociality. Three contingent but permanent features of the human condition conspire to give human social groups an inherent instability: limited resources, vulnerability and limited sympathies. We cannot avoid the competition for limited resources; we cannot make ourselves invulnerable to our competitors; and we cannot escape our inclination to gain competitive advantage by exploiting the vulnerability of others. For these reasons we are never far away from breakdowns in cooperation and outbreaks of conflict.

It is no part of this account of the human predicament that we are fundamentally self-interested or incapable of altruism. The claim that our capacity for sympathy is limited is not to be confused with the claim that we are generally unsympathetic. Hart puts it like this:

> Men are not devils dominated by a wish to exterminate each other, and the demonstration that, given only the modest aim of survival, the basic rules of law and morality are necessities, must not be identified with the false view that men are predominantly selfish and have no disinterested interest in the survival and welfare of their fellows. But if men are not devils, neither are

> they angels; and the fact that they are a mean between these two extremes is something which makes a system of mutual forbearances both necessary and possible ... As things are, human altruism is limited in range and intermittent, and the tendencies to aggression are frequent enough to be fatal to social life if not controlled.
>
> (Hart 1961: 196)

There are good evolutionary reasons why human beings should have developed inclinations to prosocial behaviour and why they should take a 'disinterested interest in the survival and welfare of their fellows'. Without such an interest, as Hart suggests, it is difficult to see how the enterprise of formulating and enforcing public standards of conduct could get off the ground in the first place. To that extent, at least, the problem-of-sociality justification for morality assumes rather than denies that human beings are altruistic.

But, crucially, we are not angels. Our capacity for altruism is limited. Education in altruism can do much to enlarge our sympathies, to increase the strength and scope of our concern for others, but it cannot free us from our inclination to secure resources for ourselves and our loved ones at the expense of those who stand in our way. The difference between someone who has and someone who lacks a full set of fully developed altruistic dispositions is not the difference between an angel and a devil; it is the difference between two points somewhere in the middle of this spectrum. The altruism of human beings is always 'limited in range and intermittent' and, though we can take steps to increase its range and reduce the frequency of lapses, we cannot aspire to the angelic state of permanent and unlimited concern for others.

What follows from this is that altruism cannot do the job of morality. It can, and does, often move us to act in ways that benefit others or avoid causing them harm; and it can, and does, enable us to see the point of formulating and enforcing public standards of conduct. But it cannot obviate the need for such standards, for it cannot rid us of the inclination to favour ourselves and our intimates in the competition for scarce resources, nor reliably outweigh that inclination in our practical reasoning. To ameliorate the problem of sociality we need not only to be well-disposed to others, to care for them and desire their well-being, but also to be obligated to others, to be bound by duty to conduct ourselves in ways that take their interests into account.

'The main task for education', says White, 'has nothing to do with entrenching our entrenched morality still further' (White 1997: 25). Main task or not, I have tried to explain why I think it is at least *one* of the tasks of education to entrench in each new generation the moral standards that are entrenched in society, at least insofar as those standards are cooperation-sustaining and conflict-averting. This entrenching of standards should not be uncritical or indoctrinatory: there is a sound rational justification for morality and no reason why this justification cannot be shared with children. Nor, of course, should it be accompanied by the impoverished idea that, once our moral obligations are discharged, the only goals worth pursuing are hedonistic ones. White offers us a coherent and compelling account of education in altruism, but we should understand it as a complement to moral education, not a replacement for it.

References

Copp, D. (2009) 'Toward a pluralist and teleological theory of normativity', *Philosophical Issues*, 19 (1): 21–37.

Gauthier, D. (1986) *Morals by Agreement*. Oxford: Oxford University Press.

Haidt, J. (2003) 'The moral emotions', in R. J. Davidson, K. R. Scherer and H. H. Goldsmith (eds), *Handbook of Affective Sciences*. Oxford: Oxford University Press, pp. 852–70.

Hart, H. L. A. (1961) *The Concept of Law*. Oxford: Clarendon Press.

Haydon, G. (1999) *Values, Virtues and Violence: Education and the Public Understanding of Morality*, Special Issue of the *Journal of Philosophy of Education*. Oxford: Blackwell.

Mackie, J. L. (1977) *Ethics: Inventing Right and Wrong*. Harmondsworth: Penguin.

Warnock, G. J. (1971) *The Object of Morality*. London: Methuen.

White, J. (1990) *Education and the Good Life: Beyond the National Curriculum*. London: Kogan Page.

White, J. (1997) 'Three proposals and a rejection', in R. Smith and P. Standish (eds), *Teaching Right and Wrong: Moral Education in the Balance*. Stoke on Trent: Trentham, pp. 15–27.

Williams, B. (1981) *Moral Luck*. Cambridge: Cambridge University Press.

Chapter 9

John White on the aims of education

Harvey Siegel

John White's contributions to philosophy of education are many and varied: in a career spanning a solid half century he has taught generations of students, many of whom have become important scholars in their own right, and published more than 20 books and more than 160 papers. His work, always clearly and engagingly written, covers an impressive span of topics, from meat-and-potatoes philosophical topics in ethics, social and political philosophy and philosophy of mind to the gritty details of curriculum and policy. His is a remarkable record of achievement and impact. I am honoured to be a part of this volume's critical celebration of White's important work in education and its philosophy. In what follows I focus on his multi-faceted views concerning the aims of education.

The "aims-vacuum" in educational thinking and practice

One striking and laudable feature of White's decades-long writing on the aims of education is his strident rejection of the "aims-vacuum" (White 1991: 10) of much curriculum and policy thinking and his concomitant insistence that the curriculum in particular, and educational activities more generally, ought to be driven by independently established educational aims. He makes the point repeatedly – a nice recent statement of it occurs in his discussion of the place of philosophy in primary education:

> My central thought is that we should not posit from the start that there should be a subject called "Philosophy" and then show what contribution it can make to school learning. This gets things round the wrong way. *We should begin with fundamental aims and see what learning requirements these bring with them.* The work that primary philosophy does in helping children to reason more adequately, and not least some of the group discussion techniques it uses, may well be useful in this. But *if so, it should find its place within a larger, aims-based, approach to schooling* and not keep itself confined to a separate slot on the timetable.
>
> (White 2012: 457, emphases added)

White has made this important point many times over the years.[1] He has urged a particular view of these fundamental aims, to which I turn next.

The aims of education

In White's view, the fundamental aims of education involve *flourishing*, *well-being* and *personal autonomy*. The relationships among these are complex, and White has devoted considerable effort over the years to clarifying these relationships. He urges that we "think of education as having a single overarching aim: the promotion of the pupil's well-being" (White 1991: 12). Well-being is in turn understood in terms of the satisfaction of a person's most important informed desires[2] (ibid.: 30–4). In his view well-being and flourishing are more or less the same thing, so that promoting students' well-being is *eo ipso* promoting their flourishing.[3] Autonomy is a crucially important component of this, not in general but in "the kind of society in which we live, that is a liberal democracy built around an advanced industrial economy" such as Great Britain (and presumably much of the so-called "First World") (ibid.: 21). In such a state education aimed at preparing their citizens for autonomy is central:

> Close to the heart of a defensible liberalism, I would argue, lies an attachment to personal autonomy – to the idea that individuals should be self-directed in the conduct of their lives, deciding on their major goals themselves and not pressurized into accepting goals laid down by custom or authority and so forth. This is to apply to everyone in the community, not just a privileged few … As applied to education, this generates the aim of providing students with whatever mental equipment they need to become autonomous individuals, bearing in mind that self-directedness can never be wholly constraint-free.
>
> (White 1999: 185)

From the aim of well-being flows the aim of promoting personal autonomy (in liberal democratic states), since autonomy contributes to well-being (in such states): "Education for personal autonomy involves aiming at promoting the autonomous person's well-being" (White 1991: 74). Autonomy's contribution to well-being in the right kind of social context makes its promotion extremely important for education and a central dimension of educational activities: "If a government is committed to the promotion of autonomy for everyone, its aim must be that everyone should be educated to enable them to exercise it" (ibid.: 23); "The main conclusion … is the extensive responsibility that liberal democratic states should have for laying down educational aims which prepare their citizens for autonomy" (ibid.: 24); "The specific contribution which education can make lies in equipping people with the various capacities, dispositions and kinds of knowledge and understanding needed both to become and remain autonomous" (ibid.: 27). White's view is admirably clear and unambiguous: autonomy is important insofar as it contributes to the well-being of people living in liberal democratic states: "The central aim of education in a liberal democracy should be to prepare its citizens for a life of autonomous well-being" (ibid.: 143). Elsewhere White reiterates his view of the relationship between these two important aims, put now in terms of "values" rather than educational aims:

> Personal autonomy is a central liberal value. It rests on an even more fundamental value in human life – personal well-being. Autonomous well-being is only one variant of the more general concept, given that people can flourish or not flourish in non-liberal – for example, traditional-tribal – as well as liberal societies.
>
> (White 1999: 193)

He is quite clear that at least some educational aims – in particular that of personal autonomy – are at least in part a function of the type of state or society in which the education in question is embedded: in a "traditional-tribal" society the overarching aim is still the promotion of well-being or flourishing, but equipping children to live autonomous lives is not an aim of education since autonomy need not (and presumably will not?) contribute to their flourishing in such a society.

The character of autonomy and the avoidance of heteronomy

It is worth noting briefly that White's depiction of personal autonomy, though complex, is in keeping with most authors' basic understanding of it. It is fundamentally a matter of self-directedness or self-government, according to which autonomous persons choose their own major goals themselves rather than deferring unreflectively to tradition, religion, family or dominating others. Their choices are as much as possible free from external constraint. White makes many insightful observations about the character and development of autonomy, noting especially that autonomous choice is not and cannot be free of all external constraint – it "can never be wholly constraint-free" – at least in part because the achievement of autonomy is a developmental process that relies on the child's education and upbringing. As White puts the point:

> Human beings cannot make themselves into whatever they like. This is not only for practical reasons, but because the ideal [of "radical choosers"] carries with it an inadequate picture of the choosing self. If the self is to determine what it is to become, it can have no fixed dispositions. These would limit it in advance, obliging it to stay forever within certain tracks. With this conception of autonomy character itself becomes another form of constraint: one must be free to make and remake oneself at will.
>
> It is doubtful whether any coherent sense can be attached to this ideal.
>
> (White 1991: 75)

White is I think importantly right about this: one's free choices cannot be completely free of constraint. The challenge to the theorist of autonomy is to establish that choices can be genuinely autonomous even though they are constrained in various ways by the chooser's biology, upbringing, culture, etc. That is, we are inevitably constrained both socially and naturally; theories of autonomy must acknowledge as much (White 1991: ch. 5). While I do not want to commit myself to all the many details of White's account of these constraints and the genuine autonomy that might result, he is I think importantly right that the constraints are genuine and must be acknowledged to be so.

The point is actually familiar in a more straightforwardly epistemological context. It is a commonplace in epistemology that we cannot judge from a "God's eye view," "view from nowhere," or "perspectiveless perspective"; there is no alternative to judging from the perspective, framework or conceptual scheme we occupy. Many writers have taken this to imply an ineliminable relativism: our judgments are inescapably relative to those schemes. This alleged implication, however, is only apparent: even though we inevitably judge from the scheme we occupy at the time of judging, we can nevertheless gain critical leverage over that scheme; from within the scheme we can recognize its flaws and biases and work to improve it. In this way we can acknowledge the perspective-boundedness of our judgments but also acknowledge that those judgments can nevertheless be objective, rational, and justified, thus upending the suspect inference from perspective-boundedness to relativism. The detailed arguments for this claim are complex and cannot be rehearsed here (cf. Siegel 2004: 754–6, 2007). Still, the lesson is clear: just as objectivity and rationality can be had in the face of the ineliminable perspective-boundedness of judgment, so can autonomous judgment be had in the face of the ineliminable constraints imposed by nature, culture, and upbringing. White, that is, is quite right: autonomy must be conceived not as without constraint but rather as operating within constraints that, though genuine, are such that we can gain critical leverage over them, thus upending the inference from constraint to heteronomy.[4]

The justification of the aim of autonomy

White devotes considerable effort to the problem of justifying the aim of autonomy, both in general and, in particular, in the face of challenges posed by societies and cultures within them in which people lead heteronomous but nevertheless fulfilled and flourishing lives (e.g. White 1991: 24–6, ch. 6). Let us consider these in turn.

Justifying autonomy as a general educational aim

On the general problem, White argues, as we have seen, that in autonomy-promoting societies autonomy is justified by its conditional relationship to well-being: "Being autonomous is a condition of achieving a life of well-being [in such societies]. Its justification lies in this relationship (White 1999: 196). Well-being is the more fundamental value; autonomy is justified by its contribution to the attainment of well-being in such societies. What about societies that do not promote autonomy, e.g. the "traditional-tribal"? White restricts his justification of autonomy to its conditional role in liberal democratic states, and does not try to justify it in non-liberal states. On the contrary, since in such states autonomy is not in general conducive to the achievement of well-being, it is not rightly regarded as a fundamental educational aim or societal value:

> The autonomous way of life is not the best way of life in *every* set of circumstances. Nearly all human beings who have ever lived have belonged to traditional societies. *Their* well-being has consisted in living, as far as good fortune has permitted them, a broadly fulfilled life according to the mores and expectations of those societies.
>
> (White 1991: 26, emphases in original; cf. pp. 96–9)

So in White's view the justification of the educational aim of autonomy depends upon the type of society in which the education takes place. There is thus no *general* justification of that aim. (This leaves open the difficult problem concerning the education of the children of heteronomous cultures residing within liberal, autonomy-promoting states, on which more below.) Is he right about this?

A Kantian alternative?

In White's view the status of personal autonomy as a legitimate educational ideal, and the appropriateness of its promotion, is *conditional* and *instrumental*: it is conditional on the type of society in which the education takes place – that is, on whether or not the society in question is liberal or autonomy-promoting – and it is instrumental insofar as the promotion of the ideal in the context in question actually contributes to the more fundamental aim of well-being or flourishing.[5] White's extended discussion of the justification of autonomy (1991: ch. 6) endorses the conditionality and instrumentality of this justification: we who live in autonomy-promoting societies "cannot help seeing our well-being as involving autonomy" (ibid.: 103), but those living in other sorts of societies see no such thing. The justification extends not to all people in all contexts but only to those living in autonomy-promoting ones; it so extends because it is only in such contexts that autonomy contributes to well-being.

This will be disappointing to those who think autonomy is a more universal ideal, applicable to all people regardless of the social context in which they live. It is therefore surprising that White does not consider a more general justification of the sort associated with or inspired by Kant. It is surprising not just because it is the obvious "universal" alternative to a conditional, contextual and instrumental view of the justification of autonomy, but also because White avails himself of Kantian universality elsewhere in his discussion. For example, in his systematic and powerful critique of the economic justification offered for the 1988 National Curriculum (roughly that economic gain will help "to bring about greater and more extensive personal well-being" (White 1991: 139; cf. ch. 8), White points out that such justifications not only leave open important questions concerning the benefits of economic growth themselves and their value in different sorts of societies, "but also, and more importantly, the Kantian principle of treating everyone as an end in himself or herself is contravened" (ibid.). And in a substantive footnote at this point in the text, White reiterates his endorsement of the Kantian view:

> It is sometimes argued, by writers opposed to making education instrumental to the economy, that education should be seen as an "intrinsic" good. (See, for example, R. S. Peters, 1967, ch 1.) There is a danger of confusion at this point. While *education should certainly treat students as ends in themselves*, it does not follow that the only legitimate content of education should be "intrinsically valuable activities" – that is activities which among other things are pursued only for their own sake. It should be clear from early chapters of the book that I am advocating an education which both makes the promotion of the pupil's well-being for its own sake the central objective, and also, as part of that promotion, encourages him or her to engage in various activities intended to serve others' well-being. These may include activities which help the economy to prosper – to do with numeracy, for instance, science, or computing.
>
> (White 1991: 182–3, emphasis added)

This is not only an admirably clear statement of White's favoured view. It also draws a helpful distinction between education itself being intrinsically valuable, on the one hand, and educational activities themselves being intrinsically valuable and "pursued only for their own sake," on the other; and points out the compatibility between an education in which students' well-being is promoted for its own sake, on the one hand, and that education's promotion of students' promoting others' well-being, in ways that might also produce economic benefit, on the other. All this is worthwhile. But I have quoted the passage at length because of its explicit, repeated endorsement of the Kantian principle that requires education, and educators, to treat students as ends in themselves. What does this requirement come to?

In White's view, we treat students as ends in themselves if we promote their well-being. That is, promoting students' well-being is a sufficient condition of treating them as ends in themselves.[6] Is it in fact sufficient?

It is unclear to me that it is. My hesitation is that in order to treat students with respect as persons, as ends in themselves, we cannot ourselves determine either that we should regard their well-being as (one of) their own end(s) or in what their well-being consists. Treating them as ends in themselves requires doing our best to enable them to determine for themselves the character of their own ends.[7] And if well-being is indeed (one of) their end(s), that is because they have chosen it for themselves. And of course it is up to them to determine in what their well-being consists.

There are, I think, two aspects to this: two related obligations we incur as their educators. First, as I have argued elsewhere, they must determine their own ends competently and *well*, on the basis of skilled critical reflection concerning the reasons that bear on candidate ends. For this, they need to be able, willing and disposed to think critically about such ends. Consequently, treating them with respect, as ends in themselves, requires us to do our best to foster the abilities and dispositions of critical thinking (Siegel 1988).

Second, and more importantly in the present context, treating students as ends in themselves requires that we do our best to foster their autonomy.[8] That is, so treating them requires that we endeavour to enable students to reason and judge self-directedly, freely and (insofar as is possible and feasible) independently of external constraint, as well as competently on the basis of their own reasoned evaluations of candidate reasons. It is possible, at least in principle, for students (and people more generally) to judge competently and yet not self-directly or autonomously. This might happen, for example, if they are educated in such a way that they master the techniques and develop the abilities and dispositions of critical thinking but are strongly discouraged from critically examining the value, desirability or justification of critical thinking itself. This possibility can be expressed in terms of indoctrination: they might be *indoctrinated into critical thinking*.[9] In such a scenario it can hardly be said that they have been educated in a way that respected them as persons or treated them as ends in themselves. In order to be so educated, their education must have been such as to have encouraged them to think critically about critical thinking itself. And this requirement involves the fostering of their autonomy as well as the various abilities and dispositions, habits of mind and character traits that together constitute the ideal of critical thinking (Siegel 1988: ch. 5; 1997: 24–5).

If this is right, we seem to have the sort of universal, general justification of the educational aim of autonomy that White eschews. It renders the aim not contextual, conditional on society-type, or instrumental with respect to a still more basic educational aim. Whether students are educated in autonomy-promoting or autonomy-rejecting societies, we are obliged, in treating them with respect, as ends in themselves, to foster their autonomy – even if doing so does not contribute to their well-being. We are so obliged even if it turns out that well-being is not in fact a more fundamental educational ideal. Whatever their society-type, whatever other educational aims there happen to be, whatever the relationships with other such aims in which autonomy happens to stand, we are obliged to promote students' autonomy, simply because doing so is required by our duty to treat them with respect as persons, as ends in themselves.

Does this mean that parents and other educators in "traditional-tribal" societies fail to honour the injunction to treat children and students with respect, as ends in themselves? This may seem a wildly ethnocentric and politically incorrect thing to say. Nevertheless, I think it is true – and that White, perhaps despite himself, agrees. The point is best made in the context of students from autonomy-rejecting cultures living within broader autonomy-promoting societies or states, so we should consider such students next.

Justifying autonomy for students being raised in autonomy-rejecting cultures within broader autonomy-promoting societies

What should we say about the more particular problem concerning the education of children raised in heteronomous cultures within liberal societies? I have argued elsewhere (Siegel 2010) that students (and their parents) who prefer to live in such societies are obliged to embrace the education that such societies offer – that is, education that is guided by the educational aims and ideals of such societies. There is obviously a tension between those aims and ideals and those of their home cultures. Moreover, we who endorse the former aims and ideals are nevertheless duty-bound to respect both those students and parents and their home cultures. Nevertheless, when conflicts arise, the latter must give way to the former. In a slogan: in liberal societies, *liberal values and ideals trump cultural difference.*[10] And this is true of educational aims, values, and ideals in particular.

I won't repeat my earlier argument here. But I must note that, gratifyingly, White agrees: "In an autonomy-supporting society *all* children must be protected against true believers who wish to impose on them a non-autonomous conception of the good life" (White 1991: 105, emphasis in original). White's discussion (pp. 103–5) makes it completely clear that the "all" expressly includes children from "tradition-directed," non-autonomy-supporting cultures being raised within autonomy-supporting broader societies. His reasons include both the evils of indoctrination, which are of course related to the failure to treat students with respect, as ends in themselves, and the practical impossibility of keeping such children from the influences of the broader society. On these reasons too we are agreed. On White's view as well as my own, the autonomy of all students living in autonomy-promoting societies, including those being raised in autonomy-rejecting cultures, must be promoted.

Justifying autonomy in autonomy-rejecting cultures

But, as we have seen, White and I disagree about promoting the autonomy of children in autonomy-rejecting cultures. Why does White think that it is obligatory to foster the autonomy of children in autonomy-promoting societies, including those whose home cultures reject autonomy, but permissible (if not obligatory) to promote the heteronomy of children in autonomy-rejecting ones? His answer is clear: both paths are intended to promote the well-being of the respective sets of children:

> … there is an important difference between them [i.e. children being raised in autonomy-rejecting cultures within broader autonomy-promoting societies] and children brought up in a tradition-directed society *not* within an open society. In the latter, their educators have no awareness of any alternative way of life, but in a minority community there *is* this awareness. This means that the educators and other community leaders of the tradition-directed society have to take steps to keep their children within the fold, to prevent their being influenced by the values of the wider society. This means that forms of indoctrination are required; these are aimed at a deliberate sequestration from the wider society and a restriction of attention on to the values and traditions of the community …
>
> How might this be justified? Can it be justified in terms of the children's well-being? But might it not have been better for them not to be indoctrinated but to be brought up as autonomous persons? Doesn't the recourse to indoctrination suggest that if the child could choose between the values of the closed and of the open society he or she might well choose the latter? The community leaders might appeal here to internal religious arguments that personal well-being is only possible via the religious belief in question …
>
> But even if it is difficult to show quite conclusively that a child's flourishing *cannot* depend on his or her being indoctrinated into a set of religious beliefs, does this imply that the community leaders should be left alone to indoctrinate? Surely no one – and this includes the religious leaders – would want to say that *anyone* has the right to bring up a child according to their own conception of human flourishing, whatever form this may take, and however convinced they are about the truth and unassailability of their conception, and willing to back up their position by acres of theological or other argument …
>
> In an autonomy-supporting society *all* children must be protected against true believers who wish to impose on them a non-autonomous conception of the good life.
>
> (White 1991: 104–5, emphases in original)

White is certainly right, I think, about the impermissibility of indoctrinating and imposing heteronomy on the children of autonomy-rejecting cultures embedded within larger autonomy-promoting societies. He suggests that it is permissible to do so for children of cultures not so embedded because in such societies: (a) it can plausibly be thought to promote their well-being; (b) their educators "have no awareness of any alternative way of life" (unlike in embedded cultures, where there is such awareness); and (c) those educators have no obligation to foster children's autonomy because doing so is not conducive to the promotion of the children's well-being. I will briefly raise a question about the first in the next section. I won't press a challenge to the second other than to note its implausibility as both a factual depiction of actual extant "traditional" cultures in the current global context and its presupposed characterization of such cultures as monolithic wholes.[11] I cannot endorse the third, however, in light of the Kantian alternative sketched above. If it or something like it is correct, then educators' obligation to treat all children with respect, as ends in themselves, and so to promote their autonomy, extends to the children of unembedded traditional cultures as much as to the children of embedded ones. White thinks that the crucial consideration is the fostering of well-being, and that because their well-being will be a function of their society-type, children of different society-types should be treated differently: where autonomy will promote well-being, autonomy should be fostered; where it will not, it should not or at least need not. But as we've seen, White also endorses the universal obligation to treat students as ends in themselves. If I am right that doing so requires promoting their autonomy, then all children, including those being raised in unembedded traditional cultures, should be educated in such a way as to promote their autonomy. If White disagrees, he will have to reconcile his positing of well-being as the single overarching aim of education with his acknowledgment of educators' obligation to treat students with respect, as ends in themselves. For these can and sometimes do conflict. When they do, it is the obligation to treat children and students with respect as persons, as ends in themselves, that takes precedence.

The justification of the aim of well-being

Finally: what should we say about the justification of the overarching aim of well-being or flourishing? How is it justified? That is, why regard well-being, or flourishing, as the ultimate human value or educational aim?

There is no question that many contemporary philosophers of education who write about the aims of education join White in taking the promotion of student flourishing or well-being to be education's overarching aim. Certainly those engaged in the contemporary enthusiasm for Aristotle do, but many not especially committed to Aristotle do as well.[12] I cannot enter into a serious critical discussion of this proposed aim here. But I do want to register a worry about it.

The worry is this: taking the promotion of children's well-being or flourishing as the overarching aim of education runs the risk of threatening student autonomy insofar as it presupposes a clear understanding of well-being – its value, substance, and character – and imposes this value, and this understanding of it, on students. It says, in effect, "We have determined that this is what is most important for you, and this is what its character consists in." It does not offer the presupposed understanding of well-being, or the predetermined judgment of its worthiness or relative importance, to students' independent judgment; it does not provide the opportunity for students to consider for themselves whether the presupposed understanding of well-being is correct or whether it correctly characterizes *their* well-being, or whether, so understood, this well-being is worth having. By imposing a pre-digested understanding of well-being on students, it runs the risk of treating students as mere means rather than as ends in themselves. In doing so it risks treating students immorally, because it fails to treat them with respect, as autonomous agents whose desires, needs and interests ought not to be subordinated to educators' imposed ends. As Israel Scheffler has argued, education should not endeavour to shape the mind or the values of the student or to prepare the student for predetermined roles in the social and economic orders. It should rather strive to *liberate* students by enabling them both to envision possibilities and to evaluate their desirability intelligently (Scheffler 1989: 143–4). In the same way, education's task should be not to predetermine either the desirability or the character of students' well-being, nor should it presuppose and impose a "one size fits all" understanding of well-being on students. Rather, it should help students develop sufficient competence that they are able to envision possible lives and possible conceptions of well-being, consider the various ways in which well-being can manifest itself in their lives, and evaluate the desirability of the conceived alternatives critically. If this or something like it is right, we should be wary of taking for granted that the overarching aim of education is the promotion of students' well-being.

Conclusion

In raising the just-rehearsed worry concerning the status of well-being as an aim of education, I don't for a moment take myself to have settled the matter or shown White's view of these things to be mistaken. On the contrary, it speaks volumes for the power of White's vision that its clarity enables the worry to be articulated. The same should be said concerning the other worries raised above. And in making my case we have seen many points of agreement and many others that I think White has clearly established. White's contribution will endure; we are all the beneficiaries of his work. I conclude by registering my admiration for and congratulating him on it.

Notes

1 Cf. White (1982, 1991, 1995 1999, 2002) for earlier statements, and White (2011) and Reiss and White (2013) for still later ones. White of course is not alone in making it; Robin Barrow makes it as well, as do Israel Scheffler, yours truly and many others. For discussion and references cf. Siegel (2013).
2 I would have thought that "informed" is by itself insufficient; for the satisfaction of desires to count towards well-being, they should be *critically* informed: my desire may be maximally well-informed, but if I have not thought critically about it the satisfaction of my desire may actually contribute to a lessening of my well-being. I won't pursue this point further here.
3 Though not exactly the same thing: White has recently glossed a flourishing life as "one filled with successful and wholehearted engagement in worthwhile activities and relationships" (White 2011: 113) The differences between them are not such as to affect the arguments that follow.

4 So, for example, we should grant that our autonomous choices are constrained by our character traits, but nevertheless insist that those traits can be subjected to critical scrutiny and, where we judge it to be necessary or appropriate, work to tweak, modify, or abandon the suspect traits. I may, for example, make choices guided by my character trait of selfishness, but on reflection come to realize that I should in fact not be so selfish, work to change or at least constrain the trait, and subsequently choose less selfishly. This realization is not "from nowhere" – White's constraints remain – but the resulting judgment, resolution to change, and subsequent change of character, trait, and choices, though constrained, are – or at least can be – perfectly autonomous.

5 White considers the idea that the ideal might be justified on the basis of autonomy's intrinsic (as opposed to instrumental) value, but rejects this proposed justification as justifying at most autarchy rather than the more demanding autonomy (White 1991: 96–8).

6 Here I assume that White believes that his favored end, the promotion of students' well-being, is sufficient to meet the Kantian duty to treat them as ends in themselves. The assumption seems justified since without it White would still have the task of showing that his view in fact satisfies the Kantian requirement he here acknowledges, a task he does not take up in the book.

7 White is clearly sensitive to this. Cf., for example, White (2006: 386).

8 The connection between autonomy and critical thinking is complex; they are clearly related but are not identical.

9 This is in keeping with White's understanding of indoctrination as involving "the intentional prevention of reflection" (White 1991: 104)

10 In the earlier piece the slogan was "democracy trumps cultural difference" (Siegel 2010: 7). There the issue concerned multicultural democratic education in the case of democracy-rejecting cultures within broader democratic societies. Insofar as liberal, autonomy-promoting societies are democratic ones and vice versa the cases are coextensive. Here I take it that democracy is only one liberal value among others and so the current discussion is in that respect more general. However, the earlier argument, if successful in the narrower context, should succeed in the broader one as well.

11 Cf. here Siegel (2010: 8) and references to the work of Seyla Benhabib, Pradeep Dhillon, and J. Mark Halstead therein.

12 The list of such authors is too long to enumerate here. For important representatives of both groups, cf. Curren (2000, 2013) and Brighouse (2006).

References

Brighouse, H. (2006) *On Education*. London: Routledge.

Curren, R. (2000) *Aristotle on the Necessity of Public Education*. Lanham, MD: Rowman & Littlefield.

Curren, R. (2013) "A neo-Aristotelian account of education, justice and the human good," *Theory and Research in Education*, 11 (3): 232–50.

Peters, R. S. (1967) *Ethics and Education*. London: Allen & Unwin.

Reiss, M. and White, J. (2013) *An Aims-Based Curriculum: The Significance of Human Flourishing for Schools*. London: Institute of Education Press.

Scheffler, I. (1989) *Reason and Teaching*. Indianapolis, IN: Hackett; first published London: Routledge & Kegan Paul, 1973.

Siegel, H. (1988) *Educating Reason: Rationality, Critical Thinking, and Education.* London: Routledge.
Siegel, H. (1997) *Rationality Redeemed? Further Dialogues on an Educational Ideal.* New York: Routledge.
Siegel, H. (2004) "Relativism," in I. Niiniluoto, M. Sintonen, and J. Woleński (eds), *Handbook of Epistemology.* Dordrecht: Kluwer, pp. 747–80.
Siegel, H. (2007) "Multiculturalism and rationality," *Theory and Research in Education*, 5 (2): 203–23.
Siegel, H. (2010) "How should we educate students whose cultures frown upon rational disputation? Cultural difference and the role of reason in multicultural democratic education," in Y. Raley and G. Preyer (eds), *Philosophy of Education in the Era of Globalization.* London: Routledge, pp. 7–14.
Siegel, H. (2013) "Robin Barrow on the aims of education," in J. Gingell (ed.), *Education and the Common Good: Essays in Honor of Robin Barrow.* London: Routledge, pp. 64–74.
White, J. (1982) *The Aims of Education Restated.* London: Routledge & Kegan Paul.
White, J. (1991) *Education and the Good Life: Autonomy, Altruism, and the National Curriculum.* New York: Teachers College Press.
White, J. (1995) *Education and Personal Well-Being in a Secular Universe.* London: Institute of Education, University of London.
White, J. (1999) "In defence of liberal aims in education," in R. Marples (ed.), *The Aims of Education.* London: Routledge, pp. 185–200.
White, J. (2002) *The Child's Mind.* London: RoutledgeFalmer.
White, J. (2006) "Autonomy, human flourishing and the curriculum," *Journal of Philosophy of Education*, 40 (3): 381–90.
White, J. (2011) *Exploring Well-Being in Schools: A Guide to Making Children's Lives More Fulfilling.* New York: Routledge.
White, J. (2012) "Philosophy in primary schools?" *Journal of Philosophy of Education*, 46 (3): 449–60.

Chapter 10

Philosophy, educational research and educational policy

David Bridges

Introduction

My first real encounter with philosophy of education and with John White was in 1967 when I embarked on a Diploma in Philosophy of Education course at the London Institute of Education. John taught Epistemology and Metaphysics, and I recall that our very first essay question was 'Are synthetic a priori truths possible?' People often say that there is no shallow end to philosophy, but there must be an easier entry point than this!

With the benefit of 45 years of hindsight and with John White's extensive writing to hand I can now see that, for him at least, the answer to this question must have been a resounding 'Yes'. His body of work over this period is substantially posited on the conviction that one can indeed draw meaningful insights into the service of educational policy and practice from philosophical analysis, reflection and argument and from the literature that records the history of such work. This conviction has animated both his academic writing from his first book, *Towards a Compulsory Curriculum* (White 1973) and his continuing engagement with this and related themes until the present. It has also found expression in John's long-standing commitment to writing in a form more accessible to teachers and to policy-makers, for example through the *Bedford Way Papers* (see White 1981, 1984) and through the *Impact* series established by the Philosophy of Education Society of Great Britain (PESGB) on John's initiative and with his own contributions (for example, his 2007a pamphlet on *What Schools Are For, and Why*) and long-standing support.

This same conviction has sustained, too, my own interest in philosophy over this same period of engagement in educational practice, policy and research in many different contexts. But philosophy requires us to question even, or especially, our most strongly held beliefs, and in this spirit I want to examine more closely in this paper the claims of philosophy, as well as other forms of educational inquiry, to inform or provide a 'basis' for educational policy.

Philosophical approaches to policy – and some hazards

The best argument for the contribution that philosophy can make to educational policy in John White's own work is that body of writing that engages directly with policy issues rather than any meta-discussion. Some of this is in a sense procedural, for example arguing for almost a logical requirement for consideration to be given to aims as a condition of designing a (rational?) curriculum (in a long succession of publications running from White (1982) to White (2008)). Some, like his earliest attempt to argue for a compulsory curriculum, develops a substantive view of what should be the key elements of a compulsory curriculum from first principles about the terms on which any such intrusion into human freedom might be justified (White 1973). Other writing argues for policy conclusions from more substantive social and political principles, e.g. about how democratic principles might bear upon the shaping of a national curriculum or about socialist principles and education (White 1992, 1997).

Such writing brings philosophical sources and argument close to contemporary policy debate. Strictly, however, it tends to generate often quite complex 'if ... then ...' equations, e.g. 'if you broadly endorse democratic principles ... and if you interpret these to mean ... and if you take these to apply to this particular sphere of human activity ..., then you will probably conclude with me that ...' But of course there are some quite big 'ifs' in such equations, and it is precisely disagreement on one or more of the conditionals that leads to argument and debate about the conclusion. The difficulty with engaging with philosophy of education in territory which is close to policy and practice is that one is always exposed to critique of some of the premises on which this engagement is inevitably based. At the other extreme, if one really insists on starting, as we did in that 1967 course on metaphysics, by establishing that, after all, (1) the author is not alone in a solipsistic universe, (2) there are other people in the world, (3) we can have at least some understanding of their minds and behaviour and (4) we can communicate with them in a meaningful way – all premises that philosophers can spend an entire academic career exploring – then we shall take a very long time to approach educational philosophy let alone educational policy or practice.

If this seems a rather far-fetched train of argument, the literature of philosophy of education quickly illustrates the way in which even what on the face of it are more substantive principles can lead to very different conclusions about educational policy. Different readings of the principle of equality can be invoked in favour of a highly interventionist state seeking to use educational provision as a means to rectify underlying social injustice, but also in favour of non-intervention and open meritocratic competition. It can be used in support of racially integrated comprehensive schools and in favour of 'free schools' which any minority group can run on their own terms. Swift argues, similarly: 'You won't find a single politician who is against equality of opportunity. So all politicians agree about something? No. The same words stand for a range of different things. There may be a common concept, but there are very different conceptions of it. The concept is contested' (Swift 2001: 42). Swift goes on to point out that even Rawls had to acknowledge that his elucidation of the principle of justice still left it 'indeterminate between capitalist and socialist ways of organising the economy' (Swift 2001: 43). 'Liberal democratic' principles, similarly, can be invoked in support of parents' rights to bring up children in their own beliefs and the state's obligation to protect those same children from indoctrination. Of course, even cursory analysis will quickly reveal that these arguments are rooted not only in different uses of the same word, but in different traditions of thought and social practice.

This indicates a caution about policy-close philosophy of education: even if the starting point for 'near policy' philosophy of education is not way back in the metaphysics but in more widely recognisable domains of ethics or social political principles, the work has to start at places that other philosophers have come to, perhaps not uncontroversially, after they have done a lot of other work. This is one reason why some philosophers of education construct a volume of writing on the back of other philosophers' 'mainstream' philosophical work – for example Michael Fielding's use of Macmurray, Carr's use of Aristotle, Pring's recurrent referencing of Dewey and the use by almost everyone who has written about justice in the last 25 years of Rawls. Life is really not long enough to do all the fundamental work *and* to work out all the educational applications, and certainly few readers in the policy or practice fora – or even academia – will have time to wade through both.

Of course one can approach educational policy and practice from a slightly different direction, though I desperately want to avoid setting these up as dichotomous. One can start not with applied social science or philosophy, but with the way in which policy and practice are articulated in educational circles, with the 'educational theory' that is represented in the professional beliefs, conversations and writing of teachers and other educational practitioners and of policy-makers (see multiple references in John Elliott's work (for example 1991 and 2007) and also Whitehead (1993)), and one can begin to apply to them both the investigative tools of empirical research and the analytic and critical tools, the insights and the argument, that philosophy of education offers to these discourses. For Elliott, of course, action research is the practice which joins all these things together: 'Action research integrates teaching and teacher development, curriculum development and evaluation, research and philosophical reflection, into a unified conception of a reflective educational practice' (Elliott 1991: 53–4).

While White, a 'purer' philosopher perhaps, has not taken the action research route, he has, as much as any philosopher of education, engaged directly with contemporary policy debates and discourses in particular, and taken these as the starting point for many of his discussions and critiques. It is an approach that is perhaps particularly accessible to a wider research and educational readership because it foregrounds *educational* debates and relies very largely on a vocabulary shared with educational communities. This is the case with most of White's scholarly writing as well as, for example, *Impact* pamphlets written for a wider audience. If it is accessible, however, this is because the author goes to strenuous efforts to make it so, not because it lacks either scholarship or rigour.

Even this brief discussion highlights four of the problems for philosophers seeking to engage in what we might think of as publicly accessible fora of educational policy debate.

1 If they start in places too deeply embedded in philosophical argument they may never reach their educational destinations. (I recall when I was conference programme chair for the PESGB many submitted papers that failed on this count.)
2 Even if they start with ethical and social principles more visible in educational argument (like autonomy, democracy, equality, parents' rights, etc.), they will be forced to acknowledge not only the multiplicity of policy directions which any one such principle might support but also the additional complication of seeking to reconcile more than one such principle.
3 If they short circuit some of this complexity in the interests of, for example, producing some realisable policy recommendations, they expose themselves very visibly to charges of over-simplification and of failure to recognise the contested nature of their premises.

But also:

4 If they try to short circuit some of these issues by relying on a particular philosophical source for the philosophical groundwork, they are faced with the challenge that I recall Richard Peters addressing to one hapless student after he had repeatedly invoked Aristotle in response to question after question: 'Yes, but was Aristotle right?'

It gets worse ...

Policy-makers, philosophy and research: what does inform policy?

Even when philosophy of education is written in ordinary language without too much that is either technical or elusive, this is no guarantee that it will be read by the policy-makers it seeks to reach, let alone that it will influence the policies they are forming. John White claims at least one success in getting consideration of educational aims reinstated in National Curriculum planning in England but, more generally, philosophers share with other educational researchers a sense that, with rare exceptions, policy-makers are really not interested in what they produce and that in practice they pay little regard to what the educational research community might have to contribute.

Empirical studies of policy formation suggest that politicians rely for their ideas primarily on trusted experts and ideologically sympathetic think tanks, and that academic research sits below the media, lobbyists, constituents and consumers as a source of influence on their priorities (see, for example, Edwards *et al.* 2007). Whitty's account of New Labour's relationship with educational research supports these observations and concludes that 'in reality, policy is driven by all sorts of considerations, of which the findings of educational research are likely on some occasions to be pretty low down' (Whitty 2006: 168). The evidence cited here is from England, where government is notoriously anti-intellectual. Our Scottish neighbours still revere their Enlightenment tradition and continue to engage more wholeheartedly with their research community. The concerns about the lack of engagement between policy and research have not, however, been limited to the UK. In France (Prost 2001) and Australia (McGaw *et al.* 1992) there have been reviews similar to those referred to above, bewailing the gap between research and policy. In the United States a Department of Education website observes in familiar terms:

> Our nation's failure to improve its schools is due in part to insufficient and flawed educational research. Even when rigorous research exists, solid evidence rarely makes it into the hands of practitioners, policymakers and others who need it to guide their decisions.
>
> (Cited in Levin 2004: 3)

Thus researchers including philosophers complain that policy-makers ignore their research, and policy-makers complain that the research that is produced is irrelevant to policy.

This state of affairs is especially ironic at a time when the discourse of 'evidence-based policy' has established global significance, albeit on the basis of a highly restricted view of what might count as evidence. At its worst, for example, in the case of the What Works Clearing House in the USA 'evidence' is assessed against the 'gold standard' of the randomised controlled trial – a requirement which not only excludes philosophy from consideration but which also ignores all the work in philosophy of social science about how educational and other social practices might be understood. Even the reviews of educational research developed by the EPPI centre at the London Institute of Education offer almost no consideration of the contribution that philosophy – or, if it comes to that, the more critical forms of sociology – might make to policy. (See Bridges *et al.* 2009 and Bridges 2008). Thus even in a climate in which (some) political leaders sign up to the international discourse of 'evidence-based policy' there is little indication that this opens the door to philosophers of education or to the more critical end of the wider research community.

But are we expecting too much? Is the domain of 'policy' one in which research and philosophical considerations can and should play the central role that philosophers and researchers would like to think?

I will explore this question, first by looking at policy and the considerations that we might argue should or might legitimately enter into its formation, and then by reflecting on my own recent experience of working in the policy-making domain.

What is policy and what considerations might legitimately enter into educational policy decisions?

In a brief discussion, I am going to have to take some shortcuts through the substantial literature that today constitutes the educational policy literature, noting, perhaps, that even the meta-discussion of policy is derived primarily from sociological sources concerned mainly with distinguishing different types of policy research (see, for example, Gordon *et al.* 1977; Maguire and Ball 1994; Ozga 2000; Gale 2010) rather than philosophical ones. Ball (1994: 15) complained that the largest problem many analysts face is the failure to define conceptually what is meant by 'policy' (bring back the analytic philosophers?), so let me at least contribute the following thoughts on the matter (and see, more fully, Bridges and Watts 2009):

1 We can talk about policy at a number of different levels. We might be primarily concerned as philosophers with the wider stage of national policy, but policy is part of what defines subordinate administrative structures, voluntary organisations, individual schools or consortia, right down to classroom-level policies on the teaching of reading or engagement with parents. 'Policy research can be done within institutions or classrooms, as well as within local education authorities or government departments' (Ozga 2000: 2). This noted, I will focus for the remainder of this article on, loosely, government or national political party policy.
2 Though by extension an individual may have a policy, it is more usually an expression of collective intention (e.g. of a government, a political party, a school) – 'statements of prescriptive intent' as Kogan defined it (Kogan 1975: 55). McLaughlin similarly defines educational policy as 'a detailed prescription for action aimed at the preservation or alteration of educational institutions or practices' (McLaughlin 2000: 442).
3 Policy normally suggests a relatively sustained set of intentions, though in recent years teachers in the UK have become used to regular shifts in such intentions. Perhaps education will soon follow the example of the notice-board in my local hospital clinic, which has a space for 'This Week's Policy'! (Does the fact that the space is currently empty reflect someone's deep sense of irony or merely the inability of hospital managers to keep up?)
4 The intentions may relate to goals, aims, purposes (e.g. to help students to become more autonomous, to integrate children with special needs and disabilities (SEND) into mainstream classrooms) and also to the means taken (to teach critical thinking skills across the curriculum, to train all teachers to enable them to meet the needs of SEND in the classroom).
5 But we know that a crude means/ends dichotomy is misleading so we have also elements of policy, derived from aims and the values that underpin them, which, in the context of curriculum development, Lawrence

Stenhouse called 'procedural principles' (Stenhouse 1975, and see Elliott 2001: 558 and 560). Thus an aim 'to teach for personal autonomy' might impact on the means taken to achieve this end, because it would require ways of proceeding that were consistent with the goal.

The policy sociology literature draws a variety of distinctions between different elements of policy which it may be useful to note here. Gordon *et al.* (1977: 27) observed a commonly drawn distinction between analysis *for* policy and analysis *of* policy. More finely they distinguish:

- *analysis for policy advocacy* – preoccupied with specific policy recommendations;
- *information for policy* – the main function of which is to revise actual policies;
- *analysis of policy determination and effects* – which examines the factors and processes shaping policies, i.e. the policy formation stage;
- *analysis of policy content* – which examines the values, assumptions, ideologies and discourses that underpin policies.

The first of these clearly has to be underpinned by aims, goals or values. The last category clearly provides for (critical) analysis of the values that underpin any recommendations. The second category points more towards the sort of (mainly empirical) research that policy-makers seem to be most interested in. They have decided to pursue a particular aim and now need technical advice about how to succeed with this. This tends to be the focus of, for example, official ministry research commissions and other calls on the research community. The third category of policy research invites history, narrative, case study, etc. of a more spectatorial or critical kind with which policy-makers are less enamoured and of which philosophers are especially fond.

Clearly one very obvious feature of policy on these accounts is the way in which values and normativity are deeply embedded in it. As Winch and Gingell have argued:

> Education is at least partly about the overall aims that society has for itself and how these aims are realised in practice. It cannot, therefore, be a neutral technical exercise, but is invariably a deeply ethical, political and cultural one bound up with ideas about the good society and how life can be worthwhile.
>
> (Winch and Gingell 2004: preface)

Philosophers of education *do* values, aims, goals, the good life, the good society, human flourishing, etc., all of which are deeply rooted in moral, social and political philosophy, so this should be open season for philosophical contributions. But while philosophers can certainly occupy themselves in the domain of aims and values and the good life, there are limits to what they can finally offer.

First, though the history of philosophy as well as contemporary discussion will provide us with plenty of examples of visions of the good society, the good person, the life that is worth living and, with these, visions of the aims of education, philosophy itself will not provide a single conclusion as to what vision of society, humanity or education should in fact be pursued in any particular setting at any particular time. Philosophy can offer a kind of ethical connoisseurship ('look at this as a way of life'; 'see its merits'; 'marvel at its internal coherence'; 'see how it enhances humanity'!). But more typically, perhaps, philosophical argument problematises, critiques and challenges such visions.

John White of course turned the inconclusiveness of arguments about the good life etc. to his own purpose, arguing in *Towards a Compulsory Curriculum* in classically liberal terms that since there was no 'knock-down argument' for an education orientated to a single vision of what sort of life was worth living, then education had to equip young people to make their own choices between such visions.

But few political leaders are so pusillanimous when it comes to social values. They do have, often very strongly drawn, visions of what society should look like, how people should live and what children should be introduced to through a state system of schooling. Such visions, values, principles and aspirations feature strongly in political rhetoric, in party political manifestos and in the public pronouncements of those who aspire to lead the next phase of policy. Few politicians feel the need to be supplied with such visions (they can trot them out in bucketfuls), and few welcome attempts to unsettle their confidence in the vision they have. This after all is the political role of those – like Her Majesty's Opposition in the UK – seeking to unseat them from power.

And here is a further difficulty for the philosopher/policy-maker. For political leaders the justification for honouring certain social-political values and pursuing certain aims or policies, is not so much that they can provide a compelling philosophical rationale for them which will trump all others (though in their campaigns they will have offered arguments of a kind), but simply that in a democratic setting these have won popular approval: the politicians have a mandate for the pursuit of the goals and policies they have set out, which philosophers cannot claim. Richard Smith acknowledges as much in his opening editorial to a special issue of the *Journal of Philosophy of Education* on 'Philosophy and Educational Policy':

> Education as a public activity is inescapably political. There are different and competing views about what constitutes the good life, about human nature, about justice and equality, about what is worth learning and why, and about the purposes of education in relation to these. Accordingly it is entirely proper in a democracy that education policy should be created by the people's elected representatives in parliament, even if the thought that it would be good to keep politics out of education from time to time holds its attractions.
>
> (Smith 2012: iii)

So, one way in which political policy-makers act and policy gets established is for the politician to set out his or her political vision, embracing aims, values and the policies emanating from them, and then to seek election on this basis. Successful election is taken as providing a political mandate for the policies laid out in their party manifesto.

But within this framework, something else may be going on which, as Richard Smith describes it, has less to do with policy formation than with political game-playing in the interests of retaining office or power. For some politicians the important thing is less to advance certain policies or principles to which they have a deep-seated attachment and more to do with hanging on to office or power. One way to do this is to be responsive to what the public wants, as evidenced for example in reports from focus groups or media campaigns or trusted lobbyists from different sectoral interests, and to offer them these things as policy. Market research into what people want thus takes the place of philosophical inquiry into what might be desirable or empirical inquiry into what might have what effects. Political integrity becomes measured by reference to the consistency between promised policies and those actually implemented rather than consistency between what politicians say and do and what they deeply believe to be right.

Clearly few philosophers – except perhaps those of the Machiavellian school – are going to condone what can easily be presented as an unprincipled pursuit of power. But it is surely also the case that political policy-makers (even head teachers) can legitimately take into account in formulating policy the likely reactions of key stakeholders or the wider public. If a particular educational policy that I favour in principle because I have good philosophical argument and empirical evidence to support my position is one that is likely to result in a general strike among teachers, my removal from office and the fall of the government, then I think I would be entitled as a rather significant matter of prudence to hold back from pursuing it. But, less dramatically, is a policy-maker's willingness to bend his or her own views to public opinion an indicator of unprincipled political opportunism or of a democratic spirit?

Either way the point that can be made, I think, is that intelligent, indeed rational, policy-making legitimately takes into account considerations to do with likely stakeholder and public response to what is proposed. There are practical arguments for taking this into account (politics is after all 'the art of the possible'), but also principled considerations to do with people's entitlement to a stake in decision-making in a democratic society even if their opinions are ill informed and philosophically naive.

There is a good deal more to policy-making than can ever be offered by philosophy even in conjunction with some solid empirical research. Let us suppose, for example, that philosophical argument points to the moral and social good of an education which is focused on the goal of personal autonomy. Further philosophical work identifies the sort of knowledge and understanding that might contribute to that personal autonomy. On this basis the philosopher makes a set of recommendations to policy-makers. Even if we leave aside contestations of what is proposed of an ideological character and/or on the basis of competing value systems, we are still a long way away from knowing what we should do, how to proceed. For example:

- We still do not know whether as a matter of fact teaching the knowledge and understanding referred to would indeed enhance personal autonomy. We would have to conduct some trials or empirical research over quite a long period to find out the actual as distinct from the intended outcomes of the intervention.
- We do not know whether the system is capable of delivering the sort of changes indicated in the policy proposal or what would need to happen (to teachers, to learning resources, to classrooms, to infrastructure) to achieve what is desired.
- We do not know how the proposals will be received, not just by students and the teaching profession, but also by parents and other stakeholders. What sort of public reaction will there be to the proposals (and what sort of political response)?
- We do not know the financial cost of introducing the changes – especially if they require new investment to deal with the issues indicated above.
- We do not know how many other changes are being proposed, how compatible these are (or how contradictory). We do not know the opportunity cost of pursuing this innovation.

My argument is that all these things are not just irritating diversions from some purer and more philosophical thought process aimed at the determination of policy, rather they are the very stuff of policy. The epistemology of policy rests upon just such considerations, without which it is pipe dreaming. So either philosophers and empirical researchers have to engage with this wider range of considerations or they have to acknowledge that their own arguments are insufficient for policy and their conclusions may legitimately be undermined by those who are in a position to take all these other things into account. A report for the OECD produced by the Centre for Educational Research and Innovation speaks of 'the essential indeterminacy of educational R&D as a producer of operational solutions' (CERI 1995: 31). The report continues in terms that apply as much to the contribution of philosophy as to other forms of educational research:

> Educational research cannot deliver the kind of independent, authoritative knowledge that directly suits the needs of educational policymakers and practitioners ... It cannot decide normative issues, which severely limits its ability to procure a consensus on practical questions ... It is the very nature of research to raise more questions than it can answer, or to seek to answer questions that have not been formulated yet. Thus, although research can expose a complex and contradictory set of issues, it is unable of itself to lend them operational reality.
>
> (CERI 1995: 30)

None of what I have argued means that philosophical thought and argument cannot enter policy-making processes. Rather it suggests that we need perhaps a more nuanced, less obvious account of how this might happen. I will conclude by reflecting on some recent experience in policy-making to see if this has anything to offer towards such an account.

A philosopher at court?

As I have been struggling to write this article, I have simultaneously been struggling with another task, leading the development of a 2015–20 strategy for the reform of school-level education in Kazakhstan. In this role a small team of four local and four international advisors have been reporting directly to the Deputy Prime Minister who has overall responsibility for Health, Education and Social Care. The leader of the project in Kazakhstan, Aslan Sarinzhipov, who brought the international team together, was appointed part way through the planning process as Minister of Education. The scope of the plan extends from the provision of school toilets and drinking water to broadband connectivity; from pre-school to university entrance; from curriculum, pedagogy and assessment to school inspections; from the structure of teachers' pay to the introduction of more equitable finance for rural schools; from inclusive education for children with special needs and disabilities to the role of Olympiads in measuring school and student achievement; from the implementation of trilingualism to citizenship education. There is a lot of policy in and around the plan, but how much philosophy? How, if at all, can and does philosophy enter into the multi-level processes of policy formation?

Reflection on my experience in this environment (a philosopher at court, so to speak, if not a philosopher king!) prompts the following observations about philosophy and policy.

Underpinning the whole reform agenda were really quite different philosophies (in the sense of world, or at least educational, views) derived from Kazakh tradition, in which the nineteenth-century philosopher and poet Abai plays an iconic role (Abai 2005 edn), Russian Imperial and Soviet traditions and the discourses of 'the global educational space', themselves on closer inspection by no means as homogenous as is sometimes supposed (see Bridges 2014). Part of the policy challenge is to find a way to play to the strengths of all three, and this calls for at least some measure of sensitive understanding of the different traditions.

Conroy *et al.* captured rather nicely a role which we can recognise from our own experience working across cultural divides that we nevertheless sought to respect. They suggest that though the philosopher of education might be tempted to step back from normative prescription, it might nevertheless be that:

> it is precisely here that a philosophical disposition may come into its own … in the form of an ethical engagement the effect of which is to subject intended prescriptions to an interrogation that receives its authority from an acquaintance with, and understanding of a country's ethical traditions and its vision of 'a good society' …

And then:

> the philosophic attitude can critically reacquaint policy makers with the resources of their own ethical tradition and in doing so enable them to test proposed prescriptions against those traditions.
>
> (Conroy *et al.* 2009: 173)

In the case of our work in Kazakhstan it was precisely this kind of thinking that led us to make a case for the protection of the element of schooling referred to as 'upbringing' (elements of a Russified *Bildung* combined with good old-fashioned Kazakh personal and social values) against the incursions of an education couched in much narrower academic terms.

Educational and more broadly social values – mainly around issues of equity and inclusion, but also intellectual capacities and the scope for school-level initiative and creativity – were central, and we ensured that they remained so. In some cases, however, they were not deeply problematic at an ethical level, as in the requirement under a principle of *equity* to close the gap in funding between relatively poor rural schools and richer urban ones – a situation arising because the schools were supported out of local taxation. In other cases, such as arguments for greater 'school *autonomy*', there was some wisdom at this particular historical moment in not pressing too far the distinction between schools' ability to raise money from non-government sources and their ability to enjoy other freedoms from government control. Those who experienced life in the Soviet period learned to exploit ambivalences in language to create space for their own preferences and this remains a highly developed form of policy game-playing. My colleague Olena Fimyar writes not just of trilingual policy but of 'policy trilingualism' whereby people exploit the gaps in the translation of terms between Russian, Kazakh and English to present one picture of what they are doing to an international audience while presenting another to different local audiences (Fimyar 2014).

Over and over again in this and other work in Kazakhstan we (and our UK-educated Kazakhstani colleagues) encountered what were in a sense conceptual issues. 'They just don't get it', wailed one Kazakhstani colleague after trying to explain to a group of teachers and head teachers (and later a group of parliamentarians) the principles of collaborative action research. We began to unpick the presuppositions that they would have to grasp in order to 'get it' – how they would have to understand 'research' which they were used to having done to them by academics from the university; 'collaboration' in an environment in which teachers had to compete with each other to show their innovative contributions in return for higher salaries; 'teacher professionalism' in a context in which teachers received all their instructions from on high and even fairly innocuous questions about educational policy and practice elicited the response 'that is above my wage packet'. Similarly another UK colleague working on preschool education struggled to convey a view of 'childhood' as something to be valued and protected for its own sake and of young 'children as self-actuating learners' in any environment that provided them with the stimulus and opportunity to be so. A third colleague struggled to insert a belief in the capabilities of children with special educational needs and disabilities who are defined by reference to their incapacities by what is known in the Soviet tradition as 'defectology'. You do not need great familiarity with the philosophical canon to observe or grapple with these educationally significant distinctions, but in a sense they are about different philosophies of education, and a philosophical training gives you some useful tools with which to analyse and tease apart different understandings and misunderstandings and to appreciate the interdependence of some of these central educational concepts.

But clearly a philosophical understanding or orientation or direction is not enough. In our work we were required not only to diagnose problems and make high-level recommendations but also to develop an action plan for achieving change – a plan with timelines; identification of those tasked to see the actions through; identification of stakeholders who might need to be brought on board; identification of risks and how these might be mitigated; and of course costs (though we did not attempt to do more than indicate the scale of these), i.e. many of the sorts of things that I identified in the previous section as key elements of policy. Not only this, but we also had to take into account an assessment of the chances of securing support among parliamentarians for some key proposals.

But what does a philosopher draw on in trying to develop policy recommendations in this more complex territory and with the rather awesome realisation that here, at least, they might actually issue in some action affecting hundreds of thousands of children? I am tempted to answer 'common sense', but perhaps *phronesis* or practical wisdom would be more philosophically acceptable and more accurate. In settings like the one I have described, philosophical reflection, research experience and reading, experience of classrooms and teachers' conferences, some travel and conversations with different sections of Kazakhstan's own community, experience of educational reform in other countries, critical reflection on all or any of the above – these things do not sit as separate points of reference but get joined together, assimilated into what gives you the framework of understanding you bring to the policy-making task and in an important sense makes you who you are. Philosophy is in the mix in its various forms: a somewhat disjointed worldview, some social and ethical principles and values, some epistemological beliefs, some educational concepts and principles, some analytic and argumentative tools – and these are important. We just have to acknowledge that while these may be necessary, they are not sufficient.

Of course, there is another and appealing role for philosophy which avoids the complexities that come with direct engagement with policy, a more detached, slower-moving role captured in the phrase that Richard Smith borrowed from Galbraith in the introduction to the special issue of the *Journal of Philosophy of Education* on 'Philosophy and Educational Policy' where he writes about it being the function of philosophy 'to keep open the flow of thought and widen the sphere of admissible debate' (Smith 2012: vi). This echoes an earlier suggestion by Terry McLaughlin that the role of philosophy in relation to educational policy was 'to illuminate complexities, sharpen dilemmas, undermine grounds for practical compromise and encourage further discussion and argument rather than decision' (McLaughlin 2000: 451) – all nice work, but can anyone really be surprised if this is not on the whole what a politician is going to be seeking with the clock ticking away on their brief time in office? Still less will there be any enthusiasm for encouraging further discussion and argument '*rather than decision*', or undermining practical compromise in a country in a hurry, a country like Kazakhstan, mindful of the old Kazakh proverb: 'Yesterday was too soon; tomorrow is too late!'

The trouble is that in Kazakhstan and elsewhere there is no shortage of those – reminiscent of the snake oil salesmen of the Wild West – offering answers and quick-fix solutions while philosophers pursue their reflective discussions: 'outcomes based education', 'payment by results', 'hand it over to the private sector', 'target setting', etc. Can philosophers offer no more than a critique of such proposals, or are there embedded in the grounds for such a critique at least the beginnings of an argument for alternative policies? Lawrence Stenhouse used to irritate teachers' conferences by claiming 'I have nothing to recommend'. He did have something to recommend, of course, but the point that he was making was that whatever he might recommend had to be treated as a hypothesis to be tested against teachers' own experience in the classroom (and hence classroom action research). I suggest that, provided they can speak with the same humility, it is a proper contribution of philosophy and philosophers to advance well argued views about how we might go on in education even while they remain open to debate about whether these views are right.

Conclusion

My reflections on my own experience, albeit a rather eccentric one, and the considerations mapped out in earlier sections of this article both suggest that if philosophical considerations are to enter policy-making and policy in a more direct way than is suggested by either Smith or McLaughlin, then one of two conditions have to be met – and Plato, of course, anticipated both of these in his ambition for philosophers to become kings or kings to become philosophers. The first is that philosophers have to enter the policy arena ('knowledge' it is sometimes said 'transfers best on two legs'), taking with them their philosophical understanding but recognising that they need to engage with very much more, though even philosophical commentators retain some scepticism about this option. Swift observes, perhaps rather unkindly, that 'Because many philosophers have difficulty remembering where they left their bicycle, the thought of a philosopher being in Downing Street rightly fills us with horror' (Swift 2001: 40). Alternatively, those actively involved in the multi-dimensional domain of policy-making have to be coaxed and tutored into taking philosophical considerations into account. Most indications are that few of those in policy arenas have the time or motivation for such tutoring, but I do not imagine that John White will give up trying, and perhaps the rest of us should not give up either.

Acknowledgment

I am grateful for guidance received from my colleague Dr Olena Fimyar on sources for the literature on policy sociology.

References

Abai, Q. (2005 edn) *Book of Words*. Semey: Abai International Club.

Aristotle (1980) *The Nicomachean Ethics*, trans. D. Ross. Oxford: Oxford University Press.

Ball, S. J. (1994) *Education reform: A Critical and Post-structural Approach*. Buckingham: Open University Press.

Bridges, D. (2008) 'Evidence-based reform in education: a response to Robert Slavin', *European Educational Research Journal*, 7 (1): 129–33.

Bridges, D. (2014) *Educational Reform and Internationalisation: The Case of School Reform in Kazakhstan*. Cambridge: Cambridge University Press.

Bridges, D., Smeyers, P. and Smith, R. D. (eds) (2009) *Evidence-based Educational Policy: What evidence? What Basis? Whose Policy?* London: Wiley Blackwell.

Bridges, D. and Watts, M. (2009) 'Educational research and policy: epistemological considerations', in D. Bridges, P. Smeyers and R. D. Smith (eds), *Evidence-based Educational Policy: What Evidence? What Basis? Whose Policy?* London: Wiley Blackwell, pp. 36–57.

Centre for Educational Research and Innovation (1995) *Educational Research and Development: Trends, Issues and Challenges*. Paris: Organisation for Economic Cooperation and Development.

Conroy, J., Davis, R. and Enslin, P. (2009) 'Philosophy as a basis for policy and practice: what confidence can we have in philosophical analysis and argument?', in D. Bridges, P. Smeyers and R. D. Smith (eds), *Evidence-based Educational Policy: What Evidence? What Basis? Whose Policy?* London: Wiley Blackwell, pp. 157–74.

Edwards, A., Sebba, J. and Rickinson, M. (2007) 'Working with users: some implications for educational research', *British Educational Research Journal*, 33 (5): 647–61.

Elliott, J. (1991) *Action Research for Educational Change*. Milton Keynes: Open University Press.

Elliott, J. (2001) 'Making evidence-based practice educational', *British Educational Research Journal*, 27 (5): 555–74.

Elliott, J. (2007) *Reflecting Where the Action Is: The Selected Writings of John Elliott*, World Library of Educationalists. London: Routledge.

Fimyar, O. (2014) '"Soviet", "Kazakh" and "world-class" in the contemporary construction of educational understanding and practice in Kazakhstan', in D. Bridges, *Educational Reform and Internationalisation: The Case of School Reform in Kazakhstan*. Cambridge: Cambridge University Press.

Gale, T. (2010) 'Critical policy sociology: historiography, archaeology and genealogy as methods of policy analysis', *Journal of Education Policy*, 16 (5): 379–93; available online at: http://www.tandfonline.com/toc/tedp20/16/5#.UqmvCPRdXuI.

Gordon, I., Lewis, J. and Young, K. (1977) 'Perspectives on policy analysis', *Public Administration Bulletin*, 25: 26–35.

Kogan, M. (1975) *Education Policy Making*. London: Allen & Unwin.

Levin, B. (2004) 'Making research matter more', *Education Policy Analysis Archives*, 12 (56): 1–20.

McGaw, B., Boud, D., Poole, M., Warry, S. and McKechnie, P. (1992) *Educational Research in Australia: Report of the Review Panel of Research in Education*. Canberra: Australian Government Publishing Service.

McLaughlin, T. H. (2000) 'Philosophy and education policy: possibilities, tensions and tasks', *Journal of Education Policy*, 15 (4): 441–57.

Maguire, M. and Ball, S. J. (1994) 'Researching politics and the politics of research: recent qualitative studies in the UK', *International Journal of Qualitative Studies in Education*, 7 (3): 269–81.

Ozga, J. (2000) *Policy Research in Educational Settings: Contested Terrain (Doing Qualitative Research in Educational Settings)*. Buckingham: Open University Press.

Prost, A. (2001) *Pour un programme stratégique de recherche en education*. Paris: Ministère de l'Education Nationale.

Smith, R. D. (2012) 'Editorial', *Journal of Philosophy of Education*, 46 (4): i–vi.

Standish, P. (2007) 'Rival conceptions of philosophy of education', *Ethics and Education*, 2 (2): 154–77.

Stenhouse, L. (1975) *An Introduction to Curriculum Research and Development*. London: Heinemann.

Swift, A. (2001) 'Politics v philosophy', *Prospect*, 66: 40–4.

White, J. (1973) *Towards a Compulsory Curriculum*. London: Routledge & Kegan Paul.

White, J. (1980) 'Socialist perspectives on the curriculum', in D. Rubinstein (ed.), *Education and Equality*. London: Penguin.

White, J. (1981) *No Minister: A Critique of the DES Paper 'The School Curriculum'*, Bedford Way Papers 4. London: University of London Institute of Education.

White, J. (1982) *The Aims of Education Restated*. London: Routledge & Kegan Paul.

White, J. (1984) *Education plc? Head Teachers and the New Training Initiative*, Bedford Way Papers 20. London: University of London Institute of Education.

White, J. (1992) 'Can education for democracy rest on socialist foundations?', *Journal of Philosophy of Education*, 26 (1): 19–27.

White, J. (1997) 'National myths, democracy and education', in D. Bridges (ed.), *Education, Autonomy and Democratic Citizenship*. London: Routledge.

White, J. (2007a) *What Schools Are For and Why*, IMPACT Paper No. 14. London: Philosophy of Education Society of Great Britain.

White, J. (2007b) *The Aims of School Education* (pdf). London: IPPR; available online at: http://www.ippr.org/uploadedFiles/research/projects/Education/The%20Aims%20of%20School%20Ed%20FINAL.pdf (accessed 12 December 2013).

White, J. (2008) 'Aims as policy in primary education', Research Survey 1/1, in R. Alexander (ed.), *The Primary Review*. Cambridge: University of Cambridge.

White, J. (2010) 'Elusive rivalry? conceptions of the philosophy of education', *Ethics and Education*, 5 (2): 135–45.

White, J. (2012) 'Why our curriculum should be aims-based (the last word)', *Languages Today*, 11 (Summer): 34.

Whitehead, J. (1993) *The Growth of Educational Knowledge: Creating Your Own Living Educational Theories.* Poole: Hyde Publications.

Whitty, G. (2006) 'Education(al) research and education policy making: is conflict inevitable?', *British Educational Research Journal*, 32 (2): 159–76.

Winch, C. and Gingell J. (2004) *Philosophy and Educational Policy: A Critical Introduction.* London: Routledge.

Chapter 11

Education, justice and the limits of statism

Penny Enslin and Mary Tjiattas

Introduction

John White has defended the promotion of national sentiment as an educational aim that is compatible with liberal democracy (White 1996, 1997). Among the benefits he has attributed to national feeling has been a willingness to support redistribution to ensure that the basic needs of all are met:

> Only by fellow-feeling for the poor ... will the rich have a motive for accepting redistributive policies within their own country. Attachment to one's national community thus underpins one's civic responsibilities.
>
> (1997: 16)

While our earlier debate with John White about the place of nationality in the aims of education was largely about the defensibility of myth-making in nation-building (Enslin 1994; White 1997), our own work has moved on to an extended defence of the cosmopolitan sphere in preference to the nation state as a context for justice and democracy in both political philosophy and philosophy of education (Enslin and Tjiattas 2008, 2012). In this tribute to John White we defend a cosmopolitan conception of justice against those that favour the nation state as the locus of justice. Cosmopolitan accounts of justice argue that moral and political duties are not confined to compatriots; they are global in scope (Moellendorf 2002) and require a more equal global distribution of education (Enslin and Tjiattas 2008). Under the conditions of association created by globalisation, justice in education implies that rich countries and their citizens have duties to share resources and responsibilities for education in developing countries. If education plays a role in creating the conditions necessary for socio-economic development and the full exercise of democratic citizenship, these conditions extend by implication to a common global interest in education for all, transnationally. But can we treat questions of justice in education that are global in scope as questions of *social justice*?

Recent developments in political philosophy include significant work that implicitly challenges our stance on global justice in education. David Miller, whose earlier work John White drew on in his defence of national sentiment (1996, 1997) has continued to develop what we call a statist conception of justice, arguing that social justice 'refers to the distribution of rights, opportunities and resources among the members of large societies' (2007: 12) through social and political institutions capable of regulating the distribution among their citizens of goods that include education. Miller resists the claim that questions of justice that are global in scope could be treated as questions of *social justice*. So does Thomas Nagel (2005), who argues that obligations of socio-economic justice are owed only to fellow members of a political community held together by centralised coercion in that community.

We aim here to defend our claim that in education global justice should be regarded as social justice with a wider scope, basing our conception of social justice on a principle of association that extends beyond the boundaries of the nation state. Although we are sympathetic to the stronger cosmopolitan view that treating all fellow human beings equally directly implies duties of justice, we shall not assume it for the purposes of establishing any of our conclusions. Like other cosmopolitan discussions (*inter alia* Pogge 2002; Moellendorf 2002; Beitz 1979), we shall instead, in adopting a cosmopolitan position with respect to the scope of justice, take existing and emerging global cooperative practices and institutions as grounding obligations of social justice. In contrast with statist positions, such practices and institutions need not be nationally defined and do not require national identity or solidarity. It is becoming increasingly evident that demands of justice arise from contexts of interaction beyond nation states, and as several cosmopolitan theorists have argued, the case for the existence of a world basic structure is accordingly becoming increasingly indefeasible. We thus locate our account of social justice in the middle ground (Daniels 2008) between statism and a strong cosmopolitan appeal to unmediated universal rights of persons as requiring principles of justice and hence equal global distribution of social goods. This permits us to build into our deliberation and to take as regulative Daniels' important insight that the area of global justice is both new and hotly contested – and that much work is needed before reflective equilibrium can be reached.

With our primary focus on the distribution of educational goods, we defend our argument for an expansive construal of social justice that embraces global as well as domestic justice.

After exploring the ways in which Miller's and Nagel's work defend statist positions (section 2), our argument will address two central features of statism in turn. In asking 'how special is the nation state?' (section 3), we will first draw on recent developments in political philosophy that challenge the view that the state is the sole locus of authority for principles of social justice and then apply the argument to the development of multilateral transnational norms, policies and actors in the global pursuit of universal primary education. We then argue (section 4) that Miller's own principles of global justice reflect a loosening of the boundaries of the nation state as boundaries for moral obligations, with particular reference to global provision of more equal access to education as a component of social justice. In doing so we are aware that John White qualified his defence of national sentiment by allowing that global justice could properly count as a value alongside others like friendship and our personal projects (White 1996: 328). We do not assume that White would necessarily endorse all elements of the statist stance that has emerged since he wrote in defence of national sentiment, and later we will suggest that his recent discussion of education for global citizenship could contribute to opening up the middle ground between statism and cosmopolitanism.

Statist challenges to cosmopolitan theories of justice

Central to Miller's challenge to cosmopolitan theories of justice is his assertion that questions of global justice cannot be assumed to be questions of social justice with a wider scope. Social justice as the distribution of rights, opportunities and resources among members of large societies is a concept that emerged with 'institutions capable of delivering policies for regulation of industry, education, health care, pensions and the like' (2007: 12–13), i.e. the possibility of a fair allocation among all citizens presupposes the existence of institutions characteristic of those constituting the nation state.

Indeed, Miller describes the nation state as *the* context for social justice

> ... if we are to understand what differentiates social justice from the forms of justice (if any) that may apply at global level, we must take account of the fact that social justice applies within political communities that are indeed communities, in the sense that their members normally identify with each other and recognize special obligations to fellow-citizens as a result of their identification.
>
> (2008: 390)

For Miller the nation state is special in at least three ways (2008: 390):

- Its members are subject to a common set of laws, coercively imposed on all who belong to it.
- Their cooperative practices are regulated by a common set of institutions.
- They are bound by a shared national identity giving rise to particular domestic obligations

In the context of an extended and complex account of national responsibility, Miller acknowledges the extent of global material inequality as well as unequal civil liberties and political rights. But he urges that we should not automatically see these inequalities as unjust. Acknowledging the dilemma of how to resolve two apparently conflicting intuitions – huge differences in standards of living between rich and poor countries, and the value of national self-determination – he argues that global inequalities do not require that we jump to the conclusion that justice requires a form of global equality.

> Provided that we attach *some* value to the idea that, in a culturally diverse world, political communities should be able to determine their own futures, we have good reason to allow significant departures from global equality.
>
> (2007: 74)

Moreover, even when we judge existing distributions of life expectancy, education and income to be unjust, our reasons 'might not be egalitarian reasons' (2007: 52), and therefore the injustice does not qualify as social injustice.

What, for Miller, do we owe the world's poor? The cosmopolitan view is that, in principle, our responsibilities to the world's poor are the same as those to fellow citizens. But

> We do not ... owe them everything that we owe our compatriots as a matter of social justice. In particular, whatever global justice means, it does not mean global equality – of resources, opportunity, welfare etc. – so we are not required to change the global order in such a way that inequalities between societies are levelled completely.
>
> (2008: 231)

All are entitled to a global minimum as a matter of justice, which may impose obligations, especially on rich nations (2007: 166): '... when basic human rights go unprotected, any agent, individual or collective, who is able to help protect them may in principle bear remedial responsibilities' (2007: 164). But beyond basic needs, i.e. those required to live a decent life anywhere, needs vary according to and are shaped by social context (2007: 182).

Like other statist theorists (including Nagel 2005, whose position we discuss below), Miller argues that there are humanitarian obligations to members of other states. But he also emphasises the importance of treating victims of human tragedies as agents who can take charge of their lives and as members of collectives. Aid, he insists, can make matters worse and does not necessarily effect change. Thus the global poor should take responsibility for bad choices and decisions; the international order alone is not responsible for the extreme poverty suffered in some developing nations. Miller highlights the complexities involved in allocating remedial responsibilities for global poverty. His recent work (2008: 390–1) proposes a theory of global justice comprising two principles: the protection of basic human rights and that interaction between political communities should be on fair terms.

Nagel's treatment of what differentiates domestic obligations of justice to compatriots from obligations to non-compatriots is both more abstract and starker than Miller's. While recognising a universalist humanitarian morality, he nonetheless insists on a strong statist position (see Cohen and Sabel 2006): it is only from strong centralised control that a political society is able to exert through its institutions that its members 'can claim a right of democracy, equal citizenship, non-discrimination, equality of opportunity, and the amelioration through public policy of unfairness in the distribution of social goods' (Nagel 2005: 127), in other words norms beyond basic humanitarian ones.

For Nagel duties of justice are restricted to relations within a state; justice is owed to fellow members of the political community, while relations to persons outside the political community are governed by 'minimal humanitarian morality' (ibid.: 131). The institutional connections between us and those outside the state enable us to meet the duty of rescue to those in dire circumstances and to address human rights violations in other parts of the world. In a move similar to Miller's, Nagel argues that while we are obliged to recognise the equal moral status of fellow members of our 'strong and coercively imposed political community' as a unit (ibid.: 135), we owe it to individuals elsewhere to recognise their autonomy. So we have a duty to allow them to exercise collective self-help and may have a duty to assist them to do so. We do not owe them equality, as collective moral units.

Having outlined the challenge that the statist position poses to our stance on cosmopolitan justice in education, we take up in the next two sections the two features of statism we identified earlier, i.e. the nation state as the locus of legitimacy and authority, and as the boundary of obligations of justice.

How special is the nation state?

The statist position: common underlying assumptions

We turn, in addressing Miller's and Nagel's sceptical concerns about the plausibility of global justice, to a closer examination of the assumptions underlying the statist position. As we have suggested, its proponents assume that normative considerations are on their side. But with Sen (2009: 143) we suspect that this is largely attributable to the 'tyranny of ideas' generated by the prevalent picture of 'the political divisions of states ... as being ... fundamental.' This picture, Sen continues, has led to political divisions being seen not only as 'practical constraints to be addressed, but as divisions of basic significance in ethics and political philosophy.' Commitment to statism (as Moellendorf 2009: 19 points out) thus obscures a fundamental presumption of the moral point of view, namely that 'If the moral requirement of equal respect for all persons dictates some kind of an egalitarian distributive principle domestically, then surely it has similar implications globally.'

Nagel (2005) is only one of a number of theorists who have recently either ignored or attempted to block this presumption and, accordingly, narrow the scope of justice. As we have noted, his argument rests on the claim that necessary conditions for obligations of justice are provided only within the state. Or as

Julius (2006: 177) expresses the point, the justice relation between persons, for Nagel 'supervenes on co-membership in states'. The distinguishing feature of Nagel's non-global conception of distributive justice, as many commentators have noted, is the way in which it relates justice to the 'involvement of will'. As members of a political society its citizens play a dual role: they are both subjects to and participants in general will formation and thus the coercive laws of the state. Citizens are responsible to one another for the laws made in their name – and this is the basis on which the exceptional, positive obligations of justice between citizens arise (Nagel 2005: 129 n. 14, p. 130). Correlatively, institutions that speak in people's names incur special obligations (Julius 2006: 187), foremost among which is the duty to justify to citizens laws that implicate their will; one important implication is that non-egalitarian laws would not gain a foothold (since citizen-subjects, members of the state, would not accept them).

Arguably, the 'involvement of will' theory captures a central component of the very idea of democratic legitimacy.[1] But on its own it cannot establish (as Nagel seems to assume) that *only* nation states exhibit the kind of will formation that authorises regulations required by just institutions. Nagel's conclusion that a moral presumption against arbitrary (morally undeserved) inequalities is warranted *only if* they exist between persons who are co-members in a state, 'subject-sovereigns',[2] does not follow from his premises without the statist assumption that *only* the state can speak in the name of the general will, i.e. only members of a state can be affected or subjected in the kind of way that generates norms (rights and obligations) beyond humanitarian ones (which Nagel does not count as norms of justice). And this assumption is clearly problematic.

Even if, for the moment, we grant the 'subject-sovereign' condition as necessary for norms of justice to apply, why, as Cohen and Sabel ask, should forms of governance in the global world not involve the co-authorship required to trigger norms of justice and democratic participation in an exactly parallel way (Cohen and Sabel 2006: 166)? Nagel does consider this question but dismisses the suggestion that global institutions have the required features to accommodate sovereign-subjects. His reason is that global forms of governance do not involve individuals directly: their relations to the supranational bodies are mediated by governments. Since these bodies do not speak in the name of all, their conduct is not authorised by individuals, and the wills of those individuals are not implicated.

Cohen and Sabel find this response unsatisfactory. First, it is not obviously true, even in the case of formally intergovernmental organisations like the World Trade Organisation (WTO), that there is only mediated interaction between citizens and these organisations. Instead, '... there is a direct rule-making relationship between the global bodies and the citizens of different states. In an attenuated but significant way, our wills – the wills of all subject to the rule-making authority – have been implicated, sufficiently much that rules of this type can only be imposed with a special justification ...' (Cohen and Sabel 2006: 168). Some international institutions impose conditions in a manner that is coercive and that involves the wills of those in the participant states. When the WTO sets standards citizens of nation states can't opt out. Further evidence of direct involvement by citizens is furnished by protests against free trade agreements. As Daniels (2008: 351) notes: 'In effect, these protestors of the WTO and other associations and agreements believe there is a need to justify the terms of the agreements to all affected by them.'

Rule-making with global reach occurs in several areas, including economic security, labour regulation, environment, education; it has an impact on the conduct of individuals, firms and states, e.g. by providing standards for coordinated action, and a transnational politics of movements and organisations that contest the activities of supranational rule-making bodies is increasingly evident. Thus there already exist forms of connection between global bodies and inhabitants of the world that suffice to trigger norms beyond humanitarianism, such as those expressed in labour codes.

Global politics is thus not an occasional matter of sparse agreements; it is increasingly 'enduring and institutionally dense' (Cohen and Sabel 2006: 166; Julius 2006), providing the scope for an increasing degree of involvement of will. Principles of affectedness, interdependence, cooperativism and institutionalism applied to the current condition of global politics clinch the case for global norms of justice.

Nagel would not find such activity dispositive. His take on international treaties or conventions is that they have a quite different moral character from a contract between self-interested parties within a sovereign state because the latter is likely to be part of a just socio-economic system constituted by collectively imposed property and tax law, whereas trade agreements among sovereign states are '"pure" contracts, and nothing guarantees the justice of their results' (Nagel 2005: 141). But again, this statist claim that there exists no normative terrain beyond a humanitarian baseline can be resisted.[3] We reiterate that the world no longer consists of unconnected closed societies; although it is not fully interconnected, it is clear that the density of interactions is continuously increasing, providing sufficient ground for an associative principle of justice to take hold. With growing interdependence, there is increasing intrusion of transnational activities on what Julius (2006: 190) calls 'inward-looking domains of policy and association'.

Firstly, as Cohen and Sabel suggest, international bodies like the WTO have come to recognise the applicability of norms extending beyond trade rules, e.g. process norms and commitments to individual rights. Their deliberations, deficient as they may be from a democratic point of view, are increasingly triggering norms beyond the basic humanitarian. As Daniels (2009) argues, global institutions provide 'functionally equivalent conditions with the same moral import' as the nation state. Second, the weight Nagel gives to international trade agreements in this argument (to the exclusion of almost any other considerations) renders his conclusions questionable. As Pendlebury (2007: 54) argues, he fails to persuade us that there is a warrant for restricting the '... ideal of government for and by the people, according to which the legitimacy of government depends somehow on the authority of the governed ... to general terms of citizenship in a state,' rendering his conclusion that it cannot be applied to international or cosmopolitan institutions merely question-begging. Julius (2006: 191) calls for flexibility in deciding whether to apply domestic or global principles of justice, suggesting that 'We could decide to switch standards when we pass a critical point in some measure of connectivity.' In so doing, we would do justice both to global and national projects. Statists have not met the burden of showing that conceptual tensions in the conception of global justice are unresolvable.

Thus far we have granted Nagel's 'subject-sovereign' condition of social justice. Moellendorf, however, urges us to take a closer look at the role of the 'subject-sovereign' condition in Nagel's argument. He points out that for Nagel's rejection of duties of social justice to non-compatriots to work he needs to establish that co-membership in a state (allowing for the dual status of citizens as both subject and sovereign) is a *necessary* condition for establishing duties of distributive justice. His argument, however, only attempts to show that it is sufficient. Even if we grant that only state institutions satisfy the subject-sovereign condition, this would not show that a presumption against arbitrary inequalities applied only to such institutions (Moellendorf 2009: 29–30). This follows only if we grant that the only justification for egalitarianism is as a compensatory measure for coercion, and this assumption is implausible to say the least. Thus, Moellendorf continues, Nagel fails to rule out the possibility that the global economic association generates duties of justice. On this point, Cohen and Sabel (2006: 153–4) consider different types of international relationships that might give rise to obligations of justice beyond the humanitarian. For example, the United Nations Educational, Scientific and Cultural Organisation (UNESCO) would be considered unfair if it ignored the education of some and favoured others, since its Constitution commits it to 'full and equal opportunities for education for all' (UNESCO 1948) – within and across countries.

Miller expresses similar reservations about Nagel's strategy, albeit in different terms. While sympathetic to Nagel's statist project, and in particular to Nagel's attempt to confine social justice to the nation state, he worries that his argument for restricting social justice to the nation state is inadequately grounded. Citing the second and third of the characteristics that make the state 'special' (see above), he says that '... if we look at what distinguishes the nation state as a context of justice from the world as a whole, we find more than just the fact of subjection to a common sovereign authority ...' (Miller 2008: 390). Further distinguishing features are: (1) shared principles for sharing benefits of cooperative practices that '... do not depend on the idea that the rules of the practice are coercively enforced; they would apply in much the same form to a system of voluntary co-operation' (Miller 2008: 390); and (2) the existence of the nation state as a community '... with which members identify themselves, again quite apart from its coercive nature' (ibid.). Coercion is not, then, necessary for principles of social justice to apply.

A non-statist principle of association

We undertook, earlier on, to provide a conception of social justice based on a principle of association that extends beyond the boundaries of nation states. This would be congruent with analyses (e.g. Cohen and Sabel, Beitz) that point to empirical evidence of emerging international institutions, agencies and rule-making bodies. The latter can be marshalled to support the claim that a global basic structure, even if not as yet fully in place, is progressively being realised.

The principle of association widely construed (i.e. in such a way that it extends beyond the boundaries of nation states) is compatible with the requirement that duties of justice are relational or membership-dependent. Cosmopolitan positions are not restricted to non-relational varieties that eschew consideration of the 'circumstances of human engagement'. Many cosmopolitans resist the view that justice is specifiable independently of institutions and relations. Moellendorf, for example, explicitly asserts that '... justice is a property of social and political institutions so duties of egalitarian distributive justice don't exist between persons merely in virtue of their personhood' (2009: 32). Duties of social justice, including duties to construct and support egalitarian institutions, do not follow automatically from rights to inherent dignity, but depend on the kind of association that generates them (ibid.: 75).

As we construe it, the principle of association supports a wide range of relations enumerated and described by Cohen and Sabel (2006: 153–5) based on membership of institutions, schemes of cooperation and interdependence. Not all associations that entail duties of justice are coercive, nor are they restricted to nation states. Persons may owe duties of justice to one another in the absence of coercive institutions if they are 'co-participatants in an association of the requisite kind: relatively strong, largely non-voluntary, constitutive of a significant part of the background rules for the various relationships of their public lives, and governed by institutional norms that may be subject to human control' (Moellendorf 2009: 33). Duties of justice are generated by the basic rules of association, and equal respect for all persons requires that they be egalitarian. For Moellendorf, the prime instance of such an association is the global economic association which affects core interests: economic, educational, health-related.

Thus commitment to global justice need not deny that duties of justice are special moral duties, extending beyond humanitarian ones and requiring justification that goes beyond that required for basic negative ones. But the principle of association allows us to provide, given the existence of institutions and cooperative schemes of the right kind, the required justification. We attempt to illustrate how it might do so by addressing the question of what should be required of global institutions, as a matter of justice, with respect to problems of gross international inequalities by examining the global campaign for Universal Primary Education.

Universal primary education as a goal of global justice

Global developments in education since the mid-twentieth century reflect a shift away from the authority of the nation state depicted by statists as comprising citizen-sovereigns generating and enforcing norms in closed societies of all affected and all subjected. This shift began with the emergence of UNESCO after the Second World War as the United Nations' specialised agency for education, given the role from 1948 of promoting global peace and security through education as a human right. It had long been assumed that: 'A nation could gain for itself a more stable and prosperous future by educating its citizens in the principles of democracy, citizenship and social collaboration. By extension, a similar route could be taken to build peace and prosperity on a world level' (Jones 2007: 327). Alongside other agencies like the United Nations Children's (Emergency) Fund (UNICEF) and the United Nations Development Programme (UNDP), UNESCO's mission was to support educational development and embed education in a wider global development agenda, including poverty reduction and reducing childhood mortality.

In its design, constitutional foundation and early practices UNESCO (UNESCO 1948) embraced the principle of multilateral collaboration to solve common problems – involving governments and specialised agencies of the UN, as well as the many non-governmental agencies that emerged later. Nonetheless, the early achievements of bodies like UNESCO have been mixed and sometimes controversial. A standard criticism of the international educational regime in the decades of the late twentieth century has been domination of the development agenda by western governments and agencies, like the World Bank, alongside a limited role for the governments and people of developing countries who were more usually depicted as recipients of aid rather than active participants (Mundy 2006: 28), or the agents of their own fate rightly preferred by Miller. Mundy describes the post-war regime as highly decentralised, with national governments responsible for educational development, with some support from international organisations and bilateral donors offering western expertise and uncoordinated approaches. But Mundy argues that since the 1990s a new and very different regime has emerged:

> The idea of 'education for all' has become part of a broadly based consensus about 'what works' among bilateral and multilateral development agencies. It is also a rallying call for heads of state and international financial institutions, a focus for transnational advocacy, and an arena of expanding development practice characterized by widespread experimentation with new modes of aid delivery, new kinds of donor-recipient relationships and relatively high volumes of aid spending.
>
> (Mundy 2006: 24)

The agenda established at the World Education Forum in Dakar in 2000 was centred on a shared commitment to universal basic education for all citizens in all societies, with its emphasis on education as a human right and the central goal of free, compulsory, primary education for all children by 2015 (UNESCO 2000).

> Education is a fundamental human right. It is the key to sustainable development and peace and stability within and among countries, and thus an indispensable means for effective participation in the societies and economies of the twenty-first century, which are affected by globalisation.
>
> (UNESCO 2000: Art. 6)

In urging that education must be made 'universally available', the earlier Jomtien Declaration had cast the meeting of basic needs for learning as a universal responsibility, requiring the redress of economic disparities.

The EFA campaign initiated at the World Congress on Education for All at Jomtien in 1990 leaves no doubt that unequal distribution of resources is central to global educational inequalities. The funding constraints on extending the right to education to all were noted at Jomtiem, whose declaration called on the global community to increase resources for basic education in the poorest countries. Although inadequate resources continued to be highlighted in UNESCO's global monitoring reports (e.g. UNESCO 2010), one of the changes observed by Mundy (2006) is an *increase in official development aid*, especially for basic education. For our purposes, the other recent trends she observes are even more significant.

The dramatic shift towards an international *consensus on a common set of development priorities*, with education receiving growing attention (e.g. in the Millennium Development Goals and the Global Campaign for Education) 'signals the establishment of a global-level consensus about the role of basic education in development that is unprecedented in terms of scope, density, consistency and persistence' (Mundy 2006: 33). The EFA campaign reflects a global set of norms of justice, strongly informed by principles of human rights. These shared priorities have led to the establishment of *monitored targets* that are both measurable and time-bound, most notably universal primary education (UPE) itself.[4] New mechanisms for *donor coordination* suggest, for Mundy, that 'UPE is steadily being recognised by rich governments as a global public good in need of collective rather than unilateral action' (Mundy 2006: 38). The biggest shift for our purposes is the emergence in educational development of *new actors in new forms of collaboration* in an unprecedented degree of multilateralism. These include, alongside national governments and international organisations like UNESCO, civil society bodies, the private sector, advocacy networks, teacher unions and international non-governmental organisations (NGOs) like Oxfam. Policy formulation and monitoring are now shared across a wide range of organisations. Jones describes the emerging reconfigured 'global architecture of education' as follows:

> Multilateral agencies, non-governmental organisations, the professions and scientific communities have all combined in a complete system of global

> influence and engagement ... Just one of many examples was the series of international conferences convened by the UN through the 1990s on themes actively promoted by NGOs and civil society: education for all, children's rights ... All of these were monitored through the organisations of political multilateralism ... culminated in turn of the century summits that produced the Millennium Development goals reflecting commitments by broad international communities, not just collaborating nation states.
>
> (Jones 2007: 330)

Some of these developments may still prove to be fragile and temporary. The 2010 Global Monitoring Report, while restating observations in previous assessments of progress towards UPE by 2015, warns that the global financial and economic crisis threatens further progress towards the 2015 goals, as education budgets are under pressure and both global food prices and poverty levels rise. The Report not only calls for improved funding from private sources and donor countries; it notes that the poorest countries will pay a higher price for a crisis that began in the financial systems of the most developed – though it also argues that there is room for lower-income countries to make additional funds available to finance the EFA goals. '... the world is not on track to meet the universal primary education goal. Current trends will leave some 56 million children out of school in 2015' (UNESCO 2010: 6).

It is important for our purposes to note that the EFA goals are modest; they do not call for removal of educational disparities between richest and poorest nation states. The Report emphasises instead the huge variations in participation, quality and achievement – in a global economy that is more and more knowledge-based. These concerns aside, the 2010 Report is striking in the ways it invokes Miller's features of social justice. Apart from ongoing attention to inadequate financial *resources* for education in poorer countries, it continues the tradition of invoking the principle of education as a human *right*. Governments are exhorted to do much more to 'extend *opportunities* to hard-to-reach groups such as ethnic minorities, poor households in slums and rural areas, those affected by armed conflict and children with disabilities' (ibid.: 8, emphasis added). Educational opportunity is described as 'a condition for advancing social justice' (ibid.). Educational marginalisation demands 'sustained political commitment to social justice, equal opportunity and basic rights' (ibid.).

Yet the shifts in the global architecture of educational development still prompt Mundy to observe:

> Our initial sense is that what we are seeing is the opening up of an important and active phase in the re-structuring of governance at a global level. It is a phase that will almost certainly involve the redefinition of the appropriate scale, modes, and extent of global action in the field of education.
>
> (2006: 45)

Modern mass education systems had been made possible by the emergence of national states and their capacity to collect and distribute the resources necessary to fund formal schooling – and had also been a means for consolidating the authority of the state and supplying a workforce with suitable skills and attitudes. But by the early twenty-first century domestic institutions have also become an instrument of achieving global objectives; the nation state is no longer definable as a closed society unconnected with others when it comes to provision of education as a social good, even if it retains primary responsibility for its delivery.

Shifting moral boundaries: education in global justice as social justice

Having focused so far on the nation state as the locus of political authority and so the context for social justice, we turn now to Miller's third 'special' characteristic of the nation state, i.e. shared national identity as binding members of the nation state together as a community, so underpinning obligations of justice to fellow nationals. Miller put the entailment of the very idea of social justice in the nation state emphatically in his (1999) book:

> ... if we do not inhabit bounded societies, or if people's shares of goods and bads do not depend ... on a determinate set of social institutions, or if there is no agency capable of regulating that basic structure, then we no longer live in a world in which the idea of social justice has any purchase.
>
> (1999: 6)

The egalitarian distribution of rights, opportunities and resources that Miller excludes from his account of global justice are thus feasible only in the domestic context of a bounded state.

Our response questions both Miller's location of the possibility of egalitarian solidarity only in the circumstances of the bounded state and the coherence between the set of principles which his constrained account of global justice proposes should apply to human relationships at a transnational rather than a national level, and the claims he makes concerning their application.

Firstly then, we question Miller's attempt to confine the feasibility of citizens' sharing the goods and bads with fellow nationals. Available evidence does not support this claim, in two respects. As Gould (2010) observes, there is evidence that transnational solidarity plays a role in motivating people's commitment to the realisation of global justice. This is apparent in the actions of at least some of the agencies now participating in what Gould calls transnational 'solidarity networks' in campaigns for universal primary education, such as Oxfam – and also in public responses to appeals for aid at times of disaster elsewhere on the globe like floods in Pakistan and the Haiti earthquake. Similarly, Kuper (2004: 123) observes that '... global civil society is denser and more efficacious than ever before, generating a host of common platforms and garnering active and sustainable support.' And as he plausibly concludes, this is generating among participants strong allegiances beyond nationalistic ones. Miller's suggestion that national identity delimits the bounds of obligations to one another is questionable on empirical grounds. It is also questionable on moral grounds. As has been noted (e.g. Moellendorf, Singer, Kuper) it hardly goes without saying that belonging to a group should necessarily entail a moral duty or exempt one from a prior obligation; even where the group is the nation this fails to be self-justifying. As Moellendorf argues, where there exists a global basic structure, nation states do not have inbuilt rights to act contrary to demands of justice; indeed the right to self-determination is only morally tenable when constrained by considerations of justice.

Conversely, we have to question the assumption that within states the distribution of goods – especially education – comes anywhere near equality for all citizens, especially in rich liberal democracies where ongoing critiques decry unequal access and achievement in education (see, for example, National Equality Panel 2010).

Let us turn to the second of our two grounds for questioning the moral boundary that Miller draws around the state in his account of global justice. For the statist what we owe to members of other political communities – i.e. to those living in developing countries by contrast with wealthier liberal democracies like the USA and the UK – is the protection of basic human rights and sometimes a duty of humanitarian rescue, under dire circumstances. While Miller allows that rich countries may sometimes owe remedial responsibilities, he sets the further condition that the terms of interaction and cooperation between nation states should be fair. But he resists global arrangements that limit inequalities on the grounds that such limits generate pervasive incentives to shirk responsibility. Both Miller and Nagel stress the importance of treating members of other states as agents whose efforts to take charge of their own destinies should be supported but who are ultimately responsible for their own fates. But here lies a problem. If Miller thinks that responsibility is an important moral value, finding ways to enable people to take responsibility for their welfare by developing and supporting their own agency so that they can enjoy self-determination looks like a criterion for global justice with problematic implications for his own position.

What conditions are necessary for states to exercise collective self-help as autonomous political communities, especially under conditions of global association? Proponents of cosmopolitan justice would point out that the very circumstances of interaction are far from fair – whether the lingering effects of colonialism, including postcolonial dependency, or the result of a global economy in which rich states and multinationals operating beyond effective regulation have dictated the rules of interaction to serve their own competitive interests. On this uneven playing field poorer states and those with weak government and civil society will need more than the meeting of their citizens' basic humanitarian needs and rights to exercise the kind of agency prized by the statists. While meeting these humanitarian conditions would be an advance towards greater global justice, they are hardly sufficient to create the kind of collective agency needed for poor countries to interact on fair terms with the richer states and their citizens. Creating the circumstances for equal agency takes the kinds of opportunities and resources whose allocation Miller ties to social justice, restricted by definition to the domestic sphere, and more likely to be available in richer countries. Education is an obvious example for us, providing as it does resources and hence opportunities for the literacy, numeracy and information skills and critical perspectives a society needs to develop and sustain its authorship of rules, laws and institutions for involvement of the collective will, as well as viable economies and interactions on equal terms with global associates.

If we distinguish between humanitarian obligations on the one hand and promoting human rights on the other, receiving support for basic humanitarian needs, e.g. for food security or after natural disasters, however gratefully received and especially if in the form of aid that does not exacerbate dependency, is not to exercise collective agency. Asserting individual or collective human rights expresses agency in a way that having them defended by others on one's behalf does not. Again, however much international promotion of human rights is appropriate to global justice, it is different from being in a position to assert them for oneself. Education is necessary to ensure that citizens know about human rights and how to claim them. If distribution of resources and opportunities for education is a matter of social justice, can Miller's principles be restricted to a domestic issue within a nation state? On Miller's own terms, education is a social justice issue and a necessary condition for the global poor to take responsibility for themselves.

Thus, although Miller proposes an account of global justice that excludes egalitarianism, his two principles of global justice, protection of human rights and fair terms of interaction, in association with his insistence on treating those outside the bounded nation state as responsible agents, opens the door to a reinterpretation of the meaning of social justice as necessary to global justice. For this reason, although he places cosmopolitan interpretations of global justice at an extreme egalitarian end of the spectrum in current debates, Miller's own position shifts towards the middle ground between thoroughly universalist cosmopolitanism and Nagel's purer statism.

Miller has consistently and with good reason called for a historically informed interpretation of social justice, locating the emergence of social justice in the late nineteenth century with the expanding responsibilities of the state (1999: 3), the growth of the market economy and the state's role in developing policies for distributing social resources. The nation state as a bounded society became the 'universe of distribution' that prevailed until the latter half of the twentieth century. But as we have shown, new structures, norms and policies mean that local and global are now imbricated (Benhabib 2004), as new spaces that stretch the political imagination have opened up. Especially in education, social justice now has global scope. How we now attempt to reconcile the pull of the cosmopolitan and the particular demands ongoing analysis in the middle ground between the two. While John White's earlier stance on national feeling as underpinning and, we assume, the context for, civic responsibilities seems to have endorsed Miller's statist stance, we welcome a recent comment that appears to open the way for a more global and less statist conception of both citizenship and of justice, in the middle ground between statism and cosmopolitanism. In considering whether students should be encouraged to regard themselves as global citizens, White suggests that 'students' political virtues should take them beyond their own national frontiers' (Reiss and White 2013: 30). An established global commitment to universal primary education falls far short of a redistribution of resources that would remove global inequalities. It is a modest beginning that is likely to fall short of meeting Miller's own criteria for global justice.

Notes

1 As a number of commentators have noted, Nagel's view that demands for justification are triggered only when one has (independently) a moral reason to comply with a coercive rule has a very troubling implication, namely that the most tyrannical states of affairs are excluded from the scope of justice, and thus that Nagel's theory 'cannot find injustice in their situation' (Julius 2006: 183). Perhaps tyranny is a clear but far-fetched case. The same observation holds, however, for non-citizens, slaves, the disenfranchised – all who are subjects but not citizens (see Pendlebury 2007: 53).

2 In Nagel's view, this is also what makes the nation state 'uniquely propitious for solidarity' (Cohen and Sabel 2006: 158). (Compare Miller's condition 3, which Miller takes to be a *separate* ground of egalitarian duties owed to co-nationals.)

3 Buchanan (2004: 205–6) refers to the work of Thomas Franck who describes areas of recent international law and provides evidence that '… in all of these areas appeals to distributive justice are prominent and actually influence the character of the law' (Buchanan 2004: 206) and who concludes that '… in all of these areas on international law, explicit recognition of the demands of justice, not charity or the *noblesse oblige* of the more fortunate states, has become an accepted component of argumentative discourse' (ibid.: 207).

4 UPE is but one aspect of international multilateral activity in education. Jones goes so far as to observe 'global constructions of educational values and techniques … education around the world is seen to become increasingly standardised … Global systems of evaluation are adopted, testing the extent to which national systems are conforming to privileged global standards and reform agenda' (2007: 331).

References

Beitz, C. R. (1979) *Political Theory and International Relations*. Princeton, NJ: Princeton University Press.

Benhabib, S. (2004) 'Reclaiming Universalism: Negotiating Republican Self-Determination and Cosmopolitan Norms', Tanner Lecture on Human Values. Available online at: http://www.tannerlectures.utah.edu/lectures/documents/volume25/benhabib_2005.pdf (last accessed 1 August 2013).

Buchanan, A. (2004) *Justice, Legitimacy, and Self-Determination: Moral Foundations for International Law*. Oxford: Oxford University Press.

Cohen, J. and Sabel, C. (2006) 'Extra republicum nulla justitia?', *Philosophy and Public Affairs*, 34 (2): 147–75.

Daniels, N. (2008) *Just Health: Meeting Health Needs Fairly*. Cambridge: Cambridge University Press.

Enslin, P. (1994) 'Should nation building be an aim of education?', *Journal of Education*, 19 (1): 23–36

Enslin, P. and Tjiattas, M. (2008) 'Cosmopolitan justice: education and global citizenship', in M. Peters, A. Britton and H. Blee (eds), *Global Citizenship Education: Philosophy, Theory and Pedagogy*. Rotterdam: Sense Publishers, pp. 491–501.

Enslin, P. and Tjiattas, M. (2012) 'Democratic inclusion and lifelong learning in a globalising world', in D. Aspin, J. Chapman, K. Evans and R. Bagnall (eds), *Second International Handbook of Lifelong Learning*. Dordrecht: Springer, pp. 77–90.

Fraser, N. (2008) *Scales of Justice: Reimagining Political Space in a Globalizing World*. Cambridge: Polity.

Gould, C. (2010) 'Does Global Justice Presuppose Global Solidarity?' Online at: http://www.philosophy.utah.edu/.../Papers2010/Gould%20Justice,%20 Solidarity.Doc (last accessed 31 December 2010).

Jones, P. (2007) 'Education and world order', *Comparative Education*, 43 (3): 325–37.

Julius, A. J. (2006) 'Nagel's atlas', *Philosophy and Public Affairs*, 34 (2): 176–92.

Kuper, A. (2004) *Democracy Beyond Borders. Justice and Representation in Global Institutions*. Oxford: Oxford University Press.

Miller, D. (1999) *Principles of Social Justice*. Cambridge MA: Harvard University Press.

Miller, D. (2007) *National Responsibility and Global Justice*. Oxford: Oxford University Press.

Miller, D. (2008) 'National responsibility and global justice', *Critical Review of International Social and Political Philosophy*, 11 (4): 383–99.

Moellendorf, D. (2002) *Cosmopolitan Justice*. Boulder, CO: Westview Press.

Moellendorf, D. (2009) *Global Inequality Matters*. Basingstoke: Palgrave Macmillan.

Mundy, K. (2006) 'Education for All and the new development compact', *International Review of Education*, 52 (1/2): 23–48.

Nagel, T. (2005) 'The problem of global justice', *Philosophy and Public Affairs*, 33 (2): 113–47.

National Equality Panel (2010) *An Anatomy of Economic Inequality in the UK: Report of the National Equality Panel*. London: Government Equalities Office.

Pendlebury, M. (2007) 'Global justice and the specter of Leviathan', *Philosophical Forum*, 38 (1): 43–56.

Pogge, T. (2002) *World Poverty and Human Rights*. Cambridge: Polity Press.

Reiss, M. and White, J. (2013) *An Aims-Based Curriculum: The Significance of Human Flourishing for Schools*. London: Institute of Education Press.

Sen, A. (2009) *The Idea of Justice*. London: Allen Lane.

UNESCO (1948) 'The Constitution'. Online at: http://www.unesco.org/new/en/unesco/about-us/who-we-are/history/constitution/ (last accessed 1 August 2013).

UNESCO (2000) *Dakar Framework for Action: Education For All: Meeting Our Collective Commitments, Including Six Regional Frameworks for Action*. Online at: http://unesdoc.unesco.org/images/0012/001211/121147e.pdf (last accessed 28 February 2008).

UNESCO (2008) *EFA Global Monitoring Report: Education for All by 2015, Will We Make It?* Online at: http://unesdoc.unesco.org/images/0015/001548/154820e.pdf (last accessed 27 February 2008).

UNESCO (2010) *EFA Global Monitoring Report: Reaching the Marginalised*. Online at: http://www.unesco.org/new/en/education/themes/leading-the-international-agenda/efareport/reports/2010-marginalization/ (last accessed 28 January 2011).

White, J. (1996) 'Education and nationality', *Journal of Philosophy of Education*, 30 (3): 327–43.

White, J. (1997) 'National myths, democracy and education', in D. Bridges (ed.), *Education, Autonomy and Democratic Citizenship*. London: Routledge, pp. 15–22.

Chapter 12

Integration as stealth assimilation

Eamonn Callan

I

The extraordinary breadth of John White's work in the philosophy of education makes it difficult to say just where that contribution has been the greatest. For my money, however, his efforts in developing a distinctively liberal political philosophy of education may turn out to be his most durable legacy. The inspirational effect of those efforts on many of my own contemporaries has been great.

But except for one short, suggestive piece (White 1987), John has not addressed a topic that has seriously engaged other liberal philosophers in recent years: multicultural education. And that particular piece looks a little dated now because it was written before any rigorous arguments were on the table for multicultural education. Since then, sophisticated arguments and counter-arguments have emerged. My main purpose in this chapter is to clarify and justify one important claim in the multicultural debate – namely that multiculturalism offers immigrants full citizenship on terms that are morally distinctive and cogent. But to make good on that claim we need to reject the way these terms have been typically framed as an alternative to assimilation.

II

The substitution of "integration" for "assimilation" as the name of the morally preferred avenue for immigrants into receiving societies became widespread during the late twentieth century. In both Europe and North America, assimilation was condemned as an oppressive vehicle of ethnocentric nation-building[1] while "integration" rose to prominence as part of a new vocabulary of valorized abstractions that inspired social movements, entered political scholarship with a bang, and penetrated the constitutional discourse, or at least the respectable political mainstream, in many countries. Diversity, difference, inclusion, and recognition are its allied abstractions. All are sometimes loosely bundled together under the aegis of "multiculturalism." But within that bundle integration is unique in its ecumenical appeal. In fact, among its exponents are many who disdain the leftist tinge that colours other concepts in the multicultural vocabulary.[2]

I suspect that what makes integration so widely alluring is the double reassurance it apparently offers.[3] First of all, by its means social fragmentation and discord are averted. Whatever else it signifies, integration by definition brings us all together as one united people. Second, by marking a sharp contrast with assimilation, immigrants are also promised that they can avoid the stigmatization and wrenching cultural loss that has so often been the fate of cultural minorities in the West. But the sheer conceptual elasticity of integration should prompt us to ask whether it merely disguises assimilation in a more difference-friendly rhetorical package. That worry motivates Peter Li's animadversions on multicultural integration in Canada. He suggests that in practice it amounts to nothing other than assimilation (Li 2003: 315–33).

A scholar far more favourably disposed to Canadian practice than Li comes to roughly the same point. In her comparative study of immigrant incorporation in the USA and Canada, Irene Bloemraad notes that:

> In some ways the integrationist thrust of government-sponsored multiculturalism means that Canadians embrace more of a "melting pot" approach to diversity than Americans. Canadian multicultural policy ... [pushes] for immigrants' incorporation into the social, economic, and political fabric of Canadian society. The project has more similarities with old-fashioned assimilation than many Canadians might be ready to admit.
>
> (Bloemraad 2006: 141)

We might call this the problem of stealth assimilation: on the one hand, liberal multiculturalists in Canada and elsewhere renounce assimilation; on the other, what they say about integration as the laudable alternative to assimilation suggests that it might just be a way of assimilating without really knowing that one is doing it. My use of the word "stealth" is thus not intended to imply that its practitioners are complicit in some covert operation to deceive immigrants about their likely fate; on the contrary, I think this is merely a familiar case of well-meaning but unfortunate conceptual confusion in public policy.

My interest is not in the particulars of Canadian practice but in the general conceptual and ethical questions raised by Li's and Bloemraad's observations on that practice. These questions are applicable to all liberal democracies where multiculturalism has had some political influence on the treatment of immigrants, and that makes a very long list. Is multicultural integration a real alternative to assimilation? And if it is, is it ethically better? On the other hand, if integration were merely assimilation in disguise, would that reveal anything morally amiss with multicultural integration? I argue that the rights to accommodation that make multicultural integration distinctive are in fact assimilative. We misrepresent its character if we depict integration as a freestanding alternative to assimilation rather than a diversification of the forms that assimilation can appropriately take under liberal democratic conditions.

The integration that liberals espouse protects no one against cultural loss. But then the justification of liberal multiculturalism becomes more challenging because it must give us good reason to accept all the costs that successful integration is likely to exact, including this one. One way to approach the challenge is by asking whether a more radical conception of multiculturalism could insulate immigrants against the threat of unwanted cultural loss by extending rights to accommodation beyond the limited sphere acceptable to liberals. These would predictably include rights to forms of education that would insulate children against the influence of the wider society. I sketch some reasons in the final section for thinking that no such conception could be consistent with the mutual understanding and respect among citizens that befits membership in a democratic society.

III

The integration of immigrants is usefully regarded as a subclass within a wider category that has to do with incorporating newcomers into existing cooperative ventures of some kind. That wider category might be aptly labeled "social integration," and examples would range from the inclusion of new countries in a trading bloc to the recruitment of a new cellist for a string quartet. The following conditions mark what might be called the circumstances of social integration: some ongoing, collective practice is to be measured against the right standards of success, whatever these might be; inducting new members into the collectivity creates new risks of failure as well as opportunities for greater success; and finally, some process of social coordination between veteran participants and newcomers must be planned or improvised to exploit the opportunities and to distribute fairly the burdens of effort and the benefits of success. Integration as an outcome is a more or less stable cooperative dispensation in which new members take their place alongside veterans in the common pursuit that unites them; integration as a process encompasses the businesses of negotiation, mutual learning, and adaptation by which that stable dispensation is brought about.

The concept of integration as I have described it necessarily has a conservative tilt. If newcomers are to be incorporated into an ongoing social practice, a presumption holds that keeping it going is desirable, and thus the burden of adaptation falls preponderantly on newcomers to learn and emulate the ways things have already been done by veterans. There is a difference between integrating a new cellist into an established string quartet and creating a wholly new quartet, even if the new quartet includes three musicians who used to play together in a different ensemble. In the case of recent immigration in Western democracies, the conservative tilt of the concept is increased by two additional factors. First, the motivation for the policies that opened the door to new immigrants had nothing to do with any desire for political renewal, and second, the scale of integration has been contained so as to minimize any serious threat to business as usual. The motivation for the policies came primarily from the demand for cheap labour or professional expertise that the domestic labour market could not supply. A more or less grudging willingness to extend citizenship to some inhabitants of former colonies was also in play in the Netherlands, the UK, and France. In either case, the politicians who opened the doors were careful to reassure their voters that what they were doing augured no significant social change. Had they not done so, political support for opening the doors would likely have been negligible.

Still, the constitutional setting in which the idea of multicultural integration took hold was liberal democracy, and we have as many ways to give content to the relevant conception of integration as we have ways to interpret the idea of equal citizenship in that setting. "Equal citizenship" is here understood as an ethical concept; it captures what I take to be the content and value of full membership in a well functioning free society. But fully to capture its value is to specify the rights and duties that befit democratic citizens, the public virtues they should cultivate among themselves and in their children, and the vices they will suppress or at least discourage. A fully developed conception of integration would take sides on numerous ethical disputes about what equal citizenship on its best interpretation requires, including the relevance or irrelevance of shared nationality, the duties of voters, and many other disputed questions as well. My aim here is much less ambitious. Rights to accommodation for cultural minorities are typically invoked to explain the distinctiveness of *multicultural* integration. I offer a parsimonious account of what these rights are and why they matter. Along with the analysis of assimilation in the following section, it will be enough to reveal the assimilative thrust of multicultural integration.

IV

The demands for accommodation by ethnic minorities have animated multicultural politics from its beginnings. They were spurred by the experience of subordination under the particular ideology of civic incorporation that prevailed in Anglophone settler societies during the nineteenth and for much of the twentieth centuries. The core idea of "assimilationism" was that integration could only succeed when immigrants were indistinguishable from respectable members of the dominant majority, bereft of all ancestral ethnic markers. The touchstone of assimilationism's success in Anglophone countries was a norm of "Anglo-conformity," constituted by the manners and ideals of the hegemonic elite (Gordon 1964: 127–8).

According to Will Kymlicka, the advent of multiculturalism fundamentally changed this:

> [Canadian multiculturalism] explicitly rejected the previous history of assimilationism, which required that immigrants not only learn English but also

> assimilate as completely as possible to the culture of English Canada; and ... explicitly affirmed that immigrants – those who are not descended from the original British or French colonists – had made a vital contribution to Canadian life, and that their distinctive identities were a defining feature of Canadian society that must be reasonably accommodated.
>
> (Kymlicka 1998: 56)

What makes assimilationism so deplorable? First, it falsely denies that citizens whose ancestry is outside the privileged ethnic category have contributed anything to the cultural and material prosperity of the receiving society, or could ever to do so without the erasure of their culture. Immigrants are thus victims of the kind of *mis*recognition that Charles Taylor famously described in which a group suffers "real damage, real distortion ... [because] the people or society around them mirror back to them a confining or demeaning or contemptible picture of themselves" (Taylor 1992: 25).

Second, assimilationism ruled out any indulgence of distinctive minority claims in the workplace or other public institutions. The misrecognition motivated the refusal to accommodate. If minorities are unworthy of recognition, then refusing to accommodate their unworthy practices must also be justified. Multiculturalism seeks to correct both these evils.

The practice of accommodation in liberal societies antedates multiculturalism, and regardless of our ethnicity, many of us will be its grateful beneficiaries at some point in our lives.[4] The consideration of illness, disability, family crises, and minority religious customs in employment laws; the provision of ballots in Braille for the blind or in multiple languages for recent immigrants; conscientious objector status for religiously motivated pacifists: all these are familiar practices in liberal societies. In such cases we revise established public role expectations or make case-based exceptions in order to enable individuals to act on reasons central to their identity without bearing prohibitive personal costs or disengaging from public institutions. Although particular instances of accommodation will be controversial, any self-styled liberal democracy that rejected accommodation wholesale must be arbitrarily rigid and unresponsive to deep human needs. Multiculturalism merely extends accommodation in two directions: language rights to help an increasingly polyglot citizenry, many of whom cannot yet speak the main or official language of the receiving society; and expanded religious accommodation to honor the place of non-Western faiths in citizens' lives.

The multicultural expectation is that by overcoming the evils of assimilationism we enable minorities to participate in public institutions on an equal footing with their majority peers and without compromising their dignity. And by enabling participation on such terms, minorities will be more likely to opt for participation. That expectation shapes what counts as appropriate recognition and reasonable accommodation. In fact, wherever recognition or accommodation is claimed for reasons that would militate against participation in mainstream public institution, they are necessarily repugnant to the ends of multicultural integration. Taking the expectation of integration seriously in the way that recognition and accommodation are construed makes them into assimilative practices, or so I shall argue in the following section.

V

As a term of art in contemporary sociology "assimilation" is focused primarily on the decline of boundaries between ethnic groups. Such groups are constituted by beliefs about common ancestry and by shared cultural practices – distinct languages, forms of worship, etc. The relevant beliefs and practices enable members to differentiate themselves from outsiders and enable outsiders to identify the group. Group assimilation occurs to the extent that changes on either side of the ethnic boundary diminish its importance for group members across multiple generations (see Alba and Nee 2005: 11; Brubaker 2004: 128–31; Bean and Stevens 2003: 94–5).

The particular boundary that matters most with respect to civic integration is between the mainstream culture of public institutions and the culture of the ethnic subgroups and enclaves to which many immigrants tend to gravitate on arrival. That mainstream culture may bear the heavy impress of a settler ethnic group – the British in North America, for example – but the assimilation of other groups will predictably diversify the mainstream itself as minority cultural practices are selectively appropriated by individuals and subgroups, and norms regarding respectable attire, accents, or even family structure become more permissive.

A resentful toleration will be the attitude of some to the cultural diversification that assimilation precipitates within mainstream institutions. But part of what distinguishes the ethos of multiculturalism is its celebratory and trusting embrace of difference and novelty. New people bring cuisines, ideas, aesthetic traditions, and the like from which we pick and choose in trying to make our lives better. That attitude is altogether different from the misrecognition of assimilationism. But it does not necessarily make it any easier for immigrants to sustain their way of life across generations. In fact, the warm and welcoming embrace of the multicultural ethos might make it harder to sustain ethnic boundaries, which is just another way of saying that it might make assimilation harder to resist.

Still, assimilation is not co-extensive with the sheer loss of ethnic difference. Ethnicity can thrive, after a fashion, in a society where its role as a boundary marker between groups has almost disappeared. To see this possibility we need Herbert Gans's distinction between practised and symbolic ethnicity (Gans 1979). Ethnicity as shared cultural practice prevails where co-ethnics organize their daily lives through common institutions that largely exclude outsiders. With the momentum of assimilation across generations, ethnicity as shared practice recedes. Yet what can persist in its aftermath is a still vivid ethnic identity sustained by the way individuals publicly define who they are, the sacred and secular holidays in which they participate, the food they eat, the news or sports they follow from an ancestral homeland, and the like. This is symbolic ethnicity:

> Symbolic ethnicity, however, does not require functioning groups or networks; feelings of identity can be developed by allegiances to symbolic groups that never meet, or to collectivities that meet only occasionally, and exist as groups only for the handful of officers that keep them going. By the same token, symbolic ethnicity does not need a practiced culture, even if the symbols are borrowed from it.
>
> (Gans 197: 12)

Symbolic ethnicity was the substance of the so-called revival of ethnicity among third- and fourth-generation immigrants in the USA during the 1970s (Jacobsen 2008). The revival did not signal any reversal to the assimilation of immigrants: all it meant was some enlargement to the range of respectable ways of being American to which they could assimilate.

What becomes hard, perhaps impossible, to see at this point is how group integration could differ much from group assimilation. First of all, the accommodation rights that accrue to immigrants in a multicultural regime presuppose that their bearers will become exponents of symbolic ethnicity who participate fully in mainstream institutions. Kymlicka says that such rights "are intended to help ethnic groups and religious minorities express their cultural particularity and pride without it hampering their success in the economic and political institutions of the dominant society" (Kymlicka 1995: 31). But the fact that accommodation rights enable the expression of cultural pride and particularity is consistent with immigrants having to conform to established norms of performance in economic and other institutions so far as they participate in them. If I am a Sikh I can proudly wear my turban and kirpan as a police officer, a professor, or a member of parliament. But it does not follow that the other criteria of role performance to which I am expected to adhere will be different than they would if I were a WASP or a Hindu. In fact, any other expectation would be inconsistent with impartial assessment of my performance. And no sensible multiculturalism could be repugnant to that.

Because symbolic ethnicity enables citizens publicly to evince a proud sense of continuity between the self before and after assimilation, it may ease scruples that would otherwise retard the process. The post-assimilation self can depict itself as keeping faith with the ethnic particularity of its pre-assimilation precursor, and inhibitions about assimilation that might be prompted by the imperative of ethnic loyalty are thereby allayed. The American literature on symbolic assimilation depicts it as a retrospective appropriation in the third generation and later of elements from a culture that has already been nearly lost. But under multiculturalism, symbolic ethnicity also has a prospective value for some newcomers who may have to contemplate the emotional costs of an assimilation that has yet to occur. By enabling a transformative process in which the self who emerges is symbolically the same as the one who arrived unassimilated (e.g. proudly Sikh) the anticipated emotional cost of the decision to assimilate may be lowered. We have some evidence that group assimilation is accelerated when the receiving society becomes more welcoming to immigrants (Alba and Lee 2005: 60), and a friendly attitude to symbolic ethnicity is a good example of the kind of hospitality likely to have that effect.

The vaporous character of the distinction between assimilation and integration is also apparent in the evidence that Kymlicka adduces for saying that under official multiculturalism immigrant integration in Canada has been expedited: higher naturalization rates; increased intermarriage and residential dispersal; widespread political participation through established, pan-ethnic political parties; greater educational success among immigrant children (Kymlicka 1998: 21). Kymlicka does not indicate how the phenomena he identifies could coincide with durably salient ethnic differences between ethnic subgroups in Canada and its French and English mainstreams. In other words, he does not show that what Canada has instituted is a form of integration that could be appropriately contrasted with group assimilation; it would seem rather to be a variant of the latter that is distinctive merely in its luxuriant display of symbolic ethnicity.[5] Kymlicka certainly has good reason for saying that integration has been a notable success under Canadian multiculturalism. But he has equally good reason for saying that group assimilation has been a triumph. Both claims seem to amount to the same thing.

As immigrants lose the language, liberalize the religion of their ancestors, marry outside the group, move into multi-ethnic suburbs, and exceed the educational attainment of their parents, they traverse the same boundaries whose gradual recession counts as group assimilation. These crossings constitute individual assimilation (Alba and Nee 2005: 60). Thus if group assimilation and integration are much the same thing, so too are individual assimilation and integration. To be sure, the immigrant who arrives already equipped with the human and cultural capital to flourish in the receiving society shows how one can integrate without having to assimilate. But if we set that case aside, the more familiar phenomenon is surely a process of integration that thrusts us into new roles with new rules and pressures to conform that deeply refashion who we are.

That point deserves some emphasis because it tends to be understated in the rhetoric of liberal multiculturalism. The magnetic power of cultural conformity cannot be wholly erased in the immigrant's experience, even when integration is offered on fair terms. Consider the following evocative passage from Yan Martel's novel, *The Life of Pi*:

> The first time I went to an Indian restaurant in Canada I used my fingers. The waiter looked at me critically and said. "Fresh off the boat, are you?" I blanched. My fingers, which a second before had been taste buds savoring the food a little ahead of my mouth, became dirty under his gaze. They froze like criminals caught in the act. I didn't dare lick them. I wiped them guiltily on my napkin. He had no idea how deeply these words wounded me. They were like nails being driven into my flesh. I picked up the knife and fork. I had hardly ever used such instruments. My hands trembled. My sambar lost its taste.
>
> (Martel 2001: 7)

Table manners in North American restaurants seem to me rather more indulgent nowadays. But Martel's wonderfully exact account of Pi's reaction evokes the familiar pull of assimilation once our incompetence or sheer eccentricity as cultural outsiders is exposed for all to see. He will not be caught eating with his hands in public again. He will eat like the natives eat. No one wants to be caught on the wrong side of the local distinction between civilized dining and the bestial ingestion of food, however that distinction is made. (The same goes for the convention-laden distinctions between being friendly and being overbearing, disagreeing respectfully or rudely, etc.) And for any immigrant whose integration into a new society requires learning new norms, such moments of instructive failure will not be rare and they will be long remembered.

The waiter's scorn in Pi's narrative reveals him to be an anti-multicultural villain, ready to trample on the hero's dignity when a more considerate soul would turn a blind eye. But then again we do not need the scornful waiter to ascribe a susceptibility to humiliation in the situation Martel describes. Merely noticing that one is failing to eat as a normal adult is supposed to eat in any public setting is humiliation enough. And that is the crucial point. Pi's humiliation might be mitigated, but it would not disappear, if the waiter and his fellow diners were all paragons of multicultural sensitivity who studiously overlooked his faux pas.

One might be endowed with an unusual resistance to humiliation. Still, induction into the labour market will still require conformity to the norms that constitute roles within that market or that prepare one for induction in schools or universities. I must learn to perform the role of student, say, or engineer in a way that comports with extant and sometimes arbitrarily parochial criteria of successful performance. And the transformative changes to the self that ensue are instances of assimilation. They are just what we should expect in people's lives whenever the challenge of integration is to learn roles that require modes of conduct (and concomitant forms of thought and feeling) that depart substantially from the self's established repertoire of habits and capabilities.

I have argued that multicultural integration is assimilative whether we apply the concept at the group or the individual level. Further, the challenge of integration – or assimilation, if you will – frequently requires individuals to undergo quite radical personal changes as they learn new roles. What does this imply about how liberals should interpret their multicultural project? And what can we say to those who demand accommodations to countervail assimilative pressures?

VI

It is high time for liberal multiculturalists to give up the stealth in the stealth assimilation that the rhetoric of integration currently obscures. At the very least, that would make for more transparent public policy. To whatever degree cultural loss is the likely fate of immigrants under a multicultural regime, they should be told about that. Furthermore, at a time when a backlash in Europe associates all multiculturalism with escalating cultural segregation, it becomes politically urgent to insist that a liberal multiculturalism endorses no such thing. Clarity on that point is forfeit so long as we pretend that immigrants are empowered to preserve their culture by virtue of multicultural politics. Finally, liberal multiculturalists should worry that confusion about the character of the integration they espouse will invite a return to assimilationism. If people are gulled into thinking that they have to choose between a society ethnically fractured by segregation or unified through assimilationism, that invitation will be hard to resist.

My argument thus far might also evoke a very different response. If integration exacts so much cultural loss, one might well ask if liberal multiculturalism is not itself oppressive and that some more radical politics of difference is what we need. I have had something to say about that in a different venue (Callan 1998). Here I only try to allay some of the worries about oppressive policies with respect to religious education that my argument might provoke.

Immigrants have a duty to integrate only to the extent that they must contribute their fair share to making the new society they live in a just and decent place for everyone who lives there. Fulfilling that duty is compatible with exercising their right to freedom of association in some social settings to favour contact with co-ethnics. What the duty to integrate is not compatible with is a determination wholly to shun contact with others who do not share their tradition, language, or religion. To insulate oneself culturally so as to avoid contamination bespeaks contempt for fellow citizens who are unlike oneself and militates against the mutual understanding and respect that creating just and decent institutions demands of us all. The accommodation of such contempt may sometimes be a necessary evil. I am at a loss to see how it could be morally justified as a general policy.

This point is deeply relevant to demands for state-supported religiously separate schooling by Muslims (or other religious groups, whether or not they mainly comprise immigrants) who worry that their faith is threatened without such schools. For reasons I have rehearsed elsewhere (Callan 2004: 162–91), it would be wrong to assume that religious schooling must be repugnant to the integration that an adequate common citizenship requires. And if I can be taught to be a devout Catholic or Jew in denominational schools that also cultivate good citizenship, only sheer prejudice could dispose me to think that religious and civic educational ends could not be similarly reconciled in Islamic schools.

Still, it would be reckless to assume that civic educational goals will be given their due without judicious state regulation in *any* school. This is not the place for an exhaustive consideration of what kind of regulatory regime that would be fitting, but one important consideration is surely this. Children who come from ethnic minorities are denied adequate opportunity for civic integration unless they are frequently immersed in social settings where they can engage with children from the majority ethnic group on terms of mutual respect. (Of course, just the same point could be made backwards: the other children lack vitally important civic educational opportunities without substantial and respectful interaction with fellow citizens from minority ethnic groups.) This gives us a strong prima facie reason to try to ensure that all schools, whether they are religious or not, exhibit an ample level of ethnic diversity, and ethnic diversity will almost inevitably bring religious differences in its wake. A Muslim school in the north of England, say, could hardly diversify its ethnic composition merely by attracting ethnic English converts to Islam. The need for the state to require such diversity in schools, whether they are religious or not, was one of the wise but controversial recommendations of the UK's Cantle Report (Cantle 2001). Unfortunately, it was not implemented.

The resilience of Catholicism and Judaism across many generations in the USA suggests that faith can prevail despite many changes that assimilation induces in the lives of its adherents. Perhaps multiculturalism will make the retention of minority religions easier because it destigmatizes retention. No doubt there are some historical variants of any of the great religions whose perpetuation requires that the children of the faithful be systematically insulated from other children's influence. But if their erosion under a multicultural regime is inevitable, it is not clear why that counts as a reason against liberal multiculturalism.[6]

Notes

1 The very word "assimilation" has taken on such invidious overtones in Western Europe that it is now almost universally avoided for purposes other than denunciation (see Kastoryano 2002: 30–1). On the other side of the Atlantic after the 1960s, assimilation came to be seen "as an ethnocentric and patronizing imposition on minority peoples struggling to retain their cultural and ethnic integrity" (Alba and Nee 2007: 124).

2 Thus it is not surprising that integration has its detractors on the far left (see Young 2000: 219).

3 The double reassurance is not a defining feature of multicultural political theory. Jeff Spinner-Halev has been refreshingly blunt about the inevitability of cultural loss under what he calls "pluralistic integration" (Spinner-Halev 1996: 60–85). Will Kymlicka, perhaps the most influential liberal theorist, has consistently acknowledged that immigrants have no right to recreate their own societal culture in the receiving society. But Kymlicka, like so many theorists writing about multiculturalism, persistently depicts assimilation and multicultural integration as polar opposites (e.g. Kymlicka 1995: 15, 113–15; 1998: 40–59). That depiction fosters the illusion that even if immigrants cannot wholly recreate the society from which they came, their way of life can still be substantially replicated in the receiving society.

Joseph Heath is to my knowledge the only theorist who has explicitly considered whether pressures of cultural conformity under a multicultural regime might make integration effectively tantamount to assimilation. But in the end he concludes that what is superficially deemed assimilation is more aptly described as *liberalization* "which we can use to denote an endogenous transformation that renders cultural value systems institutionally compatible with a plurality of other cultural forms" (Heath 1997: 359). But the pressures to conform to which immigrants will inevitably be exposed extend far beyond liberalization, and in very many cases, liberalization will not be needed at all. A refugee to Canada who knows no English or French and has little human capital may be an ardent and knowledgeable believer in liberal democracy. But if she is to be integrated into the receiving society, she must still learn a great deal in social settings where assimilative influences are predictably powerful.

If we turn from theoretical to untheoretical, vernacular multiculturalism, the double reassurance quickly rears its head. When Prime Minister Elliott Trudeau first announced the policy of multiculturalism, he presented it as an instrument of cultural preservation: "Every ethnic group has the right to preserve and develop its own culture and values within the Canadian context" (Canada, *House of Commons Debates* (October 8, 1971), VIII, 8580, quoted in Forbes 2007: 41). The same story is told nowadays on the website of Citizenship and Immigration Canada. Prospective immigrants viewing the site are falsely assured that they will experience "no pressure to assimilate and give up their culture" (http://www.cic.gc.ca/english/multiculturalism/citizenship.asp (accessed July 19, 2012)).

The purpose of my essay is to debunk the double reassurance but also to show that in doing so we do not debunk multicultural integration itself. The moral appeal of the latter lies not in any avoidance of assimilation but in its distance from assimilationism.

4 The most important work on accommodation in recent political philosophy is Seana Shiffrin's, though Shiffrin has no particular interest in the multicultural species of the genus (see Shiffrin 2000: 205–50; 2004: 270–302). Shiffrin argues (persuasively in my view) that the importance of accommodation derives from its role in enabling the exercise and development of personal autonomy.

5 I do not say that he wants to show this. The point is that he needs to show this if multicultural integration in Canada can be rightly contrasted with assimilation.

6 This paper was made possible through a generous grant from the Spencer Foundation. I am also grateful for Rebecca Taylor's exemplary research assistance. I was helped to improve the paper by Penny Enslin's incisive commentary at the PESGB's annual conference in 2013. Thanks also to Christian Joppke for wise thoughts.

References

Alba, R. and Nee, V. (2005) *Remaking the American Mainstream: Assimilation and Contemporary Immigration.* Cambridge, MA: Harvard University Press.

Alba, R. and Nee, V. (2007) "Assimilation," in M. C. Waters and R. Ueda (eds), *The New Americans: A Guide to Immigration Since 1965.* Cambridge, MA: Harvard University Press.

Bean, F. D. and Stevens, G. (2003) *America's Newcomers and the Dynamics of Diversity.* New York: Russell Sage Foundation.

Bloemraad, I. (2006) *Becoming a Citizen: Incorporating Immigrants and Refugees in the United States and Canada.* Berkeley, CA: University of California Press.

Brubaker, R. (2004) *Ethnicity Without Groups.* Cambridge, MA: Harvard University Press.

Callan, E. (1998) "The politics of difference and common education," in D. Carr (ed.), *Education, Knowledge and Truth: Beyond the Postmodern Impasse.* London: Routledge.

Callan, E. (2004) *Creating Citizens: Political Education and Democracy.* Oxford: Oxford University Press.

Cantle, T. (2001) *Community Cohesion: A Report of the Independent Review Team.* London: Home Office.

Forbes, H. D. (2007) "Trudeau as the first theorist of Canadian multiculturalism," in S. Tierney (ed.), *Multiculturalism and the Canadian Constitution*. Vancouver: University of British Columbia Press.
Gans, H. (1979) "Symbolic ethnicity: the future of ethnic groups and cultures in America," *Ethnic and Racial Studies*, 2 (1): 1–20.
Gordon, M. (1964) *Assimilation in American Life: The Role of Race, Religion, and National Origins*. New York: Oxford University Press.
Heath, J. (1997) "Immigration, multiculturalism, and the social contract," *Canadian Journal of Law and Jurisprudence*, 10: 359.
Jacobsen, M. F. (2008) *Roots Too: White Ethnic Revival in Post-Civil Rights America*. Cambridge, MA: Harvard University Press.
Kastoryano, R. (2002) *Negotiating Identities: States and Immigrants in France and Germany*. Princeton, NJ: Princeton University Press.
Kymlicka, W. (1995) *Multicultural Citizenship: A Liberal Theory of Minority Rights*. Oxford: Oxford University Press.
Kymlicka, W. (1998) *Finding Our Way: Rethinking Ethnocultural Relations in Canada*. Toronto: Oxford University Press.
Li, P. (2003) "Deconstructing Canada's discourse on immigrant integration", *Journal of International Migration and Integration*, 4: 315–3.
Martel, Y. (2001) *The Life of Pi*. New York: Harcourt Books.
Shiffrin, S. (2000) "Paternalism, unconscionability doctrine, and accommodation," *Philosophy and Public Affairs*, 29 (3): 205–50.
Shiffrin, S. (2004) "Egalitarianism, choice-sensitivity, and accommodation," in R. J. Wallace, P. Pettit, S. Scheffler, and M. Smith (eds), *Reason and Value: Themes from the Moral Philosophy of Joseph Raz*. Oxford: Oxford University Press.
Spinner-Halev, J. (1996) *The Boundaries of Citizenship*. Baltimore, MD: Johns Hopkins University Press.
Taylor, C. (1992) *Multiculturalism and the "Politics of Recognition"*. Princeton, NJ: Princeton University Press.
White, J. (1987) "The quest for common values," in G. D. Haydon (ed.), *Education for a Pluralist Society: Philosophical Perspectives on the Swann Report*, Bedford Way Paper 30. London: University of London Institute of Education.
Young, I. M. (2000) *Inclusion and Democracy*. Oxford: Oxford University Press.

John White – publications

Books and monographs

(1973) *Towards a Compulsory Curriculum*. London: Routledge & Kegan Paul.

(1975) (with Keith Thompson) *Curriculum Development: A Dialogue*. London: Pitman.

(1979) (with Peter Gordon) *Philosophers as Educational Reformers*. London: Routledge & Kegan Paul.

(1982) *The Aims of Education Restated*. London: Routledge & Kegan Paul.

(1990) *Education and the Good Life: Beyond the National Curriculum*. London: Kogan Page.

(1991) *Education and the Good Life: Autonomy, Altruism and the National Curriculum*, Advances in Contemporary Educational Thought, Vol. 7, New York: Teachers College Columbia University (American edition of *Education and the Good Life*).

(1992) (with P. O'Hear) *A National Curriculum for All: Laying the Foundations for Success*, Institute for Public Policy Research.

(1992) *The Arts 5–16: Changing the Agenda*, London File series. London: Institute of Education.

(1992) (with P. Lee, J. Slater and P. Walsh) *The Aims of School History: The National Curriculum and Beyond*. London File series. London: Institute of Education.

(1995) *Education and Personal Well-Being in a Secular Universe*, inaugural lecture, Institute of Education (reprinted in J. White, *The Curriculum and the Child*. London: Routledge, 2005).

(1997) *Education and the End of Work: A New Philosophy of Work and Learning*, London: Cassell.

(1998) (with Richard Aldrich) *The National Curriculum Beyond 2000: The QCA and the Aims of Education*. London: Institute of Education.

(1998) *Do Howard Gardner's Multiple Intelligences Add Up?* London: Institute of Education.

(1998) *The Road Towards a Worthwhile National Curriculum in England and Wales 1944–1988–2000* (in English and Japanese), UK–Japan Education Forum Monograph No. 3. Tokyo.

(2000) (with Steve Bramall) *Will the New National Curriculum Live Up to Its Aims?*, IMPACT Paper No. 6. Philosophy of Education Society of Great Britain.

(2002) *The Child's Mind*. London: RoutledgeFalmer.

(2005) *The Curriculum and the Child: The Selected Works of John White*. London: RoutledgeFalmer.
(2005) *Howard Gardner: The Myth of Multiple Intelligences*, Viewpoint No. 16. London: Institute of Education.
(2006) *Intelligence, Destiny and Education: The Ideological Roots of Intelligence Testing*. London: Routledge.
(2007) *What Schools Are For and Why*, IMPACT Paper No. 14. Philosophy of Education Society of Great Britain.
(2011) *Exploring Well-being in Schools: A Guide to Making Children's Lives More Fulfilling*. London: Routledge.
(2011) *The Invention of the Secondary Curriculum*. London: Palgrave Macmillan.
(2013) (with Michael Reiss) *An Aims-based Curriculum: The Significance of Human Flourishing for Schools*. London: Institute of Education Press.

Edited books and journals

(1981) *No Minister: A Critique of the DES Paper 'The School Curriculum'*, Bedford Way Papers 4. London: ULIE.
(1984) *Lessons before Midnight: Educating for Reason in Nuclear Matters*, Bedford Way Papers 19. London: ULIE.
(1984) *Education plc?: Head teachers and the New Training Initiative*, Bedford Way Papers 20. London: ULIE.
(1985) *Psychology and Schooling: What's the Matter?*, Bedford Way Papers 25. London: ULIE.
(1990) (with N. Nickandrov, USSR) Special Issue of *International Review of Education* (UNESCO) on 'Aims and Content of General Education'.
(1993) (ed. with P. O'Hear) *Assessing the National Curriculum*. London: Paul Chapman.
(1997) (ed. with M. Barber) *Perspectives on School Effectiveness and School Improvement*. London: Institute of Education.
(2001) (ed. with F. Heyting and D. Lenzen) *Methods of Philosophy in Education*. London: Routledge.
(2004) (ed.) *Rethinking the School Curriculum: Values, Aims and Purposes*. London: RoutledgeFalmer.

Articles and book chapters

(1967) 'Indoctrination', in R. S. Peters (ed.), *The Concept of Education*. London: Routledge & Kegan Paul; reprinted in I. Snook (ed.) (1972) *Concepts of Indoctrination*. London: Routledge & Kegan Paul.
(1968) 'Creativity and education', *British Journal of Educational Studies*, XVI (2); reprinted in: (1) J. R. Martin (ed.) (1970) *Readings in Philosophy of Education: The Curriculum*. Boston: Allyn & Bacon; (2) R. F. Dearden, P. H. Hirst and R. S. Peters (eds) (1970) *Education and the Development of Reason*. London: Routledge & Kegan Paul.
(1969) (with R. S. Peters) 'The philosopher's contribution to educational research', *Educational Philosophy and Theory*, Vol. 1, No. 2.

(1970) 'The concept of the school counsellor', *Education for Teaching*, No. 82.
(1970) 'Indoctrination: reply to I. M. M. Gregory and R G Woods', *Proceedings of the Philosophy of Education Society*, Vol. IV; reprinted in I. Snook (ed.) (1972) *Concepts of Indoctrination*. London: Routledge & Kegan Paul.
(1971) 'A note on creativity', *British Journal of Educational Studies*, Vol. XIX, No. 1.
(1971) 'The concept of curriculum evaluation', *Journal of Curriculum Studies*, Vol. 3, No. 2.
(1972) 'Learning: reply to S. Brown', *Proceedings of Aristotelian Society* (Supp. Vol. 1972).
(1974) 'Intelligence and the logic of the nature-nurture issue', *Proceedings of the Philosophy of Education Society*, Vol. VIII, No. 1; reprinted in P. H. Hirst and P. A. White (eds) (1998) *Philosophy of Education: Major Themes in the Analytic Tradition*. London: Routledge, Vol. 2; reprinted in J. White (2005) *The Curriculum and the Child*.
(1974) 'The moral objectives of a uniform curriculum', in M. Taylor (ed.) *Progress and Problems in Moral Education*. NFER.
(1974) 'The end of the compulsory curriculum: a historical investigation', in *The Curriculum: The Doris Lee Lectures*, University of London Institute of Education; reprinted in J. White (2005) *The Curriculum and the Child*.
(1974) 'Instruction in obedience', in R. Bell and W. Prescott, *The Schools Council: A Second Look* (Ward Lock, 1975); reprinted from *New Society*, May 1968.
(1976) (with M. F. D. Young) 'A dialogue on the sociology of knowledge', *Education for Teaching*, No. 99.
(1976) (with P. A. White) 'A programme for political education: a critique', *Teaching Politics*, Vol. 5, No. 3.
(1976) 'Teacher accountability and school autonomy – a reply to Hugh Sockett', *Proceedings of the Philosophy of Education Society of Great Britain*, Vol. X.
(1976) (with P. White) 'Barr Greenfield and organisational theory: a symposium', *Educational Administration*, Vol. 5, No. 1.
(1976) 'Authenticity, autonomy and compulsory curriculum: a reply to Michael Bonnett', *Cambridge Journal of Education*, Vol. 6, No. 3.
(1977) 'The impossibility of a core curriculum: a reply to Alan Harris', *Oxford Review of Education*, Vol. 3, No. 2.
(1978) 'The aims of education: three legacies of the British Idealists', *Journal of Philosophy of Education*, Vol. 12.
(1979) 'Towards a philosophy of comprehensive education', *Teach*, Vol. 2, Summer Term.
(1979) 'The primary teacher as servant of the state', *Education 3–13*, Vol. 7, No. 2; reprinted in C. Richards (ed.), *New Directions in Primary Education*. London: Falmer Press, 1982.
(1979) 'Aims and curricula: have heads and teachers got the right to decide?', *NUT Primary Education Review*, No. 7.
(1979) 'Comments on articles by John Clark and Helen Freeman', *Journal of Further and Higher Education*, Vol. 3, No. 3.
(1980) 'Socialist perspectives on the curriculum', in D. Rubinstein (ed.), *Education and Equality*. London: Penguin.
(1980) 'Conceptions of individuality', *British Journal of Educational Studies*, Vol. XXVIII, No. 3.

(1980) (with P. White) 'David Cooper's illusions', *Journal of Philosophy of Education*, Vol. 14, No. 2.

(1981) 'In defence of state-controlled curricula', *Journal of Philosophy of Education*, Vol. 15, No. 2.

(1982) 'Three perspectives on a National Curriculum', *Forum for the Discussion of New Trends in Education*, Vol. 24, No. 3.

(1983) 'Sir Percy Nunn', in A. Bullock and R. B. Woodings (eds), *The Fontana Biographical Companion to Modern Thought*. London: Fontana.

(1984) 'Compulsion and the curriculum', *British Journal of Educational Studies*, Vol. XXXII, No. 2.

(1984) 'A reply to Raymond Godfrey', *Journal of Philosophy of Education*, Vol. 18, No. 1.

(1984) 'The education of the emotions', *Journal of Philosophy of Education*, Vol. 18, No. 2. Reprinted in P. H. Hirst and P. A. White (eds) (1998) *Philosophy of Education: Major Themes in the Analytic Tradition*, Vol. 2.

(1985) (with P. White) 'Improving quality through INSET', in F Slater (ed.), *The Quality Controllers*, Bedford Way Papers 22. London: ULIE.

(1985) 'The compulsory curriculum and beyond: a reply to Peter Gardner', *Journal of Philosophy of Education*, Vol. 19, No. 1.

(1985) 'The importance of educational psychology', in *Psychology and Schooling* (see Books edited).

(1986) (with P. White) 'Education, liberalism and human good', in D. E. Cooper (ed.), *Education, Values and Mind*. London: Routledge & Kegan Paul; reprinted in P. H. Hirst and P. A. White (eds) (1998) *Philosophy of Education: Major Themes in the Analytic Tradition*, Vol. 1.

(1986) (with P. White) 'Teachers and Political Activists: three perspectives', in A. Harnett and M. Naish (eds), *Education and Society Today*. London: Falmer.

(1986) 'On reconstructing the concept of human potential', *Journal of Philosophy of Education*, Vol. 20, No. 1.

(1986) 'The problem of self-interest: the educator's perspective', *Journal of Philosophy of Education*, Vol. 20, No. 2.

(1986) 'Philosophy and educational administration', in D. A. Howell and P. M. Ribbins (eds), *Collaborative Research in Educational Administration*. London: BEMAS.

(1987) 'The quest for common values', in G. D. Haydon (ed.), *Education for a Pluralist Society: Philosophical Perspectives on the Swann Report*, Bedford Way Paper 30. London: ULIE.

(1987) 'The comprehensive ideal and the rejection of theory' *British Journal of Educational Studies*, Vol. XXXV, No. 3.

(1987) 'The medical condition of philosophy of education', *Journal of Philosophy of Education*, Vol. 21, No. 2.

(1987) Essay review of *Philosophers on Education* (eds R. Straughan and J. Wilson), in *Journal of Philosophy of Education*, Vol. 21, No. 2.

(1988) 'Educational psychology: science or common sense?', *Educational and Child Psychology*, Vol. 5, No. 1.

(1988) 'Two National Curricula: Baker's and Stalin's. Towards a liberal alternative', *British Journal of Educational Studies*, Vol. XXXVI, No. 3.

(1988) 'Philosophy in Spanish Schools', *Cogito*, Vol. 2, No. 3.

(1988) 'An unconstitutional National Curriculum', in D. Lawton and C. Chitty (eds), *The National Curriculum*, Bedford Way Series. London: ULIE.
(1988) 'Diversity and conflict in values-education', in A. Horvath and O. Mihaly (eds), *Philosophy of Education: Bridge or Gulf between East and West.* Budapest: Orszagos Pedagogiai Intezet.
(1989) 'Values education for the age of perestroika', *Oxford Review of Education*, Vol. 15, No. 1.
(1989) 'The aims of personal and social education', in P. White (ed.), *Thinking About Personal and Social Education*, Bedford Way Series. London: Kogan Page and ULIE.
(1989) 'Bridging gulfs within and between East and West: reply to Horvath', *Paideusis*, Vol. 2, No. 2.
(1990) '"The goals are the same" (Warnock Report). Are they?', *British Journal of Special Education*, Vol. 18, No. 1.
(1990) 'The aims of education', in N. Entwistle (ed.), *Handbook of Educational Ideas and Practices.* London: Routledge.
(1990) (with N. Nikandrov) 'Introduction', in Special Issue of *International Review of Education.*
(1990) (with N. Nikandrov) 'Educational reform in Britain: beyond the National Curriculum', in Special Issue of *International Review of Education.*
(1991) 'A new National Curriculum for England and Wales', in V. Firsov (ed.), *Soviet-English Symposium on National Curriculum: Proceedings.* Moscow: Perspectiva.
(1991) 'The justification of autonomy as an educational aim', in B. Spiecker and R. Straughan (eds), *Freedom and Indoctrination in Education: International Perspectives.* London: Cassell.
(1991) 'Humanisation and education: issues for school reform', *Studies in Philosophy and Education*, Vol. I, No. 1.
(1992) 'The arts, personal well-being and education', in R. Barrow and P. White (eds), *Beyond Liberal Education: essays in Honour of Paul H. Hirst.* London: Routledge.
(1992) 'The purposes of school history', in P. Lee., J. Slater, P. Walsh and J. White (eds), *The Aims of School History: The National Curriculum and Beyond.* London: Institute of Education.
(1992) 'The roots of philosophy', in A. P. Griffiths (ed.), *The Impulse to Philosophize*, Royal Institute of Philosophy lecture series 1991–2. Cambridge: Cambridge University Press.
(1992) 'Creativity', in D. E. Cooper (ed.), *Companion to Aesthetics.* Oxford: Blackwell.
(1992) 'Morality and art', in D. E. Cooper (ed.), *Companion to Aesthetics.* Oxford: Blackwell.
(1992) 'The quadrate mind: a philosophical perspective', *New Ideas in Psychology*, Vol. 10, No. 3.
(1992) 'Can education for democracy rest on socialist foundations?', *Journal of Philosophy of Education*, Vol. 26, No. 1.
(1993) (ed. with P. O'Hear) 'Introduction' to *Assessing the National Curriculum.* London: Paul Chapman.
(1993) (ed. with P. O'Hear) 'What place for values in the National Curriculum?', in *Assessing the National Curriculum.* London: Paul Chapman.
(1994) 'The dishwasher's child: education and the end of egalitarianism', *Journal of Philosophy of Education*, Vol. 28, No. 2.

(1994) 'Education and the limits of the market', in D. Bridges and T. H. McLaughlin (eds), *Education and the Marketplace*. London: Falmer.
(1994) 'Instead of OFSTED: a critical discussion of OFSTED on spiritual, moral, social and cultural development', *Cambridge Journal of Education*, Vol. 24, No. 3.
(1994) 'Curriculum: philosophical perspectives', in T. Husen and T. N. Postlethwaite (eds), *The International Encyclopaedia of Education* (2nd edn). Oxford: Pergamon.
(1994) 'Education and recognition', *Paedeusis* (Canada), Vol. 7, No. 2.
(1994) 'The aims of school history', *Teaching History*, No. 74.
(1995) 'The concept of intelligence', Review Article, *Journal of Philosophy of Education*, Vol. 29, No. 3.
(1995) 'Beyond belief', *Nursing Times*, 1 November.
(1995) 'Peters, Richard Stanley', in T. Honderich (ed.), *The Oxford Companion to Philosophy*. Oxford: Oxford University Press.
(1995) 'Philosophy of education: problems of', in T. Honderich (ed.), *The Oxford Companion to Philosophy*. Oxford: Oxford University Press.
(1995) (with A. Bird) 'Consent and the adult patient', in J. Tingle and A. Cribb (eds), *Nursing Law and Ethics*. Oxford: Blackwell.
(1996) 'Richard Peters', in S. Brown *et al.* (eds), *Biographical Dictionary of Twentieth Century Philosophers*. London: Routledge.
(1996) 'Paul Hirst', in S. Brown *et al.* (eds), *Biographical Dictionary of Twentieth Century Philosophers*. London: Routledge.
(1996) (with P. O'Hear) 'Aims and values in the National Curriculum', in P. Woods (ed.), *Contemporary Issues in Teaching and Learning*. Buckingham: Open University Press.
(1996) 'Moral absolutes and artistic cannon-fodder', *Education*, March.
(1996) 'Liberalism, nationality and education', *Studies in Philosophy and Education*, Vol. 15.
(1996) 'Education and nationality', *Journal of Philosophy of Education*, Vol. 30, No. 3.
(1997) 'National myths, democracy and education', in D. Bridges (ed.), *Education, Autonomy and Democratic Citizenship*. London: Routledge.
(1997) 'Three proposals and a rejection' in R. Smith and P. Standish (eds), *Teaching Right and Wrong: Moral Education in the Balance*. Stoke-on-Trent: Trentham.
(1997) 'Philosophical perspectives on school effectiveness and school improvement', *Curriculum Journal*, Vol. 8, No 1.
(1997) 'Is moral education an aid or obstacle to personal well-being?', *Prospero*, Vol. 3, No. 1.
(1997) 'Education, work and well-being', *Journal of Philosophy of Education*, Vol. 31, No. 2.
(1997) 'Philosophy and the aims of higher education', *Studies in Higher Education*, Vol. 22, No. 1.
(1998) 'New aims for a new national curriculum' in R. Aldrich and J. White (eds), *The National Curriculum Beyond 2000: The QCA and the Aims of Education*. London Institute of Education.
(1998) 'Moral education', in E. Craig (ed.), *Routledge Encyclopaedia of Philosophy*. London: Routledge.
(1999) 'What is a national curriculum for?' in S. Dainton (ed.), *Take Care, Mr Blunkett*. London: ATL.
(1999) 'Response to Ronald Glasberg', *Studies in Philosophy and Education*, Vol. 18, No. 4.

(1999) Review article on A. O. Rorty *Philosophers on Education*, *Journal of Philosophy of Education*, Vol. 33, No. 3.
(1999) 'Thinking about assessment', *Journal of Philosophy of Education*, Vol. 33, No. 2.
(1999) 'In defence of liberal aims in education', in R. Marples (ed.), *The Aims of Education*. London: Routledge.
(2000) 'Moral education', in E. Craig (ed.), *Concise Routledge Encyclopaedia of Philosophy*. London: Routledge.
(2000) 'The value of education: a reply to Andrew Reid', *Journal of Philosophy of Education*, Vol. 34, No. 4.
(2000) 'Should maths be compulsory for all until 16?', in S. Bramall and J. White (eds), *Why Learn Maths?*, Bedford Way Paper. London: Institute of Education.
(2001) (with A. Davis) 'Accountability and school inspection: in defence of audited self-review', *Journal of Philosophy of Education*, Vol. 35, No. 4.
(2001) 'Philosophy with children and Howard Gardner's theory of multiple intelligences: a sceptic's reasons', in *Arista*, Vol. 1, No. 2. Association of Teachers for Philosophy with Children.
(2001) (with P. White) 'Analytic philosophy of education and children's rights', in F. Heyting, D. Lenzen and J. White (eds), *Methods in Philosophy in Education*. London: Routledge.
(2001) 'Richard Peters', in J. Palmer-Cooper (ed.), *50 Modern Thinkers on Education: From Piaget to the Present*. London: Routledge.
(2001) 'Patriotism without obligation', *Journal of Philosophy of Education*, Vol. 35, No. 1.
(2001) 'How should educational aims be decided?', in T. Yamazaki (ed.), *Personal Development in Children from the Perspective of the Twenty-first Century*. Kyoto: University of Kyoto Press.
(2002) 'The last rites for religious education?', *Ethical Record*, Vol. 107, No. 10. London: South Place Ethical Society.
(2002) 'New light on personal well-being', *Journal of Philosophy of Education*, Vol. 36, No. 4.
(2002) 'Education, the market and the nature of personal well-being', *British Journal of Educational Studies*, Vol. 50, No. 4; reprinted in W. Carr (ed.) (2005) *The RoutledgeFalmer Reader in the Philosophy of Education*. London: RoutledgeFalmer.
(2003) 'Introduction': Chapter 1 of J. White (ed.), *Rethinking the School Curriculum: Values, Aims and Purposes*. London: RoutledgeFalmer.
(2003) 'Shaping a curriculum': Chapter 2 of J. White (ed.), *Rethinking the School Curriculum: Values, Aims and Purposes*. London: RoutledgeFalmer.
(2003) 'Conclusion': Chapter 14 of J. White (ed.), *Rethinking the School Curriculum: Values, Aims and Purposes*. London: RoutledgeFalmer.
(2003) 'Five critical stances towards liberal philosophy of education in Britain', *Journal of Philosophy of Education*, Vol. 37, No. 1.
(2003) 'Dumbing down educational research: a reply to John Wilson', *Educational Research*, Vol. 45, No. 2.
(2003) "Education, well-being and the market', in M. Mangold and J. Oelkers (eds), *Demokratie, Bildung und Markt*. Bern: Peter Lang.
(2003) (with E. Callan) 'Liberalism and communitarianism', in N. Blake, P. Smeyers, R. Smith and P. Standish (eds), *The Blackwell Guide to the Philosophy of Education*. Oxford: Blackwell.

(2004) (with M. Hand) 'Is compulsory religious education justified?', *Journal of Education and Christian Belief*, Vol. 8, No. 2.
(2004) 'Reply to James Muir', *Educational Philosophy and Theory*, Vol. 36, No. 4.
(2004) 'Should RE be a compulsory school subject?', *British Journal of Religious Education*, Vol. 26, No. 2.
(2005) 'Howard Gardner: the myth of multiple intelligences', in *Formazione & Insegnamento*, Vol. III, No. 1. Lecce.
(2005) 'Reply to Andrew Stables', *Journal of Curriculum Studies*, Vol. 37, No. 6.
(2005) 'Reassessing 1960s philosophy of the curriculum', *London Review of Education*, Vol. 3, No. 2.
(2005) 'Puritan Intelligence', *Oxford Review of Education*, Vol. 31, No. 3; reprinted in J. White, *The Curriculum and the Child.*
(2005) 'Multiple intelligences: the end of the bandwagon?', *Post-16 Educator*, No. 25.
(2005) 'Reply to Andrew Wright', *British Journal of Religious Education*, Vol. 27, No. 1.
(2005) 'Educating for success', in D. de Ruyter, G. Bertram-Troost and S. Sieckelinck (eds), *Idealen, idolen en iconen van de pedagogiek.* Amsterdam: SWP.
(2006) 'The religious origins of intelligence testing', *The Psychologist*, June, Vol. 19, No. 6.
(2006) 'Autonomy, human flourishing and the curriculum', *Journal of Philosophy of Education*, Vol. 40, No. 3.
(2007) 'Education, politics and religious decline', online at: http://www.humanism.org.uk/site/cms/contentViewArticle.asp?article=2281.
(2007) 'The Aims of School Education'. London: IPPR; online at: http://www.ippr.org/.../Education/The%20Aims%20of%20School%20Ed%20FINAL.pdf.
(2007) 'The puritan origins of the 1988 curriculum in England', in A. Moore (ed.), *Schooling, Society and Curriculum.* London: Routledge.
(2007) 'Multiple invalidities?', in J. A. Schaler (ed.), *Gardner Under Fire: A Rebel Psychologist Faces His Critics.* Chicago: Open Court Publishing.
(2007) 'Education for well-being', *Education Review*, Vol. 19, No. 1.
(2007) 'How not to organize an educational system', *Primary Leadership Today*, No. 8.
(2007) 'Wellbeing and education: issues of culture and authority', *Journal of Philosophy of Education*, Vol. 41, No. 1.
(2007) 'What's wrong with Gardner's multiple intelligences?', in *Education: Ideas and Dialogue*, Vol. 2. Beijing: Educational Science Publishing House.
(2007) 'Is the traditional curriculum past its prime?', *Educational Studies in Japan: International Yearbook*, No. 2.
(2008) 'Aims as policy in primary education', Research Survey 1/1 in R. Alexander (ed.), *The Primary Review.* University of Cambridge.
(2008) 'The centrality of well-being', in L. Waks (ed.), *Leaders in Philosophy of Education: Intellectual Self Portraits.* Rotterdam: Sense Press.
(2008) 'Education' and 'Philosophy of education', in D. Crook and G. McCulloch (eds), *The Routledge International Encyclopedia of Education.* London: Routledge.
(2008) 'Illusory intelligences', *Journal of Philosophy of Education*, Vol. 42, Nos 3–4.
(2009) 'Further and higher: a philosophical divide?', in N. Garrod and B. Macfarlane (eds), *Challenging Boundaries: Managing the Integration of Post-Secondary Education.* London: Routledge.

(2009) 'Education and a meaningful life', *Oxford Review of Education*, Vol. 35, No. 1.
(2009) 'Why general education? Peters, Hirst and history', *Journal of Philosophy of Education*, Vol. 43, Supplement 1.
(2009) (with M. Reiss) 'Atheism needs to be studied in schools', *The Independent*, 16 July.
(2010) (online: forthcoming at http://www.ttrb.ac.uk/) TTRB Glossary Item on 'Curriculum aims', Teacher Training Resource Bank.
(2010) 'Turning the clock back to subject slavery', *Times Educational Supplement*, 5 February.
(2010) 'The Curriculum', in 'Much improved: should be even better?', New Visions for Education Group; available online at: http://www.newvisionsforeducation.org.uk/2010/03/31/much-improved-should-do-even-better/.
(2010) 'Equality does not come from letting subjects rule', *Questa*, No. 1, pp. 50–3.
(2010) 'Elusive rivalry? Conceptions of the philosophy of education', *Ethics and Education*, Vol. 5, No. 2.
(2010) 'The Coalition and the curriculum', *Forum*, Vol. 52, No. 3.
(2010) 'The escalator taking teens straight from school to university is a crazy way to proceed', *Times Educational Supplement*, 22 October.
(2011) 'Gove's on the Bac foot with a white paper stuck in 1868', *Times Educational Supplement*, 21 January.
(2011) 'If the young aspire only to fame and fortune, where does that leave our 19-century fact-driven curriculum?', *Times Educational Supplement*, 15 April.
(2011) 'Education and well-being', in I. Boniwell and S. David (eds), *The Oxford Handbook of Happiness.* Buckingham: Open University Press.
(2011) 'What does it mean to be well-educated?', *Think*, Summer.
(2011) 'Philosophy of education as public servant', *Bajo Palabra* (Madrid), Vol. 11 No. 6.
(2012) 'R. S. Peters', Obituary, *The Times*, 27 January.
(2012) (with M. Brown) 'An unstable framework – critical perspectives on *The Framework for the National Curriculum*', New Visions for Education Group; online at: http://www.newvisionsforeducation.org.uk/2012/04/05/an-unstable-framework/.
(2012) 'Powerful knowledge: too weak a prop for the traditional curriculum?', New Visions for Education Group; online at: http://www.newvisionsforeducation.org.uk/2012/05/14/powerful-knowledge-too-weak-a-prop-for-the-traditional-curriculum/.
(2012) 'Why our curriculum should be aims-based' [The Last Word, p. 34], *Languages Today*, No. 11, Summer.
(2012) 'Towards a new ABC of curriculum-making: a reply to John Hopkin', *Forum*, Vol. 54, No. 2.
(2012) 'Philosophy in primary schools', *Journal of Philosophy of Education*, Vol. 46, No. 3.
(2012) 'The role of policy in philosophy of education: an argument and an illustration', *Journal of Philosophy of Education*, Vol. 46, No. 4.
(2013) 'Trust in testers', *London Review of Education*, Vol. 11, No. 1; online at: http://www.tandfonline.com/eprint/4p8mKugQSeRTVdnacHfq/full.
(2013) (with Michael Reiss) 'Time for an alternative curriculum', *School Leadership Today*, Vol. 4, No. 6.

Index